Silver Poets
of the
Eighteenth Century

Edited, with an introduction, by
Arthur Pollard

Professor of English,
University of Hull

Dent, London
Rowman and Littlefield, Totowa, N.J.

© Introduction, notes and editing, J. M. Dent & Sons Ltd, 1976
Made in Great Britain
at the
Aldine Press · Letchworth · Herts
for
J. M. DENT & SONS LTD
Aldine House · Albemarle Street · London
First published in 1976
First published in the United States 1976
by ROWMAN AND LITTLEFIELD, TOTOWA, N.J.

This book is set in 9 pt Baskerville 169

Dent edition
Hardback ISBN 0 460 10085 8
Paperback ISBN 0 460 11085 3

Rowman and Littlefield edition
Library of Congress Cataloging in Publication Data
Hardback ISBN 0-87471-799-x
Paperback ISBN 0-87471-800-7

Contents

[v]

THOMAS GRAY

WILLIAM COLLINS

Introduction

Matthew Arnold considered the eighteenth century as 'our age of prose and reason'. Its poets lacked for him 'an adequate poetic criticism of life'. Only Gray had any claim to be the 'poetical classic of that literature and age', and he is the 'scantiest and frailest' of such classics. Arnold wrote on the ebb-tide of Romanticism, and we today would find it hard to accept, though we can understand, his judgment and his order of priorities. Gray a better poet than Dryden or Pope? None the less, the gold did not flow abundantly and the silver was much more in evidence in the eighteenth century. After Pope, who? Surely Swift and Johnson and Goldsmith who are included here. High-quality silver, but poets, we must remember, all of whose principal works were in prose. After them, indeed, the two precursors of the Romantics—Gray and Collins, the one, at least, admitted into the Arnoldian poetic pantheon.

While it can be said that a gulf lies between the poetic modes of the Augustans and the Romantics, it can be added that three of the poets in this selection are firmly on the hither side and the other two are crossing over. Whereas the Romantics exalted novelty, simplicity, suggestion, feeling and individuality, their eighteenth-century predecessors chose such qualities as decorum, control, sophistication and explicitness. They were writing not for themselves, but for a well-knit public. They knew what was wanted, or should have done. They had no right to particularize; as Johnson somewhat scathingly put it in *Rasselas* (chapter 10), 'the poet does not number the streaks of the tulip'. Elsewhere he wrote: 'Great thoughts are always general and consist in positions not limited by exceptions, and in descriptions not descending to minuteness' (*Life of Cowley*). The emotion of recognition was important to the eighteenth-century reader.

It made for poetry that was strongly orientated towards social and moral themes. It made, too, for a didactic inclination. It sustained, and perhaps encouraged, a conservatism of manner. Imitation of older, and especially classical, poets flourished. Certain forms like the epic and the pastoral were employed long after all the life had left them. Even newer forms like the mock-epic derived a status from their relationship to their more serious parallels and to their own classical precedents in satiric writing. The prosperity of satire itself is a mark of the dominate critical conservatism. And yet another is the heavily stylized language which persisted by a kind of prescriptive right. 'The language of the age is never the language of poetry.' Gray's remark sounds hardly credible to the astonished ears of later generations, but it would not have shocked his contemporaries. For them poetic diction with its Latinisms, compound epithets, abstractions, periphrases and the like was not only perfectly proper; as Johnson's famous dismissal of Shakespeare's evocative passage in *Macbeth* about the 'blanket of the dark' shows, anything else was likely to be perfectly improper. In this regard also the eighteenth-century poet catered for his reader's expectation and for his delight in recognition.

Our first poet may seem at times hardly to fit the strict and well-ordered pattern of Augustanism which I have summarized above. Jonathan Swift (1667–1745), as poet, belongs rather with a preceding generation, with men like Rochester and Butler, the one to whom nothing was sacred, the other the devotee of low burlesque. Swift's fearless vision and terrifying candour could not be contained within the limits of the Augustan decencies. He is, of course, best known as a prose-writer, in particular for his satirical *Tale of a Tub* and *Gulliver's Travels*. His verse, however, much of it occasional like a lot of his prose, is copious and comprehensive. The early work—around 1692—was mainly formal including exercises in the then fashionable Pindaric ode. The 'Ode to the Athenian Society' has been called 'the worst thing that Swift ever wrote', and Johnson tells us that, after looking over these and other verses, Dryden remarked, 'Cousin Swift, you will never be a poet.'
    Had Swift continued in that manner, Dryden would have been right, but fortunately the bulk of his verse is of a very different kind. The change is marked in 'The Humble Petition of Frances Harris' with its metrical virtuosity (almost to the point of ignoring metre altogether), its outrageous rhymes and its general conversational flavour so exactly representing the shallow garrulity of the supposed speaker. The ease, the informality and the fun of this poem are found again in the very different 'Baucis and Philemon' where Swift takes Ovid's story of the metamorphosis of this couple and sets it in the homely surroundings of the English countryside. The technique of reduction was of the essence of his art. In Boileau's phrase, he would have his 'Dido and Aeneas speak like fishwomen and scavengers'. Thus

> Now Aurora had left the bed of Tithonus

becomes for Swift in 'A Description of the Morning'

> Now Betty from her master's bed had flown.

One of the most appealing of the poems inspired by classical parallel is his version of the sixth satire in Horace's second book, a piece that was to be eventually finished by Pope. Swift's lines belong to his happy years when he was the confidant of statesmen and enjoyed favour and influence in the highest circles of London society in the period from 1710 to 1713. The urbane and facile manner of Horace just suited Swift's circumstances, and the whole poem manifests that good-humoured, bantering tone which, alas, was to appear less and less as the years went by.

> Three Gifts for Conversation fit
> Are Humor, Raillery and Witt,

wrote Swift in his lines 'To Delany', and it is just these qualities which we find in Swift's easy verse such as the imitation of Horace. We find it again in his several poems on Stella's birthdays. Stella was Esther Johnson, daughter of the steward at Moor Park, the seat of Sir William Temple, under whose patronage Swift had lived in the last years of the seventeenth century. She became his intimate friend, and to her is addressed his famous, even notorious, *Journal to Stella*. She was also the recipient of several birthday poems between 1718 and 1727, of which the first and last are included in this volume. The first manifests a grace and charm in compliment that is turned from the candour of

> Although thy Size and Years are doubled,
> Since first I saw thee at Sixteen.

It demonstrates not only the confidence and security that must have underlain their relationship, but also those qualities that Swift refers to in the lines to Delany quoted above. By contrast, there is a melancholy, an elegiac note even, about the 1726/7 poem, written as it was at a time of Stella's increasing illness. It was her last birthday; she died on 28th January 1727/8.

The only other woman who appears to have played any significant part in Swift's life, and that for an altogether shorter time, was Esther Vanhomrigh (Vanessa), with whose family Swift became familiar in the London years. *Cadenus and Vanessa*, his longest poem, sprang from this relationship. It is cast as an elaborate compliment to Vanessa, as the maiden endowed not only with virtue and beauty but also with knowledge, judgment and wit, created by Venus to regain the ascendancy in marriage over intrigue and money. Her tutor, Cadenus (anagram of Decanus, or Dean: Swift was Dean of St Patrick's, Dublin), deflects Cupid's arrows shot at various possible lovers, but then she falls in love with Cadenus himself. The poem ends with Venus lamenting that, though she had formed a perfect maiden, no worthy lover had appeared to deserve her. We read of Cadenus's 'Shame, Disappointment, Guilt, Surprize' when Vanessa declares her love. The poem seems to testify something of Swift's embarrassment, if not at the existence, at least at the continuance of their relationship.

Swift's pleasanter poems about women are marked by a certain condescending banter (cf. 'The Furniture of a Woman's Mind') which, one suspects, the relationship with Vanessa never allowed. She probably wanted to be too serious without being able to engage the whole of his personality, as Stella seems able to have done. His unpleasanter poems display that horror of the body that may well point to Swift's failure ever to establish a complete sexual relationship, even with Stella. His disgust with some of the baser, but necessary, physical functions is evident enough in parts of *Gulliver's Travels*. In the poems it takes the form of repulsion at the artificial mask which makes a woman's beauty and conceals the horrid reality beneath.

Swift's comprehensive and fearless view of mankind could only be sustained by a chronic compromise with life. He expressed it in his motto—'Vive la bagatelle'; and he put it again in the 'Epistle to A Lady':

> Like the ever laughing Sage
> In a Jest I spend my Rage
> (Tho' it must be understood
> I would hang them if I cou'd.)

His inability, deliberate or otherwise, at times to control his rage shows some of those he would have gladly hanged. Fifteen lines on Walpole conclude:

> Tho I name not the wretch you know who I mean
> Tis the Cur dog of Brittain & spaniel of Spain,

whilst the 'Satirical Elegy' on Marlborough is matched only in its disgust for the rotten corpse, fit symbol of a rotten life, by Byron's later and similar treatment of George III in *A Vision of Judgment*.

The chronic compromise is never better sustained than in his greatest poem, the verses on his own supposed death. With his unrelentingly low view of life he considers how his presumed friends and acquaintances will greet his demise. To some it is matter for relief, to most for gossip, only for a few regret, and even of them

> Poor POPE will grieve a Month; and GAY
> A Week; and ARBUTHNOTT a Day.

Swift knew how little each of us really matters, but he also knew and inferred that the same applies as much to those who forget as to those who are forgotten. The poem concludes with as just an estimate as ever man wrote of himself and in the final lines tells of his bequest 'To build a House for Fools and Mad'. He ended up, in a jest spending his rage. Swift's superficial triviality should never deceive us. It was an ironic means, the disguise by which alone he was able to keep within bounds the pressing intensity of his disgust for his fellow men.

Swift, it has been said, was the man of action who had to be satisfied to be the man of letters. Samuel Johnson (1709–84) had no such problem. He was the born man of letters whose roles included essayist, dramatist, novelist, lexicographer, editor of Shakespeare and writer of sermons, as well as poet—and all this is to say nothing about him as supreme talker. With Swift he embraces Augustanism in its widest possible chronological interpretation, the one born in the year that Milton published *Paradise Lost*, the other dying as Burns was about to enter upon his short-lived but phenomenal popularity.

Like Swift, Johnson was a conservative and, like him also, his views of life were pessimistic, but whereas the older writer's emotions often assumed a manic guise of anger or apparent nonchalance, Johnson's usually manifest the measured solemnity of a man who has come to terms with the enduring and irremediable realities of life. I say 'usually', because this does not hold true for his first major work, *London*, which appeared in 1738. There we have the angry young man, struggling to establish himself in the world of letters. An immense amount of bitter experience is distilled into the single, capitalized line:

SLOW RISES WORTH, BY POVERTY DEPREST.

Johnson never forgot those early struggles, either in his own regard for the poor or in his admiration of the regard that others showed. The late poem 'On the Death of Dr Robert Levet' shows the latter. Characteristically, it makes no mention of Johnson's own care for Levet in his last years of poverty.

Johnson's only two major poems are both imitations of Juvenal—*London* of the Latin author's third satire and *The Vanity of Human Wishes* of his tenth. Juvenal's third satire, the attack on life in Rome, is built on four contrasts—city *v.* country, rich *v.* poor, Roman *v.* foreigner and sincerity *v.* flattery (these categories are from Gilbert Highet's brilliant *Juvenal the Satirist*, 1954). Johnson takes over his predecessor's xenophobia to show how Britain has become 'Of France the Mimic, and of Spain the Prey', but one feels that he is going too far to be persuasive when he bids us believe that London has become 'the Common Sewer of *Paris* and of *Rome*'. Nevertheless one admires the felicity with which this renders:

iam pridem Syrus in Tiberim defluxit Orontes.

It is not just felicity, it is also amazing conflation. Latin is concise enough, and Juvenal has the gift not only for brevity but also for the deftly chosen and positioned word. We see this in

haut facile emergunt quorum virtutibus opstat
res angusta domi;

but Johnson improves even on this in his line of capitals which I quoted above.

London, however, is not wholly satisfactory. This shows in some of the contrasts. The poor man's exposure to the loss of his 'little *All*' by fire (ll. 182 ff.) seems exaggerated, as does, in spite of the undoubted dangers, 'Prepare for Death, if here at Night you roam' (ll. 224 ff.). The intermediate paragraph on the way in which the wealthy Orgilio becomes even wealthier when a fire destroys his 'palace' (ll. 194 ff.) is probably no less exaggerated, and yet it appears all the more impressive for being so. In this passage Johnson is content to state—sonorous statement though it is; whereas the other two passages introduce an element of the dramatic which verges on the melodramatic. There is, finally, a problem about the remaining paragraph (ll. 210 ff.) in this long passage. Johnson there simply extols the country life, whereas his original appears more ambiguous. When Juvenal says you can buy outright a house at some outlandish towns of Latium for the price of a year's rent of a dark hole in Rome, there may well be a reflection on

Sora, Fabrateria and Frusino as well as on Rome. The country estate is a little one, 'hortulus', and there is surely something doubtful about becoming 'unius . . . dominum lacertae', master of a single lizard. So many English poets writing on the 'Beatus ille . . .' theme ignore the fact that Horace's statesman soon gets bored and rushes back to Rome at the end of the second epode. Has Johnson made the same mistake with Juvenal? It is a piquant question of one who believed that 'he who is tired of London is tired of life'.

Juvenal's tenth satire is high moralizing. With what Highet both elegantly and powerfully calls 'the remorseless lucidity of pessimism', Juvenal examines man's aspirations for power, eloquence, military glory, long life and beauty and concludes that we should desire only health and virtue—'mens sana in sano corpore', leaving all the rest to the gods. It was a theme and an attitude exactly suited to Johnson's genius. He was always conscious of mortality; even in a *jeu d'esprit* like that on Mrs Thrale's thirty-fifth birthday we are not allowed to forget time's winged chariot hurrying near, and it is appropriate that one of his last and also his finest poems is his rendering of Horace's 'Diffugere nives', where the burgeoning spring reminds the Roman and the English poet that

> The changing year's successive plan
> Proclaims mortality to Man.

It was appropriate, too, and not surprising that A. E. Housman also translated this ode. Not for him or for Johnson the Shelleyan optimism of 'If winter comes, can spring be far behind?'; rather that another spring presages only another winter, and man's spring is but prelude to an abiding winter.

In the shadow of death what then can man's life be worth? How futile is so much of his aspiration! In the metaphor of fireworks Johnson sees men as 'They mount, they shine, evaporate and fall'. None illustrates this better than Wolsey, and the paragraph devoted to him describes the full extent of this pyrotechnic parallel. With characteristic Johnsonian concentration Wolsey is seen first with 'Law in his Voice, and Fortune in his Hand'. His relentless ambition is summarized:

> Still to new Heights his restless Wishes tow'r,
> Claim leads to Claim, and Pow'r advances Pow'r . . .;

and then 'At length his Sov'reign frowns . . .', 'Now drops at once . . .', and there follows a catalogue that reads like a ceremonial stripping of the fallen favourite. But vain though much of human activity is or turns out to be, that is not all. Lifting Juvenal's inspired common sense and ignoring the satire that intrudes even in a passage like this when the scornful sage dismisses popular religious superstition with its offering of 'exta et candiduli divina tomacula porci' (the entrails and divine sausages of a little white porker), Johnson, in lines instinct with religious feeling and yet reticent of explicit statement, concludes the poem with what can only be called the noblest sentiments of Christian Stoicism ('Thy will be done').

Though younger than either Gray or Collins, Goldsmith (1729–74) displays little evidence of being affected by the new movement in poetry, of which they were early exemplars. It is therefore both more convenient and more appropriate to consider him alongside his fellow Irishman, Swift, and his friend, Johnson, as a late but no less whole-hearted Augustan than they. Whole-hearted, but with neither their intellectual endowment nor their moral strength. By comparison with Johnson's full-bodied tones, Goldsmith's voice is lighter and less sonorous. Yet there is truth in Johnson's epitaph on him: 'There was hardly any kind of writing that he did not touch upon, and he touched none that he did not adorn.'

Like Johnson, Goldsmith wrote a few longer and more important poems and a variety of occasional verse. This latter included prologues and epilogues, songs and humorous pieces. It is said that Goldsmith was a vain man who resented criticism, but he certainly shows the capacity to enjoy a joke at his own expense, as in 'The Haunch of Venison', a poem notable also for its free-running, colloquial measure. His humour is often at its best when he can employ a contrasting and anti-climactic turn in the finale. Thus in the ironically entitled 'Elegy on that Glory of Her Sex, Mrs Mary Blaize', the compliment in every verse is annihilated by the qualification in the last line, whilst the more famous 'Elegy on the Death of a Dad Mog' neatly contradicts the exaggerated prognosis of shocked spectators with:

> The man recovered of the bite,
> The dog it was that dy'd.

This ability to see both sides of a question fills Goldsmith's work with the note of qualification. It is used to more serious purpose in other poems. Thus in *The Double Transformation*—the title itself illustrates the point I am trying to make—there are Swiftian implications, but they do not get very far. (Incidentally 'A New Simile in the Manner of Swift' is but mildly modelled on the master.) In *The Double Transformation* we read of an ill-suited pair, the retiring don and the flighty beauty. The latter's charms 'Arose from powder, shreds or lace' and we see sugges-tions in 'Insulting repartee and spleen', of the life of Phyllis and the erstwhile footman in Swift's 'Phyllis'. Very differently in Goldsmith, however, Flavia's beauty is destroyed by small-pox, her fleet of admirers desert her, the couple draw closer together, 'She finds good nature every day [and] . . . / Jack finds his wife a perfect beauty.'

This optimistic conclusion is also typical of Goldsmith. Reading *The Traveller*, for example, one finds oneself recalling Pope's *Essay on Man*. For every ill there is a compensating good; and, though the reverse also applies, it is, none the less, the best of all possible worlds. Again, we notice balance and qualifications; 'yet' and 'but' are the favoured conjunctions. The plan is simple, to compare the varieties of scenery, climate, government, religion, national character and the like between the several European countries. Goldsmith concludes that each man is an island and his mind to him a kingdom is, saying, what none now could surely say, that

> In every government, though terrors reign,
> Though tyrant kings, or tyrant laws restrain,
> How small, of all that human hearts endure,
> That part which laws or kings can cause or cure!

This suggestion of political *laissez-faire* is implicitly criticized in the preceding lines with their lament for this very freedom which in Britain 'Keeps man from man and breaks the social tie'. This topic was to be the central inspiration of Goldsmith's best and best-known poem, *The Deserted Village*. Typically, the poem is built on contrasts. One is reminded of Johnson's *London* in the opposition of city and country, but the angle of observation here is that of the country—and it is a desolate place. That introduces the other major opposition—of past and present. Goldsmith in his role of *laudator temporis acti* recalls what reads like his own boyhood in a place where it was always afternoon. Village sports and scenes and characters pass by in a nostalgic kaleidoscope: Auburn was always 'sweet' and 'lovely'. Now there are left only a barren desert and a frail old woman. The rest are gone to equally barren deserts, either physically for those who have emigrated or morally for those who have drifted to the destroying city. Goldsmith's meaning, like his verse, lacks the weight and grandeur of the great Augustans, but one detects in *The Deserted Village*, despite its rhetoric and sentimentality, a note of genuine feeling, a response to the changing conditions of life in a society rapidly becoming industrialized and commercialized. Goldsmith grasped some of the human consequences of this transformation and moralized, tritely but truthfully, when he wrote:

> Ill fares the land, to hastening ills a prey,
> Where wealth accumulates, and men decay.

The Deserted Village contains some first faint glimmerings of Romantic sentiment, but one looks in vain in Goldsmith for other evidence in that direction. His ballad of 'Edwin and Angelina', with its typical concluding reversal, has about it a whimsical, mocking air that places it alongside the two short pieces that Johnson wrote about Thomas Warton's poems. Goldsmith's hermit is a disappointed lover, re-united with his escaping beloved (who is in male disguise!); Johnson's, called upon to say where true happiness is to be found, replies to the solemn inquirer: 'Come, my lad, and drink some beer.' Solemnity and seriousness evaporate just as surely as they do with Housman's epigrammatic assertion that 'Malt does more than Milton can/To justify God's ways to man'.

For Romantic anticipations we must turn to Gray (1716–71) and to Warton's friend, Collins. Arnold complained that Gray never spoke

out. Whilst appreciating Gray's Augustan sense of restraint more care-
fully than it appears that Arnold did, we can understand why he spoke
of the poet in that manner. Not far beneath the surface there seems often
to have been more passion than Gray was willing to reveal. The com-
parative meagreness of his output may itself, to some degree, derive
from his firm capacity for self-criticism.

An early poem such as 'Ode on a Distant Prospect of Eton College'
consists of moral statements about the abiding commonplaces—fleeting
and delusive joys, the vanity of ambition, the awareness of mortality,
and the like, dear to the heart of the eighteenth century. It is a poem
full of rhetoric—alliteration, apostrophe, inversion, repetition, paral-
lelism, personification and the rest: but one must notice the differences.
The personifications, for example, have a vivid foreboding about them
that suggests a more personal, less general terror than that which, say,
Johnson might envisage. In the formal Pindaric odes we are even
closer to the 'spontaneous' overflow of 'powerful feelings', but Gray
will not allow any such spontaneity. Restraint must be maintained, and
in *The Bard* Gray does this by resort to the device of a narrator-
character. The bard is a desperate man in a wild environment,
prophesying doom on those who have destroyed his race; yet the scene
is stylized, and so is the language. In this contrast between character
and statement we can see something of the tension operating within the
poet. The very combination of a Celtic theme and a classical form is an
interesting pointer in the same direction, though we must not forget the
suggestion reported by Johnson (in the *Life of Gray*) that the poem may
be an imitation of Nereus' prophecy of the fall of Troy in Horace (Odes
I. 15). Shenstone, writing to MacGowan in 1761, declared that 'the
public has seen all that art can do, and they want the more striking
efforts of wild, original, enthusiastic genius'. *The Bard* and his other
poems on Celtic and Scandinavian themes, interesting departures from
the classical mould of high Augustanism, were Gray's own effort in
this direction.

But when all else has been said, he will be most remembered for his
Elegy in a Country Churchyard, a poem that even so unsympathetic a critic
as Johnson was constrained to praise. Whereas the Eton College ode
was condemned for suggesting nothing 'which every beholder does not
think and feel', the *Elegy* was applauded for reasons not unlike, 'with
images which find a mirror in every mind and with sentiments to which
every bosom returns an echo'. Yet the contradiction may be more
apparent than real. Is Johnson saying that the one poem merely para-
phrases the reader's ordinary reaction, whereas the other, in Keatsian
phrase, is a wording of the reader's own highest thoughts?

The melancholy of the *Elegy* is different from Johnson's; it is less
pessimistic and, in tune with its title, more elegiac. The poet is solitary,
meditative, not the Augustan man speaking to men. The twilight
setting matches his mood, as he ponders on the eternal verities whilst
the villagers pursue their customary round and rhythm of daily and
seasonal living. The churchyard reminds him of death, the leveller,

whether it be of the 'rude forefathers of the hamlet' in their narrow graves or those of a higher rank in life, now vainly commemorated by 'storied urn or animated bust'.

Gray in his awareness of the poor manifests some of the first inklings of that democratic sentiment which is part of the Romantic view of life. The poor could not choose the glorious actions of the great and proud: theirs was opportunity denied. The great and proud chose wrongly; to them opportunity was futile. If then the poor had had the chance, they too might have chosen wrongly; and in that case opportunity would have been dangerous. Theirs was then a happy ignorance: 'Along the cool sequester'd vale of life/ They kept the noiseless tenor of their way'. The tenor of Gray's own way was itself much like this. His voice is quiet, usually serious, with sometimes a flash of humour. In reading him it is not difficult to see why Lord David Cecil called him 'exquisitely civilized'.

Pre-figuring though he does certain aspects of Romanticism, Gray always displays a sense of order and control. His work conveys the impression of finished perfection. By contrast, that of Collins (1721–59) suggests exciting potentiality. His is a more definite rejection of the modes of a previous age—'From *Waller*'s Myrtle Shades retreating', as he puts it in his 'Ode on the Poetical Character'. As that poem claims, and 'Ode to Evening' with its borrowings demonstrates, Collins leaps back over the Augustans to Milton; and the one among his own contemporaries whom he celebrates is the 'Druid', Thomson, himself the closest of all Milton's eighteenth-century imitators. Milton represented sublimity, a quality which, with the revived interest in Longinus and the revelation by Lowth of the virtues of Hebrew poetry, Collins's own century came increasingly to regard. In the 'Ode on the Poetical Character' he sees poetry as the product of God and the Fancy (or Imagination), supported by Wonder and Truth. The poet must therefore approach his art with reverence and fear. The final section of the poem reads like a draft towards some pre-Romantic *Kubla Khan*. One must not press the comparison, but neither must one ignore it. After all, Coleridge himself said of the middle section that it 'inspired and whirled [him] along with greater agitation of enthusiasm than any the most *impassioned* Scene in Schiller or Shakspere'.

Collins's first work was the collection of four *Persian Eclogues* which show him attempting an exotic setting and characters and which also exhibit an unusual use of the heroic couplet, gentle and subdued. These poems contain some traces of genuine feeling, but it is really, and only, for his Odes that Collins will, or deserves to be remembered. Collins may well have chosen to write this form, believing with Young that the ode is or ought to be 'more spontaneous and more remote from prose' than other kinds of poetry. Some are elaborate like those on Liberty, the Manners and the Passions, whilst alongside these are to be found the simple two six-line stanzas of the justly famous 'How sleep the Brave'. This freedom of form, however, was dangerous where the need for self-discipline was greater than a man like Collins possessed. Syntactical carelessness, and even sheer incoherence, have presented their problems of meaning, whilst structure often appears to display no inner sense of compulsion. As Johnson put it, Collins 'designed many works, but his great fault was irresolution'. The economy and elegance of 'How sleep the Brave' are all too rare.

Collins seems to exemplify a divided mind. Perhaps there was some truth in Housman's contention that the pressures of the eighteenth century were such that its true poets went mad or at least were eccentric. Collins did go mad and Gray was eccentric, to say nothing of Smart and Cowper and Blake. Collins's own struggle in the ode on the subject of poetry itself shows his difficulty in finding a way of saying what he actually felt. Likewise, with his several odes addressed to the various qualities and emotions one senses him striving to endow his personifications with personalities. More than capital letters they may be, they yet have a hard task to escape abstraction. When he can tear himself away from turgid generalities, he revels in the freedom of the 'Popular Superstitions of the Highlands of Scotland'. He imagines his friend, Home, living in a land where fairies, strange lays, wizards and weird sisters are not just the cheats of fancy and where the natives keep their rural faith and primal innocence. Like Johnson and Juvenal, Collins is oppressed by the city and would indeed 'change the rocks of Scotland for the Strand'; but for what different reasons! Not social or political discontent, but to save his imaginative integrity, to discover 'scenes like these, which, daring to depart/From sober truth, are still to nature true'. *There* is the full length of our journey. The next stage is Romanticism proper.

NOTE ON TEXTS

The guiding principle adopted has been to choose what is regarded as the most reliable text deriving from or near the poet's own time, and the editor acknowledges the help he has received from the editions listed in the following Bibliography. The text of 'Verses on the Death of Dr Swift' has been reprinted by kind permission of the Oxford University Press, Oxford, from *The Poems of Jonathan Swift*, edited by Harold Williams (2nd edn, © Oxford University Press, 1958); and that of 'Ode on the Popular Superstitions of the Highlands of Scotland' is based on the version printed by Miss Claire Lamont in *Review of English Studies* XIX (1968), deriving from the MS. she discovered at Aldourie Castle.

The selection from Swift is necessarily a very restricted part of his voluminous output. The poetry of all the others was of much more limited extent and, whilst with the exception of Collins none is here presented complete, care has been taken to exclude only the most occasional of their verse. The poems are arranged in chronological order.

Select Bibliography

GENERAL REFERENCE

James Sutherland, *A Preface to Eighteenth-Century Poetry*, Oxford, 1948; Ian Jack, *Augustan Satire*, Oxford, 1952; Rachel Trickett, *The Honest Muse*, Oxford, 1967.

INDIVIDUAL POETS

SWIFT. WORKS: *Poems*, ed. H. Williams, 3 vols., 2nd edn, Oxford, 1958; *Poetical Works*, ed. H. Davis, Oxford, 1967. BIOGRAPHICAL AND CRITICAL: M. Johnson, *The Sin of Wit*, Syracuse U.P., 1950; H. Davis, *Jonathan Swift*, Columbia U.P., 1962.

JOHNSON. WORKS: *Poems*, ed. D. Nichol Smith and E. L. McAdam, 2nd edn, Oxford, 1974; *The Complete English Poems*, ed. J. D. Fleeman, Penguin, 1971. BIOGRAPHICAL AND CRITICAL: T. S. Eliot, 'Eighteenth-Century Poetry', *From Dryden to Johnson*, ed. B. Ford, Penguin, 1957; F. R. Leavis, 'Johnson as Poet', *The Common Pursuit*, Chatto, 1952.

GOLDSMITH. WORKS: *Works*, ed. A. Friedman, 5 vols., Oxford, 1966 (Poems in Vol. 4); *Poems and Plays*, ed. Tom Davis, Everyman's University Library, 1975; see also under Gray. BIOGRAPHICAL AND CRITICAL: A. Lytton Sells, *Oliver Goldsmith, His Life and Works*, Allen and Unwin, 1974.

GRAY. WORKS: *Complete Poems*, ed. H. W. Starr and J. R. Hendricksen, Oxford, 1966; *Poems of Gray, Collins and Goldsmith*, ed. R. Lonsdale, Longman, 1969. BIOGRAPHICAL AND CRITICAL: W. P. Jones, *Thomas Gray, Scholar*, Harvard U.P., 1937, reprinted 1965; G. Hough, *The Romantic Poets*, Hutchinson, 1953; P. M. Spacks, *The Poetry of Vision*, Harvard U.P., 1967.

COLLINS. WORKS: see under Gray. BIOGRAPHICAL AND CRITICAL: E. G. Ainsworth, *Poor Collins*, Oxford, 1937; P. M. Spacks, *The Poetry of Vision*, Harvard U.P., 1967.

Jonathan Swift (1667–1745)

Swift was probably born in Dublin, the posthumous son of an English lawyer. He was educated at Kilkenny and Trinity College, Dublin. He migrated to England in 1689 and soon afterwards became private secretary to Sir William Temple, a former diplomat and a Whig. Although ordained to Kilroot in Ireland in 1696, Swift remained at Moor Park (Surrey) with Temple until 1699, helping his patron in the latter's battle of the Ancients and Moderns against Bentley and Wotton. It was at Moor Park that Swift came to know Esther Johnson (Stella).

He was appointed prebendary of St Patrick's Cathedral, Dublin, in 1700 and spent the next fourteen years alternating between London and Ireland. He came to exercise considerable political influence, particularly after his allegiance to the Tories led by Harley (Oxford) and St John (Bolingbroke). In the later part of this period he met Esther Vanhomrigh, whom he celebrates in *Cadenus and Vanessa*.

Swift's hopes fell with the Tories at the death of Queen Anne. In 1713 he had been made Dean of St Patrick's and the rest of his life was spent in Ireland amid increasing bitterness. Some of his polemical works such as *The Drapier's Letters* demonstrate his Irish patriotism, but it is *Gulliver's Travels* (1726) for which, with his other great work, *A Tale of a Tub* (1704), he is chiefly remembered. Together they display his mordant, uncompromising view of man. After 1738 he suffered increasingly from mental illness and died in 1745.

TO THEIR EXCELLENCIES THE *LORDS JUSTICES* OF IRELAND

The Humble Petition of Frances Harris, Who must Starve, and Die a Maid if it miscarries

Anno 1700

Humbly Sheweth

That I went to warm my self in Lady *Betty*'s Chamber, because I was cold,
And I had in a Purse, seven Pound, four Shillings and six Pence, besides Farthings, in Money, and Gold;
So because I had been buying things for my *Lady* last Night,
I was resolved to tell my Money, to see if it was right:

5   Now you must know, because my Trunk has a very bad Lock,
     Therefore all the Money I have, which, *God* knows, is a very
       small Stock,
     I keep in a Pocket ty'd about my Middle, next my Smock.
     So when I went to put up my Purse, as *God* would have it, my
      Smock was unript,
     And, instead of putting it into my Pocket, down it slipt:
10   Then the Bell rung, and I went down to put my *Lady* to Bed,
     And, *God* knows, I thought my Money was as safe as my Maiden-
      head.
     So when I came up again, I found my Pocket feel very light,
     But when I search'd, and miss'd my Purse, *Lord!* I thought I
      should have sunk outright:
     Lord! Madam, says *Mary*, how d'ye do? Indeed, said I, never
      worse;
15   But pray, *Mary*, can you tell what I have done with my Purse!
     Lord help me, said *Mary*, I never stirr'd out of this Place!
     Nay, said I, I had it in Lady *Betty*'s Chamber, that's a plain
      Case.
     So *Mary* got me to Bed, and cover'd me up warm,
     However, she stole away my Garters, that I might do my self no
      Harm:
20   So I tumbl'd and toss'd all Night, as you may very well think,
     But hardly ever set my Eyes together, or slept a Wink.
     So I was a-dream'd, methought, that we went and search'd the
      Folks round,
     And in a Corner of Mrs *Duke*'s Box, ty'd in a Rag, the Money was
      found.
     So next Morning we told *Whittle*, and he fell a Swearing;
25   Then my Dame *Wadgar* came, and she, you know, is thick of
      Hearing;
     Dame, said I, as loud as I could bawl, do you know what a Loss I
      have had?
     Nay, said she, my Lord *Collway*'s Folks are all very sad,
     For my Lord *Dromedary* comes a *Tuesday* without fail;
     Pugh! said I, but that's not the Business that I ail.
30   Says *Cary*, says he, I have been a Servant this Five and Twenty
      Years, come Spring,
     And in all the Places I liv'd, I never heard of such a Thing.
     Yes, says the *Steward*, I remember when I was at my Lady
      Shrewsbury's,
     Such a thing as this happen'd, just about the time of *Gooseberries*.
     So I went to the Party suspected, and I found her full of Grief;
35   (Now you must know, of all Things in the World, I hate a Thief.)
     However, I was resolv'd to bring the Discourse slily about,
     Mrs *Dukes* said I, here's an ugly Accident has happen'd out;
     'Tis not that I value the Money three Skips of a Louse;
     But the Thing I stand upon, is the Credit of the House;

40 'Tis true, seven Pound, four Shillings, and six Pence, makes a great
    hole in my Wages,
Besides, as they say, Service is no Inheritance in these Ages.
Now, Mrs *Dukes*, you know, and every Body understands,
That tho' 'tis hard to judge, yet Money can't go without Hands.
The *Devil* take me, said she, (blessing her self), if ever I saw't!
45 So she roar'd like a *Bedlam*, as tho' I had call'd her all to naught;
So you know, what could I say to her any more,
I e'en left her, and came away as wise as I was before.
Well: But then they would have had me gone to the Cunning
    Man;
No, said I, 'tis the same Thing, the *Chaplain* will be here anon.
50 So the *Chaplain* came in. Now the Servants say, he is my Sweet-
    heart,
Because he's always in my Chamber, and I always take his Part;
So, as the *Devil* would have it, before I was aware, out I blunder'd,
Parson, said I, can you cast a *Nativity*, when a Body's plunder'd?
(Now you must know, he hates to be call'd *Parson*, like the *Devil*.)
55 Truly, says he, Mrs *Nab*, it might become you to be more civil:
If your Money be gone, as a Learned *Divine* says, d'ye see,
You are no *Text* for my Handling, so take that from me:
I was never taken for a *Conjurer* before, I'd have you to know.
Lord, said I, don't be angry, I am sure I never thought you so;
60 You know, I honour the Cloth, I design to be a *Parson*'s Wife,
I never took one in *Your Coat* for a *Conjurer* in all my life.
With that, he twisted his Girdle at me like a Rope, as who should
    say,
Now you may go hang your self for me, and so went away.
Well; I thought I should have swoon'd: *Lord*, said I, what shall I
    do?
65 I have lost my *Money*, and I shall lose my *True-Love* too.
So, my *Lord* call'd me; *Harry*, said my *Lord*, don't cry,
I'll give something towards thy Loss; and says my *Lady*, so will I.
Oh but, said I, what if after all the Chaplain won't *come to*?
For that, he said, (an't please your *Excellencies*) I must Petition
    You.

70 The Premises tenderly consider'd, I desire your *Excellencies*
    Protection,
And that I may have a Share in next *Sunday*'s Collection:
And over and above, that I may have your *Excellencies* Letter,
With an Order for the *Chaplain* aforesaid; or instead of Him, a
    Better:
And then your poor *Petitioner*, both Night and Day,
75 Or the *Chaplain*, (for 'tis his *Trade*) as in Duty bound, shall ever
    pray.

Jonathan Swift

BAUCIS AND PHILEMON

Imitated, From the Eighth Book of OVID

In antient Times, as Story tells,
The Saints would often leave their Cells,
And strole about, but hide their Quality,
To try good People's Hospitality.

5   It happen'd on a Winter Night,
(As Authors of the Legend write;)
Two Brother Hermits, Saints by Trade,
Taking their *Tour* in Masquerade;
Disguis'd in tatter'd Habits, went
10 To a small Village down in *Kent*;
Where, in the Strolers Canting Strain,
They beg'd from Door to Door in vain;
Try'd ev'ry Tone might Pity win,
But not a Soul would let them in.

15   Our wand'ring Saints in woful State,
Treated at this ungodly Rate,
Having thro' all the Village pass'd,
To a small Cottage came at last:
Where dwelt a good old honest Yeoman,
20 Call'd, in the Neighbourhood, *Philemon*.
Who kindly did the Saints invite
In his Poor Hut to pass the Night;
And then the Hospitable Sire
Bid *Goody Baucis* mend the Fire;
25 While He from out the Chimney took
A Flitch of Bacon off the Hook;
And freely from the fattest Side
Cut out large Slices to be fry'd:
Then stept aside to fetch 'em Drink,
30 Fill'd a large Jug up to the Brink;
And saw it fairly twice go round;
Yet (what was wonderful) they found,
'Twas still replenished to the Top,
As if they ne'er had toucht a Drop.
35 The good old Couple was amaz'd,
And often on each other gaz'd;
For both were frighted to the Heart,
And just began to cry;—What art!
Then softly turn'd aside to view,
40 Whether the Lights were burning blue.

The gentle *Pilgrims* soon aware on't,
Told 'em their Calling, and their Errant:
Good Folks, you need not be afraid,
We are but *Saints*, the Hermits said;
45 No Hurt shall come to You, or Yours;
But, for that Pack of churlish Boors,
Not fit to live on Christian Ground,
They and their Houses shall be drown'd:
Whilst you shall see your Cottage rise,
50 And grow a Church before your Eyes.

They scarce had Spoke; when, fair and soft,
The Roof began to mount aloft;
Aloft rose ev'ry Beam and Rafter,
The heavy Wall climb'd slowly after.

55 The Chimney widen'd, and grew higher,
Became a Steeple with a Spire.

The Kettle to the Top was hoist,
And there stood fast'ned to a Joist:
But with the Upside down, to shew
60 Its Inclination for below;
In vain; for some Superior Force
Apply'd at Bottom, stops its Course,
Doom'd ever in Suspence to dwell,
'Tis now no Kettle, but a Bell.

65 A wooden Jack, which had almost
Lost, by Disuse, the Art to Roast,
A sudden Alteration feels,
Increas'd by new Intestine Wheels:
And what exalts the Wonder more,
70 The Number made the Motion slow'r:
The Flyer, tho't had Leaden Feet,
Turn'd round so quick, you scarce cou'd see't;
Now slacken'd by some secret Power,
Can hardly move an Inch an Hour.
75 The Jack and Chimney near ally'd,
Had never left each other's Side;
The Chimney to a Steeple grown,
The Jack wou'd not be left alone,
But up against the Steeple rear'd,
80 Became a Clock, and still adher'd:
And still its Love to Houshold Cares
By a shrill Voice at Noon declares,
Warning the Cook-maid, not to burn
That Roast-meat which it cannot turn.

85   The Groaning Chair was seen to crawl
Like an huge Snail half up the Wall;
There stuck aloft, in Publick View,
And with small Change, a Pulpit grew.

    The Porringers, that in a Row
90   Hung high, and made a glitt'ring Show,
To a less Noble Substance chang'd,
Were now but Leathern Buckets rang'd.

    The Ballads pasted on the Wall,
Of *Joan* of *France*, and *English Moll*,
95   Fair *Rosamond*, and *Robin Hood*,
The *Little Children in the Wood*:
Now seem'd to look abundance better,
Improv'd in Picture, Size, and Letter;
And high in Order plac'd, describe
100   The Heraldry of ev'ry Tribe.

    A Bedstead of the Antique Mode,
Compact of Timber many a Load,
Such as our Grandsires wont to use,
Was Metamorphos'd into Pews;
105   Which still their antient Nature keep;
By lodging Folks dispos'd to Sleep.

    The Cottage by such Feats as these,
Grown to a Church by just Degrees,
The Hermits then desire their Host
110   To ask for what he fancy'd most:
Philemon, having paus'd a while,
Return'd 'em Thanks in homely Stile;
Then said; my House is grown so Fine,
Methinks, I still wou'd call it mine:
115   I'm Old, and fain wou'd live at Ease,
Make me the *Parson*, if you please.

    He spoke, and presently he feels,
His Grazier's Coat fall down his Heels;
He sees, yet hardly can believe,
120   About each Arm a Pudding-sleeve;
His Waistcoat to a Cassock grew,
And both assum'd a Sable Hue;
But being Old, continu'd just
As Thread-bare, and as full of Dust.
125   His Talk was now of *Tythes* and *Dues*,
Could smoke his Pipe, and read the News;

Knew how to preach old Sermons next,
Vampt in the Preface and the Text;
At Christnings well could act his Part,
130 And had the Service all by Heart;
Wish'd Women might have Children fast,
And thought whose *Sow* had *farrow'd* last:
Against *Dissenters* would repine,
And stood up firm for *Right Divine*:
135 Found his Head fill'd with many a System,
But Classick Authors—he ne'er miss'd 'em.

Thus having furbish'd up a Parson,
Dame *Baucis* next, they play'd their Farce on:
Instead of Home-spun Coifs were seen,
140 Good Pinners edg'd with Colberteen:
Her Petticoat transform'd apace,
Became Black Sattin, Flounc'd with Lace.
Plain *Goody* would no longer down,
'Twas *Madam*, in her Grogram Gown.
145 *Philemon* was in great Surprize,
And hardly could believe his Eyes,
Amaz'd to see Her look so Prim,
And she admir'd as much at Him.

Thus, happy in their Change of Life,
150 Were several Years the Man and Wife,
When on a Day, which prov'd their last,
Discoursing o'er old Stories past,
They went by chance, amidst their Talk,
To the Church-yard, to fetch a walk;
155 When *Baucis* hastily cry'd out;
My Dear, I see your Forehead sprout:
Sprout, quoth the Man, What's this you tell us?
I hope you don't believe me Jealous:
But yet, methinks, I feel it true;
160 And really, Yours is budding too—
Nay,—now I cannot stir my Foot:
It feels as if 'twere taking Root.

Description would but tire my Muse:
In short, they both were turn'd to *Yews*.
165 Old Good-man *Dobson* of the Green
Remembers he the Trees has seen;
He'll talk of them from Noon to Night,
And goes with Folks to shew the Sight:
On *Sundays*, after Ev'ning Prayer,
170 He gathers all the Parish there;

Jonathan Swift

Points out the Place of either *Yew*;
Here *Baucis*, there *Philemon* grew.
Till once, a Parson of our Town,
To mend his Barn, cut *Baucis* down;
175   At which, 'tis hard to be believ'd,
How much the other Tree was griev'd,
Grew Scrubby, dy'd a-top, was stunted:
So, the next Parson stub'd and burnt it.

A DESCRIPTION OF THE MORNING

The Tatler, Numb. 9. From Thursday April 28. to Saturday April 30. 1709

Now hardly here and there a Hackney-Coach
Appearing, show'd the Ruddy Morns Approach.
Now *Betty* from her Masters Bed had flown,
And softly stole to discompose her own.
5   And slipshod Prentice from his Masters Door,
Had par'd the Dirt, and Sprinkled round the Floor.
Now *Moll* had whirl'd her Mop with dext'rous Airs,
Prepar'd to Scrub the Entry and the Stairs.
The Youth with Broomy Stumps began to trace
10   The Kennel-Edge, where Wheels had worn the Place.
The Small-coal-Man was heard with Cadence deep,
'Till drown'd in Shriller Notes of *Chimney-sweep*.
Duns at his Lordships Gate began to meet,
And Brickdust *Moll* had Scream'd through half a Street.
15   The Turnkey now his Flock returning sees,
Duly let out a Nights to Steal for Fees.
The watchful Bailiffs take their silent Stands,
And School-Boys lag with Satchels in their Hands.

CADENUS AND VANESSA

The *Shepherds* and the *Nymphs* were seen
Pleading before the *Cyprian* Queen.
The Council for the Fair began,
Accusing that false Creature, *Man*.

5   The Brief with weighty Crimes was charg'd,
      On which the Pleader much enlarg'd;
      That *Cupid* now has lost his Art,
      Or blunts the Point of ev'ry Dart;
      His Altar now no longer smokes,
10   His Mother's Aid no Youth invokes:
      This tempts Free-thinkers to refine,
      And bring in doubt their Pow'r divine;
      Now Love is dwindled to Intrigue,
      And Marriage grown a Money-League.
15   Which Crimes aforesaid (*with her Leave*)
      Were (*as he humbly did conceive*)
      Against our Sov'reign Lady's Peace,
      Against the Statute in that Case,
      Against her Dignity and Crown:
20   Then pray'd an Answer, and sat down.

      The *Nymphs* with Scorn beheld their Foes:
      When the Defendant's Council rose,
      And, what no Lawyer ever lack'd,
      With Impudence own'd all the Fact.
25   But, what the gentlest Heart would vex,
      Laid all the Fault on t'other Sex.
      That modern Love is no such Thing
      As what those antient Poets sing;
      A Fire celestial, chaste, refin'd,
30   Conceiv'd and kindled in the Mind,
      Which having found an equal Flame,
      Unites, and both become the same,
      In different Breasts together burn,
      Together both to Ashes turn.
35   But Women now feel no such Fire,
      And only know the gross Desire;
      Their Passions move in lower Spheres,
      Wher-e'er Caprice or Folly steers.
      A Dog, a Parrot, or an Ape,
40   Or some worse Brute in human Shape,
      Engross the Fancies of the Fair,
      A few soft Moments they can spare,
      From Visits to receive and pay,
      From Scandal, Politicks, and Play,
45   From Fans, and Flounces, and Brocades,
      From Equipage and Park-Parades,
      From all the thousand Female Toys,
      From every Trifle that employs
      The out or inside of their Heads,
50   Between their Toylets and their Beds.

In a dull Stream, which moving slow
You hardly see the Current flow,
If a small Breeze obstructs the Course,
It whirls about for Want of Force,
55 And in its narrow Circle gathers
Nothing but Chaff, and Straws, and Feathers:
The Current of a Female Mind
Stops thus, and turns with ev'ry Wind;
Thus whirling round, together draws
60 Fools, Fops, and Rakes, for Chaff and Straws.
Hence we conclude, no Women's Hearts
Are won by Virtue, Wit, and Parts;
Nor are the Men of Sense to blame,
For Breasts incapable of Flame;
65 The Fault must on the *Nymphs* be plac'd,
Grown so corrupted in their Taste.

The Pleader having spoke his best
Had Witness ready to attest,
Who fairly could on Oath depose,
70 When Questions on the Fact arose,
That ev'ry Article was true;
Nor further those Deponents knew:
Therefore he humbly would insist,
The Bill might be with Costs dismist.

75 The Cause appear'd of so much Weight,
That *Venus*, from her Judgment-Seat,
Desir'd them not to talk so loud,
Else she must interpose a Cloud:
For if the Heav'nly Folk should know
80 These Pleadings in the Courts below,
That Mortals here disdain to love;
She ne'er could shew her Face above.
For Gods, their Betters, are too wise
To value that which Men despise.
85 And then, said she, my Son and I
Must strole in Air 'twixt Land and Sky;
Or else, shut out from Heaven and Earth,
Fly to the Sea, my Place of Birth;
There live with daggl'd *Mermaids* pent,
90 And keep on Fish perpetual *Lent*.

But since the Case appear'd so nice,
She thought it best to take Advice.
The *Muses*, by their King's Permission,
Tho' Foes to Love, attend the Session,

95   And on the Right Hand took their Places
In Order; on the Left, the *Graces*:
To whom she might her Doubts propose
On all Emergencies that rose.
The *Muses* oft were seen to frown;
100   The *Graces* half asham'd look'd down;
And 'twas observ'd, there were but few
Of either Sex, among the Crew,
Whom she or her Assessors knew.
The Goddess soon began to see
105   Things were not ripe for a Decree,
And said she must consult her Books,
The Lovers *Fleta's, Bractons, Cokes*.
First to a dapper Clerk she beckon'd,
To turn to *Ovid*, Book the Second;
110   She then referr'd them to a Place
In *Virgil* (*vide Dido's* Case:)
As for *Tibullus's* Reports,
They never pass'd for Law in Courts;
For *Cowley's* Briefs, and Pleas of *Waller*,
115   Still their Authority was smaller.

There was on both Sides much to say:
She'd hear the Cause another Day,
And so she did, and then a Third,
She heard it—there she kept her Word;
120   But with Rejoinders and Replies,
Long Bills, and Answers, stuff'd with Lies,
Demur, Imparlance, and Essoign,
The Parties ne'er could Issue join:
For Sixteen Years the Cause was spun,
125   And then stood where it first begun.

Now, gentle *Clio*, sing or say,
What *Venus* meant by this Delay.
The Goddess much perplex'd in Mind,
To see her Empire thus declin'd,
130   When first this grand Debate arose
Above her Wisdom to compose,
Conceiv'd a Project in her Head,
To work her Ends; which if it sped,
Wou'd shew the Merits of the Cause,
135   Far better than consulting Laws.

In a glad Hour *Lucina's* Aid
Produc'd on Earth a wond'rous Maid,
On whom the Queen of Love was bent
To try a new Experiment:

140   She threw her Law-books on the Shelf,
        And thus debated with herself.

            Since Men alledge they ne'er can find
        Those Beauties in a Female Mind,
        Which raise a Flame that will endure
145   For ever, uncorrupt and pure;
        If 'tis with Reason they complain,
        This Infant shall restore my Reign.
        I'll search where ev'ry Virtue dwells,
        From Courts inclusive, down to Cells,
150   What Preachers talk, or Sages write,
        These I will gather and unite,
        And represent them to Mankind
        Collected in that Infant's Mind.

            This said, she plucks in Heav'ns high Bow'rs
155   A Sprig of *Amaranthine* Flow'rs,
        In Nectar thrice infuses Bays,
        Three times refin'd in *Titan*'s Rays:
        Then calls the *Graces* to her Aid,
        And sprinkles thrice the new-born Maid.
160   From whence the tender Skin assumes
        A Sweetness above all Perfumes;
        From whence a Cleanliness remains,
        Incapable of outward Stains;
        From whence that Decency of Mind,
165   So lovely in the Female Kind,
        Where not one careless Thought intrudes,
        Less modest than the Speech of Prudes:
        Where never Blush was call'd in Aid,
        That spurious Virtue in a Maid,
170   A Virtue but at second-hand;
        They blush because they understand.

            The *Graces* next wou'd act their Part,
        And shew'd but little of their Art;
        Their Work was half already done,
175   The Child with native Beauty shone,
        The outward Form no Help requir'd:
        Each breathing on her thrice, inspir'd
        That gentle, soft, engaging Air,
        Which in old Times adorn'd the Fair;
180   And said, '*Vanessa* be the Name,
        By which thou shalt be known to Fame:
        Vanessa, by the Gods enroll'd:
        Her Name on Earth —— shall not be told.'

But still the Work was not compleat,
185   When *Venus* thought on a Deceit:
Drawn by her Doves, away she flies,
And finds out *Pallas* in the Skies:
Dear *Pallas*, I have been this Morn
To see a lovely Infant born:
190   A Boy in yonder Isle below,
So like my own, without his Bow,
By Beauty cou'd your Heart be won,
You'd swear it is *Apollo*'s Son;
But it shall ne'er be said, a Child
195   So hopeful, has by me been spoil'd;
I have enough besides to spare,
And give him wholly to your Care.

Wisdom's above suspecting Wiles:
The Queen of Learning gravely smiles,
200   Down from *Olympus* comes with Joy,
Mistakes *Vanessa* for a Boy;
Then sows within her tender Mind
Seeds long unknown to Womankind,
For manly Bosoms chiefly fit,
205   The Seeds of Knowledge, Judgment, Wit.
Her Soul was suddenly endu'd
With Justice, Truth and Fortitude;
With Honour, which no Breath can Stain,
Which Malice must attack in vain;
210   With open Heart and bounteous Hand:
But *Pallas* here was at a Stand;
She knew in our degen'rate Days
Bare Virtue could not live on Praise,
That Meat must be with Money bought;
215   She therefore, upon second Thought,
Infus'd, yet as it were by Stealth,
Some small Regard for State and Wealth:
Of which, as she grew up, there stay'd
A Tincture in the prudent Maid:
220   She manag'd her Estate with Care,
Yet lik'd three Footmen to her Chair.
But lest he shou'd neglect his Studies
Like a young Heir, the thrifty Goddess
(For fear young Master shou'd be spoil'd,)
225   Wou'd use him like a younger Child;
And, after long computing, found
'Twou'd come to just Five Thousand Pound.

The Queen of Love was pleas'd, and proud,
To see *Vanessa* thus endow'd;

230 She doubted not but such a Dame
Thro' ev'ry Breast wou'd dart a Flame;
That ev'ry rich and lordly Swain
With Pride wou'd drag about her Chain;
That Scholars wou'd forsake their Books
235 To study bright *Vanessa*'s Looks:
As she advanc'd, that Womankind
Wou'd by her Model form their Mind,
And all their Conduct wou'd be try'd
By her, as an unerring Guide.
240 Offending Daughters oft would hear
Vanessa's Praise rung in their Ear:
Miss *Betty*, when she does a Fault,
Lets fall her Knife, or spills the Salt,
Will thus be by her Mother chid,
245 ''Tis what *Vanessa* never did.'
Thus by the Nymphs and Swains ador'd,
My Pow'r shall be again restor'd,
And happy Lovers bless my Reign ——
So *Venus* hop'd, but hop'd in vain.

250 For when in time the *Martial Maid*
Found out the Trick that *Venus* play'd,
She shakes her Helm, she knits her Brows,
And fir'd with Indignation vows,
To-morrow, ere the setting Sun,
255 She'd all undo, that she had done.

But in the Poets we may find,
A wholesome Law, Time out of mind,
Had been confirm'd by Fate's Decree;
That Gods, of whatso'er Degree,
260 Resume not what themselves have giv'n,
Or any Brother-God in Heav'n:
Which keeps the Peace among the Gods,
Or they must always be at Odds.
And *Pallas*, if she broke the Laws,
265 Must yield her Foe the stronger Cause;
A Shame to one so much ador'd
For Wisdom, at *Jove*'s Council-Board.
Besides, she fear'd the Queen of Love
Wou'd meet with better Friends above.
270 And tho, she must with Grief reflect,
To see a Mortal Virgin deck'd
With Graces, hitherto unknown
To Female Breasts, except her own;
Yet she wou'd act as best became
275 A Goddess of unspotted Fame:

She knew, by Augury Divine,
Venus wou'd fail in her Design:
She study'd well the Point, and found
Her Foe's Conclusions were not sound,
280   From Premisses erroneous brought,
And therefore the Deductions nought,
And must have contrary Effects
To what her treach'rous Foe expects.

In proper Season *Pallas* meets
285   The Queen of Love, whom thus she greets,
(For Gods, we are by *Homer* told,
Can in Celestial Language scold)
Perfidious Goddess! but in vain
You form'd this Project in your Brain,
290   A Project for thy Talents fit,
With much Deceit and little Wit;
Thou hast, as thou shalt quickly see,
Deceiv'd thy self, instead of me;
For how can Heav'nly Wisdom prove
295   An Instrument to earthly Love?
Know'st thou not yet that Men commence
Thy Votaries, for Want of Sense?
Nor shall *Vanessa* be the Theme
To manage thy abortive Scheme;
300   She'll prove the greatest of thy Foes:
And yet I scorn to interpose,
But using neither Skill, nor Force,
Leave all Things to their Nat'ral Course.

The Goddess thus pronounc'd her Doom:
305   When, lo! *Vanessa* in her Bloom,
Advanc'd like *Atalanta*'s Star,
But rarely seen, and seen from far:
In a new World with Caution stept,
Watch'd all the Company she kept,
310   Well knowing from the Books she read
What dangerous Paths young Virgins tread;
Wou'd seldom at the Park appear,
Nor saw the Play-House twice a Year;
Yet not incurious, was inclin'd
315   To know the Converse of Mankind.

First issu'd from Perfumers Shops
A Croud of fashionable Fops;
They ask'd her, how she lik'd the Play,
Then told the Tattle of the Day,

320 A Duel fought last Night at Two,
 About a Lady —— You know who;
 Mention'd a new *Italian*, come
 Either from *Muscovy* or *Rome*;
 Gave Hints of who and who's together;
325 Then fell to talking of the Weather:
 Last Night was so extremely fine,
 The Ladies walk'd till after Nine.
 Then in soft Voice and Speech absurd,
 With Nonsense ev'ry second Word,
330 With Fustian from exploded Plays,
 They celebrate her Beauty's Praise,
 Run o'er their Cant of stupid Lies,
 And tell the Murders of her Eyes.

 With silent Scorn *Vanessa* sat,
335 Scarce list'ning to their idle Chat;
 Further than sometimes by a Frown,
 When they grew pert, to pull them down.
 At last she spitefully was bent
 To try their Wisdom's full Extent;
340 And said, she valu'd nothing less
 Than Titles, Figure, Shape and Dress;
 That, Merit should be chiefly plac'd
 In Judgment, Knowledge, Wit, and Taste;
 And these, she offer'd to dispute,
345 Alone distinguish'd Man from Brute:
 That, present Times have no Pretence
 To Virtue, in the Noblest Sense,
 By *Greeks* and *Romans* understood,
 To perish for our Country's Good.
350 She nam'd the antient Heroes round,
 Explain'd for what they were renown'd;
 Then spoke with Censure, or Applause,
 Of foreign Customs, Rites, and Laws;
 Thro' Nature, and thro' Art she rang'd,
355 And gracefully her Subject chang'd:
 In vain: her Hearers had no Share
 In all she spoke, except to stare.
 Their Judgment was upon the Whole,
 —That Lady is the dullest Soul—
360 Then tipt their Forehead in a Jeer,
 As who should say—she wants it here;
 She may be handsome, young and rich,
 But none will burn her for a Witch.

 A Party next of glitt'ring Dames,
365 From round the Purlieus of *St James*,

Came early, out of pure Good-will,
To see the Girl in Deshabille.
Their Clamour 'lighting from their Chairs,
Grew louder, all the Way up Stairs;
370 And Entrance loudest; where they found
The Room with Volumes litter'd round;
Vanessa held *Montaigne*, and read,
Whilst Mrs *Susan* comb'd her Head:
They call'd for Tea and Chocolate,
375 And fell into their usual Chat,
Discoursing with important Face,
On Ribbons, Fans, and Gloves and Lace;
Shew'd Patterns just from *India* brought,
And gravely ask'd her what she thought,
380 Whether the Red or Green were best,
And what they cost? *Vanessa* guess'd,
As came into her Fancy first,
Nam'd half the Rates, and lik'd the worst.
To Scandal next —— What aukward Thing
385 Was that, last *Sunday* in the Ring?
—— I'm sorry *Mopsa* breaks so fast;
I said her Face would never last.
Corinna with that youthful Air,
Is thirty, and a Bit to spare.
390 Her Fondness for a certain Earl
Began, when I was but a Girl.
Phyllis, who but a Month ago
Was marry'd to the *Tunbridge* Beau,
I saw coquetting t'other Night
395 In publick with that odious Knight.

They railly'd next *Vanessa*'s Dress;
That Gown was made for Old Queen *Bess*.
Dear Madam, Let me set your Head:
Don't you intend to put on Red?
400 A Pettycoat without a Hoop!
Sure, you are not asham'd to stoop;
With handsome Garters at your Knees,
No matter what a Fellow sees.

Fill'd with Disdain, with Rage inflam'd,
405 Both of her self and Sex asham'd,
The Nymph stood silent out of spight,
Nor wou'd vouchsafe to set them right.
Away the fair Detractors went,
And gave, by turns, their Censures Vent.
410 She's not so handsome, in my Eyes:
For Wit, I wonder where it lies.

She's fair and clean, and that's the most;
But why proclaim her for a Toast?
A Baby Face, no Life, nor Airs,
415   But what she learnt at Country Fairs;
Scarce knows what Diff'rence is between
Rich *Flanders* Lace, and Colberteen.
I'll undertake my little *Nancy*
In *Flounces* has a better Fancy.
420   With all her Wit, I wou'd not ask
Her Judgment, how to buy a Mask.
We begg'd her but to patch her Face,
She never hit one proper Place;
Which every Girl at five Years old
425   Can do as soon as she is told.
I own, that out-of-fashion Stuff
Becomes the *Creature* well enough.
The Girl might pass, if we cou'd get her
To know the World a little better.
430   (*To know the World!* a modern Phrase,
For Visits, Ombre, Balls and Plays.)

Thus, to the World's perpetual Shame,
The *Queen of Beauty* lost her Aim.
Too late with Grief she understood,
435   *Pallas* had done more Harm than Good;
For great Examples are but vain,
Where Ignorance begets Disdain.
Both Sexes, arm'd with Guilt and Spite,
Against *Vanessa*'s Pow'r unite;
440   To copy her, few Nymphs aspir'd;
Her Virtues fewer Swains admir'd:
So Stars beyond a certain Height
Give Mortals neither Heat nor Light.

Yet some of either Sex, endow'd
445   With Gifts superior to the Crowd,
With Virtue, Knowledge, Taste and Wit,
She condescended to admit:
With pleasing Arts she could reduce
Mens Talents to their proper Use;
450   And with Address each Genius held
To that wherein it most excell'd;
Thus making others Wisdom known,
Cou'd please them, and improve her own.
A modest Youth said something new,
455   She plac'd it in the strongest View.
All humble Worth she strove to raise;
Would not be prais'd, yet lov'd to praise.

The Learned met with free Approach,
Although they came not in a Coach.
460   Some Clergy too she wou'd allow,
Nor quarrell'd at their aukward Bow.
But this was for *Cadenus'* sake;
A Gownman of a diff'rent Make;
Whom *Pallas*, once *Vanessa*'s Tutor,
465   Had fix'd on for her Coadjutor.

But *Cupid*, full of Mischief, longs
To vindicate his Mother's Wrongs.
On *Pallas* all Attempts are vain;
One way he knows to give her Pain:
470   Vows, on *Vanessa*'s Heart to take
Due Vengeance, for her Patron's sake.
Those early Seeds by *Venus* sown,
In spight of *Pallas*, now were grown;
And *Cupid* hop'd they wou'd improve
475   By Time, and ripen into Love.
The Boy made use of all his Craft,
In vain discharging many a Shaft,
Pointed at Col'nels, Lords, and Beaux;
Cadenus warded off the Blows:
480   For placing still some Books betwixt,
The Darts were in the Cover fix'd,
Or often blunted and recoil'd,
On *Plutarch*'s Morals struck, were spoil'd.

The Queen of Wisdom cou'd foresee,
485   But not prevent the Fates decree;
And human Caution tries in vain
To break that Adamantine Chain.
Vanessa, tho' by *Pallas* taught,
By *Love* invulnerable thought,
490   Searching in Books for Wisdom's Aid,
Was, in the very Search, betray'd.

Cupid, tho' all his Darts were lost,
Yet still resolv'd to spare no Cost;
He could not answer to his Fame
495   The Triumphs of that stubborn Dame,
A Nymph so hard to be subdu'd,
Who neither was Coquette nor Prude.
I find, said he, she wants a Doctor,
Both to adore her and instruct her;
500   I'll give her what she most admires,
Among those venerable Sires.

Cadenus is a Subject fit,
Grown old in Politicks and Wit;
Caress'd by Ministers of State,
505   Of half Mankind the Dread and Hate.
Whate'er Vexations Love attend,
She need no Rivals apprehend.
Her Sex, with universal Voice,
Must laugh at her capricious Choice.

510   *Cadenus* many things had writ;
Vanessa much esteem'd his Wit,
And call'd for his Poetick Works;
Mean time the Boy in secret lurks,
And while the Book was in her Hand,
515   The Urchin from his private Stand
Took Aim, and shot with all his Strength
A Dart of such prodigious Length,
It pierc'd the feeble Volume thro',
And deep transfix'd her Bosom too,
520   Some Lines, more moving than the rest,
Stuck to the Point that pierc'd her Breast;
And, born directly to her Heart,
With Pains unknown increas'd the Smart.

Vanessa, not in Years a Score,
525   Dreams of a Gown of forty-four;
Imaginary Charms can find,
In Eyes with Reading almost blind;
Cadenus now no more appears
Declin'd in Health, advanc'd in Years.
530   She fancies Musick in his Tongue,
Nor further looks, but thinks him young.
What Mariner is not afraid,
To venture in a Ship decay'd?
What Planter will attempt to yoke
535   A Sapling with a falling Oak?
As Years increase, she brighter shines,
Cadenus with each Day declines,
And he must fall a Prey to Time,
While she continues in her Prime.

540   *Cadenus*, common Forms apart,
In every Scene had kept his Heart;
Had sigh'd and languish'd, vow'd, and writ,
For Pastime, or to shew his Wit;
But Time, and Books, and State Affairs
545   Had spoil'd his fashionable Airs;

He now cou'd praise, esteem, approve,
But understood not what was Love.
His Conduct might have made him styl'd
A Father, and the Nymph his Child.
550 That innocent Delight he took
To see the Virgin mind her Book,
Was but the Master's secret Joy
In School to hear the finest Boy.
Her Knowledge with her Fancy grew;
555 She hourly press'd for something new;
Ideas came into her Mind
So fast, his Lessons lagg'd behind:
She reason'd, without plodding long,
Nor ever gave her Judgment wrong.
560 But now a sudden Change was wrought,
She minds no longer what he taught.
Cadenus was amaz'd to find
Such Marks of a distracted Mind;
For tho' she seem'd to listen more
565 To all he spoke, than e'er before;
He found her Thoughts would absent range,
Yet guess'd not whence could spring the Change.
And first he modestly conjectures
His Pupil might be tir'd with Lectures;
570 Which help'd to mortify his Pride,
Yet gave him not the Heart to chide;
But in a mild dejected Strain,
At last he ventur'd to complain:
Said, she shou'd be no longer teiz'd;
575 Might have her Freedom when she pleas'd:
Was now convinc'd he acted wrong,
To hide her from the World so long;
And in dull Studies to engage
One of her tender Sex and Age.
580 That ev'ry Nymph with Envy own'd,
How she might shine in the *Grand-Monde*,
And ev'ry Shepherd was undone
To see her cloister'd like a Nun.
This was a visionary Scheme,
585 He wak'd, and found it but a Dream;
A Project far above his Skill,
For Nature must be Nature still.
If he were bolder than became
A Scholar to a Courtly Dame,
590 She might excuse a Man of Letters;
Thus Tutors often treat their Betters.
And since his Talk offensive grew,
He came to take his last Adieu.

Vanessa, fill'd with just Disdain,
595   Wou'd still her Dignity maintain,
Instructed from her early Years
To scorn the Art of Female Tears.

Had he employ'd his Time so long,
To teach her what was Right and Wrong,
600   Yet cou'd such Notions entertain,
That all his Lectures were in vain?
She own'd the wand'ring of her Thoughts,
But he must answer for her Faults.
She well remember'd to her Cost,
605   That all his Lessons were not lost.
Two Maxims she could still produce,
And sad Experience taught their Use:
That Virtue, pleas'd by being shown,
Knows nothing which it dare not own;
610   Can make us without Fear disclose
Our inmost Secrets to our Foes:
That common Forms were not design'd
Directors to a noble Mind.
Now, said the Nymph, I'll let you see
615   My Actions with your Rules agree,
That I can vulgar Forms despise,
And have no Secrets to disguise.
I knew by what you said and writ,
How dang'rous Things were Men of Wit,
620   You caution'd me against their Charms,
But never gave me equal Arms:
Your Lessons found the weakest Part,
Aim'd at the Head, but reach'd the Heart.

Cadenus felt within him rise
625   Shame, Disappointment, Guilt, Surprize.
He knew not how to reconcile
Such Language, with her usual Style:
And yet her Words were so exprest,
He cou'd not hope she spoke in Jest.
630   His Thoughts had wholly been confin'd
To form and cultivate her Mind.
He hardly knew, 'till he was told,
Whether the Nymph were Young or Old;
Had met her in a publick Place,
635   Without distinguishing her Face.
Much less could his declining Age
Vanessa's earliest Thoughts engage.
And if her Youth Indifference met,
His Person must Contempt beget.

640   Or grant her Passion be sincere,
How shall his Innocence be clear?
Appearances were all so strong,
The World must think him in the Wrong;
Wou'd say, He made a treach'rous Use
645   Of Wit, to flatter and seduce:
The Town wou'd swear he had betray'd,
By Magick Spells, the harmless Maid;
And ev'ry Beau wou'd have his Jokes,
That Scholars were like other Folks:
650   That when Platonick Flights are over,
The Tutor turns a mortal Lover.
So tender of the Young and Fair?
It shew'd a true Paternal Care—
Five thousand Guineas in her Purse?
655   The Doctor might have fancy'd worse.—

    Hardly at length he Silence broke,
And faulter'd ev'ry Word he spoke;
Interpreting her Complaisance,
Just as a Man *sans Consequence.*
660   She railly'd well, he always knew,
Her Manner now was something new;
And what she spoke was in an Air,
As serious as a Tragick Play'r.
But those who aim at Ridicule
665   Shou'd fix upon some certain Rule,
Which fairly hints they are in jest,
Else he must alter his Protest:
For, let a Man be ne'er so wise,
He may be caught with sober Lies;
670   A Science which he never taught,
And, to be free, was dearly bought:
For, take it in its proper Light,
'Tis just what Coxcombs call, *a Bite.*

    But not to dwell on Things minute,
675   *Vanessa* finish'd the Dispute,
Brought weighty Arguments to prove
That Reason was her Guide in Love.
She thought he had himself describ'd,
His Doctrines when she first imbib'd;
680   What he had planted, now was grown;
His Virtues she might call her own;
As he approves, as he dislikes,
Love or Contempt, her Fancy strikes.
Self-Love, in Nature rooted fast,
685   Attends us first, and leaves us last:

Why she likes him, admire not at her,
She loves herself, and that's the Matter.
How was her Tutor wont to praise
The Genius's of ancient Days!
690   (Those Authors he so oft had nam'd
For Learning, Wit, and Wisdom fam'd;)
Was struck with Love, Esteem, and Awe,
For Persons whom he never saw.
Suppose *Cadenus* flourish'd then,
695   He must adore such God-like Men.
If one short Volume cou'd comprise
All that was witty, learn'd, and wise,
How wou'd it be esteem'd, and read,
Altho' the Writer long were dead?
700   If such an Author were alive,
How all wou'd for his Friendship strive;
And come in Crowds to see his Face:
And this she takes to be her Case.
Cadenus answer'd every End,
705   The Book, the Author, and the Friend.
The utmost her Desires will reach,
Is but to learn what he can teach;
His Converse is a System, fit
Alone to fill up all her Wit;
710   While ev'ry Passion of her Mind
In him is center'd and confin'd.

Love can with Speech inspire a Mute,
And taught *Vanessa* to dispute.
This Topick, never touch'd before,
715   Display'd her Eloquence the more:
Her Knowledge, with such Pains acquir'd,
By this new Passion grew inspir'd.
Thro' this she made all Objects pass,
Which gave a Tincture o'er the Mass:
720   As Rivers, tho' they bend and twine
Still to the Sea their Course incline;
Or, as Philosophers, who find
Some fav'rite System to their Mind,
In ev'ry Point to make it fit,
725   Will force all Nature to submit.

Cadenus, who cou'd ne'er suspect
His Lessons wou'd have such Effect,
Or be so artfully apply'd,
Insensibly came on her Side;
730   It was an unforeseen Event,
Things took a Turn he never meant.

Whoe'er excels in what we prize,
Appears a Hero to our Eyes;
Each Girl when pleas'd with what is taught,
735   Will have the Teacher in her Thought.
When Miss delights in her Spinnet,
A Fidler may a Fortune get;
A Blockhead with melodious Voice
In Boarding-Schools can have his Choice;
740   And oft' the Dancing-Master's Art
Climbs from the Toe to touch the Heart.
In Learning let a Nymph delight,
The Pedant gets a Mistress by't.
Cadenus, to his Grief and Shame,
745   Cou'd scarce oppose *Vanessa*'s Flame;
And tho' her Arguments were strong,
At least, cou'd hardly wish them wrong.
Howe'er it came, he could not tell,
But, sure, she never talk'd so well.
750   His Pride began to interpose,
Preferr'd before a Crowd of Beaux,
So bright a Nymph to come unsought,
Such Wonder by his Merit wrought;
'Tis Merit must with her prevail,
755   He never knew her Judgment fail,
She noted all she ever read,
And had a most discerning Head.

'Tis an old Maxim in the Schools,
That Flattery's the Food of Fools;
760   Yet now and then your Men of Wit
Will condescend to take a Bit.
So when *Cadenus* could not hide,
He chose to justify his Pride;
Constr'ing the Passion she had shown,
765   Much to her Praise, more to his Own.
Nature in him had Merit plac'd,
In her, a most judicious Taste.
Love, hitherto a transient Guest,
Ne'er held Possession of his Breast;
770   So, long attending at the Gate,
Disdain'd to enter in so late.
Love, why do we one Passion call?
When 'tis a Compound of them all;
Where hot and cold, where sharp and sweet,
775   In all their Equipages meet;
Where Pleasures mix'd with Pains appear,
Sorrow with Joy, and Hope with Fear;

Wherein his Dignity and Age
Forbid *Cadenus* to engage.
780   But Friendship in its greatest Height,
A constant, rational Delight,
On Virtue's Basis fix'd to last,
When Love's Allurements long are past;
Which gently warms, but cannot burn;
785   He gladly offers in return:
His Want of Passion will redeem,
With Gratitude, Respect, Esteem:
With that Devotion we bestow,
When Goddesses appear below.

790   While thus *Cadenus* entertains
Vanessa in exalted Strains,
The Nymph in sober Words intreats
A Truce with all sublime Conceits.
For why such Raptures, Flights, and Fancies,
795   To her, who durst not read Romances;
In lofty Style to make Replies,
Which he had taught her to despise.
But when her Tutor will affect
Devotion, Duty, and Respect,
800   He fairly abdicates his Throne,
The Government is now her own;
He has a Forfeiture incurr'd,
She vows to take him at his Word,
And hopes he will not think it strange
805   If both shou'd now their Stations change.
The Nymph will have her Turn, to be
The Tutor; and the Pupil, he:
Tho' she already can discern,
Her Scholar is not apt to learn;
810   Or wants Capacity to reach
The Science she designs to teach:
Wherein his Genius was below
The Skill of ev'ry common Beau;
Who, tho' he cannot spell, is wise
815   Enough to read a Lady's Eyes;
And will each accidental Glance
Interpret for a kind Advance.

But what Success *Vanessa* met,
Is to the World a Secret yet:
820   Whether the Nymph, to please her Swain,
Talks in a high Romantick Strain;
Or whether he at last descends
To act with less Seraphick Ends;

Or, to compound the Business, whether
825 They temper Love and Books together:
Must never to Mankind be told,
Nor shall the conscious Muse unfold.

Mean time the mournful *Queen of Love*
Led but a weary Life above.
830 She ventures now to leave the Skies,
Grown by *Vanessa*'s Conduct wise.
For tho' by one perverse Event
Pallas had cross'd her first Intent,
Tho' her Design was not obtain'd,
835 Yet had she much Experience gain'd;
And, by the Project vainly try'd,
Cou'd better now the *Cause* decide.

She gave due Notice, that both Parties,
Coram Regina prox' die Martis,
840 Should at their Peril without fail
Come and appear, and save their Bail.
All met, and Silence thrice proclaimed,
One Lawyer to each Side was nam'd.
The Judge discover'd in her Face
845 Resentments for her late Disgrace;
And, full of Anger, Shame, and Grief,
Directed them to mind their Brief;
Nor spend their Time to shew their Reading;
She'd have a summary Proceeding.
850 She gather'd, under ev'ry Head,
The Sum of what each Lawyer said;
Gave her own Reasons last; and then
Decreed the Case against the *Men.*

But, in a weighty Case like this,
855 To shew she did not judge amiss,
Which evil Tongues might else report,
She made a Speech in open Court;
Wherein she grievously complains,
'How she was cheated by the Swains:
860 On whose Petition (humbly shewing
That Women were not worth the wooing,
And that unless the Sex would mend,
The Race of Lovers soon must end:)
'She was at Lord knows what Expence,
865 To form a Nymph of Wit and Sense;
A Model for her Sex design'd,
Who never cou'd one Lover find.

She saw her Favour was misplac'd;
The *Fellows* had a wretched Taste;
870   She needs must tell them to their Face,
They were a stupid, senseless Race:
And were she to begin agen,
She'd study to reform the *Men*;
Or add some Grains of Folly more
875   To *Women* than they had before,
To put them on an equal Foot;
And this, or nothing else, wou'd do't.
This might their mutual Fancy strike,
Since ev'ry Being loves its *Like*.

880   'But now, repenting what was done,
She left all Business to her Son:
She puts the World in his Possession,
And let him use it at Discretion.'

The Cry'r was order'd to dismiss
885   The Court, so made his last *O yes !*
The Goddess wou'd no longer wait;
But rising from her Chair of State,
Left all below at Six and Sev'n,
Harness'd her Doves, and flew to Heav'n.

HORACE, *LIB. 2. SAT. 6*

Part of it imitated

I often wish'd, that I had clear
For Life, six hundred Pounds a Year,
A handsome House to lodge a Friend,
A River at my Garden's End,
5   A Terras Walk, and half a Rood
Of land set out to plant a Wood.

Well, now I have all this and more,
I ask not to increase my Store,
And should be perfectly content,
10   Could I but live on this side *Trent*;
Nor cross the *Channel* twice a Year,
To spend six Months with *Statesmen* here.

I must by all means come to Town,
'Tis for the Service of the Crown.
15 '*Lewis*; the *Dean* will be of Use,
Send for him up, take no Excuse.'
The Toil, the Danger of the Seas;
Great Ministers ne'er think of these;
Or let it cost Five hundred Pound,
20 No matter where the Money's found;
It is but so much more in Debt,
And that they ne'er consider'd yet.

'Good Mr *Dean* go change your Gown,
Let my Lord know you're come to Town.'
25 I hurry me in haste away,
Not thinking it is Levee-Day;
And find his Honour in a Pound,
Hemm'd by a triple Circle round,
Chequer'd with Ribbons blew and green;
30 How should I thrust my self between?
Some Wag observes me thus perplext,
And smiling, whispers to the next,
'I thought the *Dean* had been too proud,
To jostle here among a Crowd.'
35 Another in a surly Fit,
Tells me I have more Zeal than Wit,
'So eager to express your Love,
You ne'er consider whom you shove,
But rudely press before a Duke.'
40 I own, I'm pleas'd with this Rebuke,
And take it kindly meant to show
What I desire the World should know.

I get a Whisper, and withdraw,
When twenty Fools I never saw,
45 Come with Petitions fairly pen'd,
Desiring I would stand their Friend.

This, humbly offers me his Case:
That, begs my Interest for a Place.
A hundred other Men's Affairs
50 Like Bees, are humming in my Ears.
'To morrow my Appeal comes on,
Without your Help the Cause is gone——'
The Duke expects my Lord and you,
About some great Affair, at Two——
55 'Put my Lord *Bolingbroke* in Mind,
To get my Warrant quickly signed:

Consider, 'tis my first Request.——'
Be satisfy'd, I'll do my best:——
Then presently he falls to teize,
60   'You may for certain, if you please;
I doubt not, if his Lordship knew——
And Mr *Dean*, one Word from you——'

'Tis (let me see) three Years and more,
(*October* next, it will be four)
65   Since HARLEY bid me first attend,
And chose me for an humble Friend;
Would take me in his Coach to chat,
And question me of this and that;
As, 'What's a-Clock?' And, 'How's the Wind?'
70   'Whose Chariot's that we left behind?'
Or gravely try to read the Lines
Writ underneath the Country *Signs*;
Or, 'Have you nothing new to day
From *Pope*, from *Parnel*, or from *Gay*?'
75   Such Tattle often entertains
My Lord and me as far as *Stains*,
As once a week we travel down
To *Windsor*, and again to Town,
Where all that passes, *inter nos*,
80   Might be proclaim'd at *Charing-Cross*.

Yet some I know with Envy swell,
Because they see me us'd so well:
'How think you of our Friend the *Dean*?
I wonder what some People mean;
85   My Lord and he are grown so great,
Always together, *tête à tête*:
What? they admire him for his Jokes——
See but the Fortune of some Folks!'

There flies about a strange Report
90   Of some Express arriv'd at Court;
I'm stopt by all the Fools I meet,
And catechis'd in ev'ry Street.
'You, Mr *Dean* frequent the Great;
Inform us, will the Emp'ror treat?
95   Or do the Prints and Papers lye?'
Faith Sir, you know as much as I.
'Ah Doctor, how you love to jest?
'Tis now no Secret'—I protest
'Tis one to me.—'Then, tell us, pray
100   When are the Troops to have their Pay?'

And, though I solemnly declare
I know no more than my *Lord Mayor*,
They stand amaz'd, and think me grown
The closest Mortal ever known.

105 Thus in a Sea of Folly tost,
My choicest Hours of Life are lost:
Yet always wishing to retreat;
Oh, could I see my Country Seat.
There leaning near a gentle Brook,
110 Sleep, or peruse some antient Book;
And there in sweet Oblivion drown
Those Cares that haunt a Court and Town.

ON STELLA'S BIRTH-DAY

Written A.D. 1718–[19]

Stella this Day is thirty four,
(We shan't dispute a Year or more)
However Stella, be not troubled,
Although thy Size and Years are doubled,
5 Since first I saw Thee at Sixteen
The brightest Virgin on the Green,
So little is thy Form declin'd
Made up so largly in thy Mind.
Oh, would it please the Gods to split
10 Thy Beauty, Size, and Years, and Wit,
No Age could furnish out a Pair
Of Nymphs so gracefull, Wise and fair
With half the Lustre of Your Eyes,
With half your Wit, your Years and Size:
15 And then before it grew too late,
How should I beg of gentle Fate,
(That either Nymph might have her Swain,)
To split my Worship too in twain.

PHILLIS, OR, THE PROGRESS OF LOVE

Written A.D. 1719

Desponding Phillis was endu'd
With ev'ry Talent of a Prude,
She trembled when a Man drew near;
Salute her, and she turn'd her Ear:
5   If o'er against her you were plac't
She durst not look above your Wast;
She'd rather take you to her Bed
Than let you see her dress her Head,
In Church you heard her thro' the Crowd
10   Repeat the Absolution loud;
In Church, secure behind her Fan
She durst behold that Monster, Man:
There practic'd how to place her Head,
And bit her Lips to make them red:
15   Or on the Matt devoutly kneeling
Would lift her Eyes up to the Ceeling,
And heave her Bosom unaware
For neighb'ring Beaux to see it bare.
    At length a lucky Lover came,
20   And found Admittance to the Dame.
Suppose all Partyes now agreed,
The Writings drawn, the Lawyer fee'd,
The Vicar and the Ring bespoke:
Guess how could such a Match be broke?
25   See then what Mortals place their Bliss in!
Next morn betimes the Bride was missing,
The Mother scream'd, the Father chid,
Where can this idle Wench be hid?
No news of *Phyl!* The Bridegroom came,
30   And thought his Bride had sculk't for shame,
Because her Father us'd to say
The Girl had such a Bashfull way.
    Now John the Butler must be sent
To learn the Road that Phillis went;
35   The Groom was wisht to saddle Crop,
For John must neither light nor stop;
But find her where so'er she fled,
And bring her back, alive or dead.
See here again the Dev'l to do;
40   For truly John was missing too:
The Horse and Pillion both were gone
Phillis, it seems, was fled with John.

Old Madam who went up to find
What Papers Phil had left behind,
45   A Letter on the Toylet sees
To my much honor'd Father; These:
('Tis always done, Romances tell us,
When Daughters run away with Fellows)
Fill'd with the choicest common-places,
50   By others us'd in the like Cases;
That, long ago a Fortune-teller
Exactly said what now befell her,
And in a Glass had made her see
A serving-Man of low Degree:
55   It was her Fate; must be forgiven;
For Marriages were made in Heaven:
His Pardon begg'd, but to be plain,
She'd do't if 'twere to do again.
Thank God, 'twas neither Shame nor Sin,
60   For John was come of honest Kin:
Love never thinks of Rich and Poor,
She'd beg with John from Door to Door:
Forgive her, if it be a Crime,
She'll never do't another Time,
65   She ne'r before in all her Life
Once disobey'd him, Maid nor Wife.
One Argument she summ'd up all in,
The Thing was done and past recalling:
And therefore hop'd she should recover
70   His Favor, when his Passion's over.
She valued not what others thought her;
And was—His most obedient Daughter.
    Fair Maidens all attend the Muse
Who now the wandring Pair pursues:
75   Away they rode in homely Sort
Their Journy long, their Money Short;
The loving Couple well bemir'd,
The Horse and both the Riders tir'd:
Their Vittells bad, their Lodging worse,
80   Phil cry'd, and John began to curse;
Phil wish't, that she had strained a Limb
When first she ventur'd out with him.
John wish't, that he had broke a Leg
When first for her he quitted Peg.
85   But what Adventures more befell 'em
The Muse hath now no time to tell 'em.
How Jonny wheadled, threatned, fawned,
Till Phillis all her Trinkets pawn'd:
How oft she broke her marriage Vows
90   In kindness to maintain her Spouse;

    Till Swains unwholesome spoyld the Trade,
    For now the Surgeon must be paid;
    To whom those Perquisites are gone
    In Christian Justice due to John.
95   When Food and Rayment now grew scarce
    Fate put a Period to the Farce;
    And with exact Poetick Justice:
    For John is Landlord, Phillis Hostess;
    They keep at *Staines* the *old blue Boar*,
100   Are Cat and Dog, and Rogue and Whore.

A SATIRICAL ELEGY

On the Death of a late Famous General

    His Grace! impossible! what dead!
    Of old age too, and in his bed!
    And could that Mighty Warrior fall?
    And so inglorious, after all!
5   Well, since he's gone, no matter how,
    The last loud trump must wake him now:
    And, trust me, as the noise grows stronger,
    He'd wish to sleep a little longer.
    And could he be indeed so old
10   As by the news-papers we're told?
    Threescore, I think, is pretty high;
    'Twas time in conscience he should die.
    This world he cumber'd long enough;
    He burnt his candle to the snuff;
15   And that's the reason, some folks think,
    He left behind *so great a stink*.
    Behold his funeral appears,
    Nor widow's sighs, nor orphan's tears,
    Wont at such times each heart to pierce,
20   Attend the progress of his herse.
    But what of that, his friends may say,
    He had those honours in his day.
    True to his profit and his pride,
    He made them weep before he dy'd.
25   Come hither, all ye empty things,
    Ye bubbles rais'd by breath of Kings;
    Who float upon the tide of state,
    Come hither, and behold your fate.

Let pride be taught by this rebuke,
How very mean a thing's a Duke;
From all his ill-got honours flung,
Turn'd to that dirt from whence he sprung.

30

STELLA'S BIRTH-DAY

March 13, 1726/7

This Day, whate'er the Fates decree,
Shall still be kept with Joy by me:
This Day then, let us not be told,
That you are sick, and I grown old,
Nor think on our approaching Ills,
And talk of Spectacles and Pills;
To morrow will be Time enough
To hear such mortifying Stuff.
Yet, since from Reason may be brought
A better and more pleasing Thought,
Which can in spite of all Decays,
Support a few remaining Days:
From not the gravest of Divines,
Accept for once some serious Lines.

5

10

Although we now can form no more
Long Schemes of Life, as heretofore;
Yet you, while Time is running fast,
Can look with Joy on what is past.

15

Were future Happiness and Pain,
A mere Contrivance of the Brain,
As Atheists argue, to entice,
And fit their Proselytes for Vice;
(The only Comfort they propose,
To have Companions in their Woes.)
Grant this the Case, yet sure 'tis hard,
That Virtue, stil'd its own Reward,
And by all Sages understood
To be the chief of human Good,
Should acting, die, nor leave behind
Some lasting Pleasure in the Mind,
Which by Remembrance will assuage,
Grief, Sickness, Poverty, and Age;

20

25

30

And strongly shoot a radiant Dart,
To shine through Life's declining Part.

35   Say, *Stella*, feel you no Content,
Reflecting on a Life well spent?
Your skilful Hand employ'd to save
Despairing Wretches from the Grave;
And then supporting with your Store,
40   Those whom you dragg'd from Death before:
(So Providence on Mortals waits,
Preserving what it first creates)
Your gen'rous Boldness to defend
An innocent and absent Friend;
45   That Courage which can make you just,
To Merit humbled in the Dust:
The Detestation you express
For Vice in all its glittering Dress:
That Patience under tort'ring Pain,
50   Where stubborn Stoicks would complain.

Shall these like empty Shadows pass,
Or Forms reflected from a Glass?
Or mere Chimæra's in the Mind,
That fly and leave no Marks behind?
55   Does not the Body thrive and grow
By Food of twenty Years ago?
And, had it not been still supply'd,
It must a Thousand Times have dy'd.
Then, who with Reason can maintain,
60   That no Effects of Food remain?
And, is not Virtue in Mankind
The Nutriment that feeds the Mind?
Upheld by each good Action past,
And still continued by the last:
65   Then, who with Reason can pretend,
That all Effects of Virtue end?

Believe me *Stella*, when you show
That true Contempt for Things below,
Nor prize your Life for other Ends
70   Than merely to oblige your Friends;
Your former Actions claim their Part,
And join to fortify your Heart.
For Virtue in her daily Race,
Like *Janus*, bears a double Face;
75   Looks back with Joy where she has gone,
And therefore goes with Courage on.
She at your sickly Couch will wait,
And guide you to a better State.

O then, whatever Heav'n intends,
80 Take Pity on your pitying Friends;
Nor let your Ills affect your Mind,
To fancy they can be unkind.
Me, surely me, you ought to spare,
Who gladly would your Suff'rings share;
85 Or give my Scrap of Life to you,
And think it far beneath your Due;
You, to whose Care so oft I owe,
That I'm alive to tell you so.

THE FURNITURE OF A WOMAN'S MIND

Written in the Year 1727

A set of Phrases learn't by Rote;
A Passion for a Scarlet-Coat;
When at a Play to laugh, or cry,
Yet cannot tell the Reason why:
5 Never to hold her Tongue a Minute;
While all she prates has nothing in it.
Whole Hours can with a Coxcomb sit,
And take his Nonsense all for Wit:
Her Learning mounts to read a Song,
10 But, half the Words pronouncing wrong;
Has ev'ry Repartee in Store,
She spoke ten Thousand Times before.
Can ready Compliments supply
On all Occasions, cut and dry.
15 Such Hatred to a Parson's Gown,
The Sight will put her in a Swown.
For Conversation well endu'd;
She calls it witty to be rude;
And, placing Raillery in Railing,
20 Will tell aloud your greatest Failing;
Nor makes a Scruple to expose
Your bandy Leg, or crooked Nose.
Can, at her Morning Tea, run o'er
The Scandal of the Day before.
25 Improving hourly in her Skill,
To cheat and wrangle at Quadrille.

In chusing Lace a Critick nice,
Knows to a Groat the lowest Price;
Can in her Female Clubs dispute
30   What Lining best the Silk will suit;
What Colours each Complexion match:
And where with Art to place a Patch.

If chance a Mouse creeps in her Sight,
Can finely counterfeit a Fright;
35   So sweetly screams if it comes near her,
She ravishes all Hearts to hear her.
Can dext'rously her Husband teize,
By taking Fits whene'er she please:
By frequent Practice learns the Trick
40   At proper Seasons to be sick;
Thinks nothing gives one Airs so pretty;
At once creating Love and Pity.
If *Molly* happens to be careless,
And but neglects to warm her Hair-Lace,
45   She gets a Cold as sure as Death;
And vows she scarce can fetch her Breath.
Admires how modest Women can
Be so *robustious* like a Man.

In Party, furious to her Power;
50   A bitter Whig, or Tory sow'r;
Her Arguments directly tend
Against the Side she would defend:
Will prove herself a Tory plain,
From Principles the Whigs maintain;
55   And, to defend the Whiggish Cause,
Her Topicks from the Tories draws.

O yes! If any Man can find
More virtues in a Woman's Mind,
Let them be sent to Mrs *Harding*;
60   She'll pay the Charges to a Farthing:
Take Notice, she has my Commission
To add them in the next Edition;
They may out-sell a better Thing;
So, Holla Boys; God save the King.

VERSES ON THE DEATH OF DR. SWIFT, D.S.P.D.

OCCASIONED BY READING A MAXIM IN ROCHEFOULCAULT

*Dans l'adversité de nos meilleurs amis nous trouvons quelque chose, qui ne nous
 deplaist pas.*
In the Adversity of our best Friends, we find something that doth not displease us.

As *Rochefoucault* his Maxims drew
From Nature, I believe 'em true:
They argue no corrupted Mind
In him; the Fault is in Mankind.

5   This Maxim more than all the rest
Is thought too base for human Breast;
'In all Distresses of our Friends
We first consult our private Ends,
While Nature kindly bent to ease us,
10   Points out some Circumstance to please us.'

If this perhaps your Patience move
Let Reason and Experience prove.

We all behold with envious Eyes,
Our *Equal* rais'd above our *Size*;
15   Who wou'd not at a crowded Show,
Stand high himself, keep others low?
I love my Friend as well as you,
But would not have him stop my View;
Then let me have the higher Post;
20   I ask but for an Inch at most.

If in a Battle you should find,
One, whom you love of all Mankind,
Had some heroick Action done,
A Champion kill'd, or Trophy won;
25   Rather than thus be over-topt,
Would you not wish his Lawrels cropt?

Dear honest *Ned* is in the Gout,
Lies rackt with Pain, and you without:
How patiently you hear him groan!
30   How glad the Case is not your own!

What Poet would not grieve to see,
His Brethren write as well as he?
But rather than they should excel,
He'd wish his Rivals all in Hell.

35   Her End when Emulation misses,
She turns to Envy, Stings and Hisses:
The strongest Friendship yields to Pride,
Unless the Odds be on our Side.

Vain human Kind! Fantastick Race!
40   Thy various Follies, who can trace?
Self-love, Ambition, Envy, Pride,
Their Empire in our Hearts divide:
Give others Riches, Power, and Station,
'Tis all on me an Usurpation.
45   I have no Title to aspire;
Yet, when you sink, I seem the higher.
In POPE, I cannot read a Line,
But with a Sigh, I wish it mine:
When he can in one Couplet fix
50   More Sense than I can do in Six:
It gives me such a jealous Fit,
I cry, Pox take him, and his Wit.

Why must I be outdone by GAY,
In my own hum'rous biting Way?

55   ARBUTHNOT is no more my Friend,
Who dares to Irony pretend;
Which I was born to introduce,
Refin'd it first, and shew'd its Use.

ST JOHN, as well as PULTNEY knows,
60   That I had some repute for Prose;
And till they drove me out of Date,
Could maul a Minister of State:
If they have mortify'd my Pride,
And made me throw my Pen aside;
65   If with such Talents Heav'n hath blest 'em
Have I not Reason to detest 'em?

To all my Foes, dear Fortune, send
Thy Gifts, but never to my Friend:
I tamely can endure the first,
70   But, this with Envy makes me burst.

Thus much may serve by way of Proem,
Proceed we therefore to our Poem.

The Time is not remote, when I
Must by the Course of Nature dye:
75   When I foresee my special Friends,
Will try to find their private Ends:
Tho' it is hardly understood,
Which way my Death can do them good;
Yet, thus methinks, I hear 'em speak;
80   See, how the Dean begins to break:
Poor Gentleman, he droops apace,
You plainly find it in his Face:
That old Vertigo in his Head,
Will never leave him, till he's dead:
85   Besides, his Memory decays,
He recollects not what he says;
He cannot call his Friends to Mind;
Forgets the Place where last he din'd:
Plyes you with Stories o'er and o'er,
90   He told them fifty Times before.
How does he fancy we can sit,
To hear his out-of-fashion'd Wit?
But he takes up with younger Fokes,
Who for his Wine will bear his Jokes:
95   Faith, he must make his Stories shorter,
Or change his Comrades once a Quarter:
In half the Time, he talks them round;
There must another Sett be found.

For Poetry, he's past his Prime,
100   He takes an Hour to find a Rhime:
His Fire is out, his Wit decay'd,
His Fancy sunk, his Muse a Jade.
I'd have him throw away his Pen;
But there's no talking to some Men.

105   And, then their Tenderness appears,
By adding largely to my Years:
'He's older than he would be reckon'd,
And well remembers *Charles* the Second.

'He hardly drinks a Pint of Wine;
110   And that, I doubt, is no good Sign.
His Stomach too begins to fail:
Last Year we thought him strong and hale;
But now, he's quite another Thing;
I wish he may hold out till Spring.'

115   Then hug themselves, and reason thus;
         'It is not yet so bad with us.'

         In such a Case they talk in Tropes,
         And, by their Fears express their Hopes:
         Some great Misfortune to portend,
120   No Enemy can match a Friend;
         With all the Kindness they profess,
         The Merit of a lucky Guess,
         (When daily Howd'y's come of Course,
         And Servants answer; *Worse and Worse*)
125   Wou'd please 'em better than to tell,
         That, GOD be prais'd, the Dean is well.
         Then he who prophecy'd the best,
         Approves his Foresight to the rest:
         'You know, I always fear'd the worst,
130   And often told you so at first:'
         He'd rather chuse that I should dye,
         Than his Prediction prove a Lye.
         Not one foretels I shall recover;
         But, all agree, to give me over.

135   Yet shou'd some Neighbour feel a Pain,
         Just in the Parts, where I complain;
         How many a Message would he send?
         What hearty Prayers that I should mend?
         Enquire what Regimen I kept;
140   What gave me Ease, and how I slept?
         And more lament, when I was dead,
         Than all the Sniv'llers round my Bed.

         My good Companions, never fear,
         For though you may mistake a Year;
145   Though your Prognosticks run too fast,
         They must be verify'd at last.

         'Behold the fatal Day arrive!
         How is the Dean? He's just alive.
         Now the departing Prayer is read:
150   He hardly breathes. The Dean is dead.
         Before the Passing-Bell begun,
         The News thro' half the Town has run.
         O, may we all for Death prepare!
         What has he left? And who's his Heir?
155   I know no more than what the News is,
         'Tis all bequeath'd to publick Uses.
         To publick Use! A perfect Whim!
         What had the Publick done for him!

Meer Envy, Avarice, and Pride!
160 He gave it all:—But first he dy'd.
And had the Dean, in all the Nation,
No worthy Friend, no poor Relation?
So ready to do Strangers good,
Forgetting his own Flesh and Blood?'

165 Now Grub-Street Wits are all employ'd;
With Elegies, the Town is cloy'd:
Some Paragraph in ev'ry Paper,
To *curse* the *Dean*, or *bless* the *Drapier*.

The Doctors tender of their Fame,
170 Wisely on me lay all the Blame:
'We must confess his Case was nice;
But he would never take Advice:
Had he been rul'd, for ought appears,
He might have liv'd these Twenty Years:
175 For when we open'd him we found,
That all his vital Parts were sound.'

From *Dublin* soon to *London* spread,
'Tis told at Court, the Dean is dead.

Kind Lady *Suffolk* in the Spleen,
180 Runs laughing up to tell the Queen.
The Queen, so Gracious, Mild, and Good,
Cries, 'Is he gone? 'Tis time he shou'd.
He's dead you say; why let him rot;
I'm glad the Medals were forgot.
185 I promis'd them, I own; but when?
I only was the Princess then;
But now as Consort of the King,
You know 'tis quite a different Thing.'

Now, *Chartres* at Sir *Robert*'s Levee,
190 Tells, with a Sneer, the Tidings heavy:
'Why, is he dead without his Shoes?'
(Cries *Bob*) 'I'm Sorry for the News;
Oh, were the Wretch but living still,
And in his Place my good Friend *Will*;
195 Or, had a Mitre on his Head
Provided *Bolingbroke* were dead.'

Now *Curl* his Shop from Rubbish drains;
Three genuine Tomes of *Swift*'s Remains.
And then to make them pass the glibber,
200 Revis'd by *Tibbalds*, *Moore*, and *Cibber*.

He'll treat me as he does my Betters.
Publish my Will, my Life, my Letters.
Revive the Libels born to dye;
Which POPE must bear, as well as I.

205   Here shift the Scene, to represent
How those I love, my Death lament.
Poor POPE will grieve a Month; and GAY
A Week; and ARBUTHNOTT a Day.

St JOHN himself will scarce forbear,
210   To bite his Pen, and drop a Tear.
The rest will give a Shrug and cry
I'm sorry; but we all must dye.
Indifference clad in Wisdom's Guise,
All Fortitude of Mind supplies:
215   For how can stony Bowels melt,
In those who never Pity felt;
When *We* are lash'd, *They* kiss the Rod;
Resigning to the Will of God.

The Fools, my Juniors by a Year,
220   Are tortur'd with Suspence and Fear.
Who wisely thought my Age a Screen,
When Death approach'd, to stand between:
The Screen remov'd, their Hearts are trembling,
They mourn for me without dissembling.

225   My female Friends, whose tender Hearts
Have better learn'd to act their Parts.
Receive the News in *doleful Dumps*,
'The Dean is dead, (*and what is Trumps?*)
Then Lord have Mercy on his Soul.
230   (Ladies I'll venture for the *Vole.*)
Six Deans they say must bear the Pall.
(I wish I knew what *King* to call.)
Madam, your Husband will attend
The Funeral of so good a Friend.
235   No Madam, 'tis a shocking Sight,
And he's engag'd To-morrow Night!
My Lady *Club* wou'd take it ill,
If he shou'd fail her at *Quadrill.*
He lov'd the Dean. (*I lead a Heart.*)
240   But dearest Friends, they say, must part.
His Time was come, he ran his Race;
We hope he's in a better Place.'

Why do we grieve that Friends should dye?
No Loss more easy to supply.
245 One Year is past; a different Scene;
No further mention of the Dean;
Who now, alas, no more is mist,
Than if he never did exist.
Where's now this Fav'rite of *Apollo*?
250 Departed; *and his Works must follow*:
Must undergo the common Fate;
His Kind of Wit is out of Date.
Some Country Squire to *Lintot* goes,
Enquires for SWIFT in Verse and Prose:
255 Says *Lintot*, 'I have heard the Name:
He dy'd a Year ago.' The same.
He searcheth all his Shop in vain;
'Sir you may find them in *Duck-lane*:
I sent them with a Load of Books,
260 Last *Monday* to the Pastry-cooks.
To fancy they cou'd live a Year!
I find you're but a Stranger here.
The Dean was famous in his Time;
And had a Kind of Knack at Rhyme:
265 His way of Writing now is past;
The Town hath got a better Taste:
I keep no antiquated Stuff;
But, spick and span I have enough.
Pray, do but give me leave to shew 'em;
270 Here's *Colley Cibber*'s Birth-day Poem.
This Ode you never yet have seen,
By *Stephen Duck*, upon the Queen.
Then, here's a Letter finely penn'd
Against the *Craftsman* and his Friend;
275 It clearly shews that all Reflection
On Ministers, is disaffection.
Next, here's Sir *Robert*'s Vindication,
And Mr *Henly*'s last Oration:
The Hawkers have not got 'em yet,
280 Your Honour please to buy a Set?

'Here's *Wolston*'s Tracts, the twelfth Edition;
'Tis read by ev'ry Politician:
The Country Members, when in Town,
To all their Boroughs send them down:
285 You never met a Thing so smart;
The Courtiers have them all by Heart:
Those Maids of Honour (who can read)
Are taught to use them for their Creed.

The Rev'rend Author's good Intention,
290   Hath been rewarded with a Pension:
He doth an Honour to his Gown,
By bravely running *Priest-craft* down:
He shews, as sure as GOD's in *Gloc'ster*,
That *Jesus* was a Grand Impostor:
295   That all his Miracles were Cheats,
Perform'd as Juglers do their Feats:
The Church had never such a Writer:
A Shame, he hath not got a Mitre!'

Suppose me dead; and then suppose
300   A Club assembled at the *Rose*;
Where from Discourse of this and that,
I grow the Subject of their Chat:
And, while they toss my Name about,
With Favour some, and some without;
305   One quite indiff'rent in the Cause,
My Character impartial draws:

'The Dean, if we believe Report,
Was never ill receiv'd at Court:
As for his Works in Verse and Prose,
310   I own my self no Judge of those:
Nor, can I tell what Criticks thought 'em;
But, this I know, all People bought 'em;
As with a moral View design'd
To cure the Vices of Mankind:
315   His Vein, ironically grave,
Expos'd the Fool, and lash'd the Knave:
To steal a Hint was never known,
But what he writ was all his own.

'He never thought an Honour done him,
320   Because a Duke was proud to own him:
Would rather slip aside, and chuse
To talk with Wits in dirty Shoes:
Despis'd the Fools with Stars and Garters,
So often seen caressing *Chartres*:
325   He never courted Men in Station,
Nor Persons had in Admiration;
Of no Man's Greatness was afraid,
Because he sought for no Man's Aid.
Though trusted long in great Affairs,
330   He gave himself no haughty Airs:
Without regarding private Ends,
Spent all his Credit for his Friends:

And only chose the Wise and Good;
No Flatt'rers; no Allies in Blood;
335   But succour'd Virtue in Distress,
And seldom fail'd of good Success;
As Numbers in their Hearts must own,
Who, but for him, had been unknown.

'With Princes kept a due Decorum,
340   But never stood in Awe before 'em:
And to her Majesty, God bless her,
Would speak as free as to her Dresser,
She thought it his peculiar Whim,
Nor took it ill as come from him.
345   He follow'd *David*'s Lesson just,
In Princes never put thy Trust.
And, would you make him truly sower;
Provoke him with *a slave in Power*:
The *Irish* Senate, if you nam'd,
350   With what Impatience he declaim'd!
Fair LIBERTY was all his Cry;
For her he stood prepar'd to die;
For her he boldly stood alone;
For her he oft expos'd his own.
355   Two Kingdoms, just as Faction led,
Had set a Price upon his Head;
But, not a Traytor cou'd be found,
To sell him for Six Hundred Pound.

'Had he but spar'd his Tongue and Pen,
360   He might have rose like other Men:
But, Power was never in his Thought;
And, Wealth he valu'd not a Groat:
Ingratitude he often found,
And pity'd those who meant the Wound:
365   But, kept the Tenor of his Mind,
To merit well of human Kind:
Nor made a Sacrifice of those
Who still were true, to please his Foes.
He labour'd many a fruitless Hour
370   To reconcile his Friends in Power;
Saw Mischief by a Faction brewing,
While they pursu'd each others Ruin.
But, finding vain was all his Care,
He left the Court in meer Despair.

375   'And, oh! how short are human Schemes!
Here ended all our golden Dreams.

What St John's Skill in State Affairs,
What Ormond's *Valour*, Oxford's Cares,
To save their sinking Country lent,
380   Was all destroy'd by one Event.
Too soon that precious Life was ended,
On which alone, our Weal depended.
When up a dangerous Faction starts,
With Wrath and Vengeance in their Hearts:
385   *By solemn League and Cov'nant bound*,
To ruin, slaughter, and confound;
To turn Religion to a Fable,
And make the Government a *Babel*:
Pervert the Law, disgrace the Gown,
390   Corrupt the Senate, rob the Crown;
To sacrifice old *England*'s Glory,
And make her infamous in Story.
When such a Tempest shook the Land,
How could unguarded Virtue stand?

395   'With Horror, Grief, Despair the Dean
Beheld the dire destructive Scene:
His Friends in Exile, or the Tower,
Himself within the Frown of Power;
Pursu'd by base envenom'd Pens,
400   Far to the Land of Slaves and Fens;
A servile Race in Folly nurs'd,
Who truckle most, when treated worst.

'By Innocence and Resolution,
He bore continual Persecution;
405   While Numbers to Preferment rose;
Whose Merits were, to be his Foes.
When, *ev'n his own familiar Friends*
Intent upon their private Ends;
Like Renegadoes now he feels,
410   *Against him lifting up their Heels*.

'The Dean did by his Pen defeat
An infamous destructive Cheat.
Taught Fools their Int'rest how to know;
And gave them Arms to ward the Blow.
415   Envy hath own'd it was his doing,
To save that helpless Land from Ruin,
While they who at the Steerage stood,
And reapt the Profit, sought his Blood.

'To save them from their evil Fate,
420   In him was held a Crime of State.

A wicked Monster on the Bench,
Whose Fury Blood could never quench;
As vile and profligate a Villain,
As modern *Scroggs*, or old *Tressilian*;
425   Who long all Justice had discarded,
Nor fear'd he GOD, nor Man regarded;
Vow'd on the Dean his Rage to vent,
And make him of his Zeal repent;
But Heav'n his Innocence defends,
430   The grateful People stand his Friends:
Not Strains of Law, nor Judges Frown,
Nor Topicks brought to please the Crown,
Nor Witness hir'd, nor Jury pick'd,
Prevail to bring him in convict.

435   'In Exile with a steady Heart,
He spent his Life's declining Part;
Where, Folly, Pride, and Faction sway,
Remote from St JOHN, POPE, and GAY.

'His Friendship there to few confin'd,
440   Were always of the midling Kind:
No Fools of Rank, a mungril Breed,
Who fain would pass for Lords indeed:
Where Titles give no Right or Power,
And Peerage is a wither'd Flower,
445   He would have held it a Disgrace,
If such a Wretch had known his Face.
On Rural Squires, that Kingdom's Bane,
He vented oft his Wrath in vain:
Biennial Squires, to Market brought;
450   Who sell their Souls and Votes for Naught;
The Nation stript go joyful back,
To rob the Church, their Tenants rack,
Go Snacks with Thieves and Rapparees,
And, keep the Peace, to pick up Fees:
455   In every Jobb to have a Share,
A Jayl or Barrack to repair;
And turn the Tax for publick Roads
Commodious to their own Abodes.

'Perhaps I may allow, the Dean
460   Had too much Satyr in his Vein;
And seem'd determin'd not to starve it,
Because no Age could more deserve it.
Yet, Malice never was his Aim;
He lash'd the Vice but spar'd the Name.

465   No Individual could resent,
    Where Thousands equally were meant.
    His Satyr points at no Defect,
    But what all Mortals may correct;
    For he abhorr'd that senseless Tribe,
470   Who call it Humour when they jibe:
    He spar'd a Hump or crooked Nose,
    Whose Owners set not up for Beaux.
    True genuine Dulness mov'd his Pity,
    Unless it offer'd to be witty.
475   Those, who their Ignorance confess'd,
    He ne'er offended with a Jest;
    But laugh'd to hear an Idiot quote,
    A verse from *Horace*, learn'd by Rote.

    'He knew an hundred pleasant Stories,
480   With all the Turns of *Whigs* and *Tories*:
    Was chearful to his dying Day,
    And Friends would let him have his Way.

    'He gave the little Wealth he had,
    To build a House for Fools and Mad:
485   And shew'd by one satyric Touch,
    No Nation wanted it so much:
    That Kingdom he hath left his Debtor,
    I wish it soon may have a Better.'

THE DAY OF JUDGEMENT

    With a Whirl of Thought oppress'd,
    I sink from Reverie to Rest.
    An horrid Vision seiz'd my Head,
    I saw the Graves give up their Dead.
5   Jove, arm'd with Terrors, burst the Skies,
    And Thunder roars, and Light'ning flies!
    Amaz'd, confus'd, its Fate unknown,
    The World stands trembling at his Throne.
    While each pale Sinner hangs his Head,
10   Jove, nodding, shook the Heav'ns, and said,
    'Offending Race of Human Kind,
    By Nature, Reason, Learning, blind;
    You who thro' Frailty step'd aside,
    And you who never fell—*thro' Pride*;

15   You who in different Sects have shamm'd,
      And come to see each other damn'd;
      (So some Folks told you, but they knew
      No more of Jove's Designs than you)
      The World's mad Business now is o'er,
20   And I resent these Pranks no more.
      I to such Blockheads set my Wit!
      I damn such Fools!—Go, go, you're bit.'

A BEAUTIFUL YOUNG NYMPH GOING TO BED

      Corinna, Pride of *Drury-Lane*,
      For whom no Shepherd sighs in vain;
      Never did *Covent Garden* boast
      So bright a batter'd, strolling Toast;
5   No drunken Rake to pick her up,
      No Cellar where on Tick to sup;
      Returning at the Midnight Hour;
      Four Stories climbing to her Bow'r;
      Then, seated on a three-legg'd Chair,
10   Takes off her artificial Hair:
      Now, picking out a Crystal Eye,
      She wipes it clean, and lays it by.
      Her Eye-Brows from a Mouse's Hyde,
      Stuck on with Art on either Side,
15   Pulls off with Care, and first displays 'em,
      Then in a Play-Book smoothly lays 'em.
      Now dextrously her Plumpers draws,
      That serve to fill her hollow Jaws.
      Untwists a Wire; and from her Gums
20   A set of Teeth completely comes.
      Pulls out the Rags contriv'd to prop
      Her flabby Dugs and down they drop.
      Proceeding on, the lovely Goddess
      Unlaces next her Steel-Rib'd Bodice;
25   Which by the Operator's Skill,
      Press down the Lumps, the Hollows fill,
      Up goes her Hand, and off she slips
      The Bolsters that supply her Hips.
      With gentlest Touch, she next explores
30   Her Shankers, Issues, running Sores,

Effects of many a sad Disaster;
And then to each applies a Plaister.
But must, before she goes to Bed,
Rub off the Dawbs of White and Red;
35   And smooth the Furrows in her Front,
With greasy Paper stuck upon't.
She takes a *Bolus* e'er she sleeps;
And then between two Blankets creeps.
With Pains of Love tormented lies;
40   Or if she chance to close her Eyes,
Of *Bridewell* and the *Compter* dreams,
And feels the Lash, and faintly screams;
Or, by a faithless Bully drawn,
At some Hedge-Tavern lies in Pawn;
45   Or to *Jamaica* seems transported,
Alone, and by no Planter courted;
Or, near *Fleet-Ditch*'s oozy Brinks,
Surrounded with a Hundred Stinks,
Belated, seems on watch to lye,
50   And snap some Cully passing by;
Or, struck with Fear, her Fancy runs
On Watchmen, Constables and Duns,
From whom she meets with frequent Rubs;
But, never from Religious Clubs;
55   Whose Favour she is sure to find,
Because she pays them all in Kind.
     Corinna wakes. A dreadful Sight!
Behold the Ruins of the Night!
A wicked Rat her Plaister stole,
60   Half eat, and dragg'd it to his Hole.
The Crystal Eye, alas, was miss't;
And *Puss* had on her Plumpers pisst.
A Pigeon pick'd her Issue-Peas;
And *Shock* her Tresses fill'd with Fleas.
65   The Nymph, tho' in this mangled Plight,
Must ev'ry Morn her Limbs unite.
But how shall I describe her Arts
To recollect the scatter'd Parts?
Or shew the Anguish, Toil, and Pain,
70   Of gath'ring up herself again?
The bashful Muse will never bear
In such a Scene to interfere.
Corinna in the Morning dizen'd,
Who sees, will spew; who smells, be poison'd.

ON POETRY: A RAPSODY

All Human Race wou'd fain be *Wits*,
And Millions miss, for one that hits.
Young's universal Passion, *Pride*,
Was never known to spread so wide.
5   Say *Britain*, cou'd you ever boast,——
Three *Poets* in an Age at most?
Our chilling Climate hardly bears
A *Sprig* of Bays in Fifty Years:
While ev'ry Fool his Claim alledges,
10   As if it grew in common Hedges.
What Reason can there be assign'd
For this Perverseness in the Mind?
Brutes find out where their Talents lie:
A *Bear* will not attempt to fly:
15   A founder'd *Horse* will oft debate,
Before he tries a five-barr'd Gate:
A *Dog* by Instinct turns aside,
Who sees the Ditch too deep and wide.
But *Man* we find the only Creature,
20   Who, led by *Folly*, combats *Nature*;
Who, when *she* loudly cries, *Forbear*,
With Obstinacy fixes there;
And, where his *Genius* least inclines,
Absurdly bends his whole Designs.

25   Not *Empire* to the Rising-Sun,
By Valour, Conduct, Fortune won;
Nor highest *Wisdom* in Debates
For framing Laws to govern States;
Nor Skill in Sciences profound,
30   So large to grasp the Circle round;
Such heavenly Influence require,
As how to strike the *Muses Lyre*.

Not Beggar's Brat, on Bulk begot;
Not Bastard of a Pedlar *Scot*;
35   Not Boy brought up to cleaning Shoes,
The Spawn of *Bridewell*, or the Stews;
Not Infants dropt, the spurious Pledges
Of *Gipsies* littering under Hedges,
Are so disqualified by Fate
40   To rise in *Church*, or *Law*, or *State*,
As he, whom *Phebus* in his Ire
Hath *blasted* with poetick Fire.

What hope of Custom in the *Fair*,
While not a Soul demands your Ware?
45   Where you have nothing to produce
For private Life, or publick Use?
Court, City, Country want you not;
You cannot bribe, betray, or plot.
For Poets, Law makes no Provision:
50   The Wealthy have you in Derision.
Of State-Affairs you cannot smatter,
Are awkward when you try to flatter.
Your Portion, taking *Britain* round,
Was just one annual Hundred Pound.
55   Now not so much as in Remainder
Since *Cibber* brought in an Attainder;
For ever fixt by Right Divine,
(A Monarch's Right) on *Grubstreet* Line.
Poor starv'ling Bard, how small thy Gains!
60   How unproportion'd to thy Pains!

And here a *Simile* comes Pat in:
Tho' *Chickens* take a Month to fatten,
The Guests in less than half an Hour
Will more than half a Score devour.
65   So, after toiling twenty Days,
To earn a Stock of Pence and Praise,
Thy Labours, grown the Critick's Prey,
Are swallow'd o'er a Dish of Tea;
Gone, to be never heard of more,
70   Gone, where the *Chickens* went before.

How shall a new Attempter learn
Of diff'rent Spirits to discern,
And how distinguish, which is which,
The Poet's Vein, or scribling Itch?
75   Then hear an old experienc'd Sinner
Instructing thus a young Beginner.

Consult yourself, and if you find
A powerful Impulse urge your Mind,
Impartial judge within your Breast
80   What Subject you can manage best;
Whether your Genius most inclines
To Satire, Praise, or hum'rous Lines;
To Elegies in mournful Tone,
Or Prologue sent from Hand unknown.
85   Then rising with *Aurora*'s Light,
The Muse invok'd, sit down to write;

Blot out, correct, insert, refine,
Enlarge, diminish, interline;
Be mindful, when Invention fails,
90   To scratch your Head, and bite your Nails.

    Your Poem finish'd, next your Care
Is needful, to transcribe it fair.
In modern Wit all printed Trash, is
Set off with num'rous *Breaks*——and *Dashes*—

95   To Statesmen wou'd you give a Wipe,
You print it in *Italick Type*.
When Letters are in vulgar Shapes,
'Tis ten to one the Wit escapes;
But when in *Capitals* exprest,
100   The dullest Reader smoaks a Jest:
Or else perhaps he may invent
A better than the Poet meant,
As learned Commentators view
In *Homer* more than *Homer* knew.

105   Your Poem in its modish Dress,
Correctly fitted for the Press,
Convey by Penny-Post to *Lintot*,
But let no Friend alive look into't.
If *Lintot* thinks 'twill quit the Cost,
110   You need not fear your Labour lost:
And, how agreeably surpriz'd
Are you to see it advertiz'd!
The Hawker shews you one in Print,
As fresh as Farthings from the Mint:
115   The Product of your Toil and Sweating;
A Bastard of your own begetting.

    Be sure at *Will*'s the following Day,
Lie Snug, to hear what Criticks say.
And if you find the general Vogue
120   Pronounces you a stupid Rogue;
Damns all your Thoughts as low and little,
Sit still, and swallow down your Spittle.
Be silent as a Politician,
For talking may beget Suspicion:
125   Or praise the Judgment of the Town,
And help yourself to run it down.
Give up your fond paternal Pride,
Nor argue on the weaker Side;
For Poems read without a Name
130   We justly praise, or justly blame:

And Criticks have no partial Views,
Except they know whom they abuse.
And since you ne'er provok'd their Spight,
Depend upon't their Judgment's right:
135   But if you blab, you are undone;
Consider what a Risk you run.
You lose your Credit all at once;
The Town will mark you for a Dunce:
The vilest Doggrel *Grubstreet* sends,
140   Will pass for yours with Foes and Friends.
And you must bear the whole Disgrace,
'Till some fresh Blockhead takes your Place.

      Your Secret kept, your Poem sunk,
And sent in Quires to line a Trunk;
145   If still you be dispos'd to rhime,
Go try your Hand a second Time.
Again you fail, yet Safe's the Word,
Take Courage, and attempt a Third.
But first with Care imploy your Thoughts,
150   Where Criticks mark'd your former Faults.
The trivial Turns, the borrow'd Wit,
The *Similes* that nothing fit;
The *Cant* which ev'ry Fool repeats,
Town-Jests, and Coffee-house Conceits;
155   Descriptions tedious, flat and dry,
And introduc'd the Lord knows why;
Or where we find your Fury set
Against the harmless Alphabet;
On A's and B's your Malice vent,
160   While Readers wonder whom you meant.
A publick, or a private *Robber*;
A *Statesman*, or a South-Sea *Jobber*.
A *Prelate* who no God believes;
A Parliament, or Den of Thieves.
165   A Pick-purse, at the Bar, or Bench;
A Duchess, or a Suburb-Wench.
Or oft when Epithets you link,
In gaping Lines to fill a Chink;
Like stepping Stones to save a Stride,
170   In Streets where Kennels are too wide:
Or like a Heel-piece to support
A Cripple with one Foot too short:
Or like a Bridge that joins a Marish
To Moorlands of a diff'rent Parish.
175   So have I seen ill-coupled Hounds,
Drag diff'rent Ways in miry Grounds.

So Geographers in *Afric*-Maps
With Savage-Pictures fill their Gaps;
And o'er unhabitable Downs
180   Place Elephants for want of Towns.

    But tho' you miss your third Essay,
You need not throw your Pen away.
Lay now aside all Thoughts of Fame,
To spring more profitable Game.
185   From Party-Merit seek Support;
The vilest Verse thrives best at Court.
A Pamphlet in Sir *Bob*'s Defence
Will never fail to bring in Pence;
Nor be concern'd about the Sale,
190   He pays his Workmen on the Nail.

    A Prince the Moment he is crown'd,
Inherits ev'ry Virtue round,
As Emblems of the sov'reign Pow'r,
Like other Bawbles of the Tow'r.
195   Is gen'rous, valiant, just and wise,
And so continues 'till he dies.
His humble *Senate* this professes,
In all their *Speeches*, *Votes*, *Addresses*.
But once you fix him in a Tomb,
200   His Virtues fade, his Vices bloom;
And each Perfection wrong imputed
Is fully at his Death confuted.
The Loads of Poems in his Praise,
Ascending make one Funeral-Blaze.
205   As soon as you can hear his Knell,
This God on Earth turns *Devil* in Hell.
And lo, his Ministers of State,
Transform'd to Imps, his Levee wait.
Where, in the Scenes of endless Woe,
210   They ply their former Arts below.
And as they sail in *Charon*'s Boat,
Contrive to bribe the Judge's Vote.
To *Cerberus* they give a Sop,
His triple-barking Mouth to Stop:
215   Or in the Iv'ry Gate of Dreams,
Project Excise and South-Sea Schemes:
Or hire their Party-Pamphleteers,
To set *Elysium* by the Ears.

    Then *Poet*, if you mean to thrive,
220   Employ your Muse on Kings alive;

With Prudence gath'ring up a Cluster
Of all the Virtues you can muster:
Which form'd into a Garland sweet
Lay humbly at your Monarch's Feet;
225   Who, as the Odours reach his Throne,
Will smile, and think 'em all his own:
For *Law* and *Gospel* both determine
All Virtues lodge in royal Ermine.
(I mean the Oracles of Both,
230   Who shall depose it upon Oath.)
Your Garland in the following Reign,
Change but the Names will do again.

    But if you think this Trade too base,
(Which seldom is the Dunce's Case)
235   Put on the Critick's Brow, and sit
At *Wills* the puny Judge of Wit.
A Nod, a Shrug, a scornful Smile,
With Caution us'd, may serve a-while.
Proceed no further in your Part,
240   Before you learn the Terms of Art:
(For you can never be too far gone,
In all our modern Criticks Jargon.)
Then talk with more authentick Face,
Of *Unities, in Time and Place.*
245   Get Scraps of *Horace* from your Friends,
And have them at your Fingers Ends.
Learn *Aristotle*'s Rules by Rote,
And at all Hazards boldly quote:
Judicious *Rymer* oft review:
250   Wise *Dennis*, and profound *Bossu.*
Read all the *Prefaces* of *Dryden*,
For these our Criticks much confide in,
(Tho' meerly writ at first for filling
To raise the Volume's Price, a Shilling.)

255   A forward Critick often dupes us
With sham Quotations *Peri Hupsous*:
And if we have not read *Longinus*,
Will magisterially out-shine us.
Then, lest with *Greek* he over-run ye,
260   Procure the Book for Love or Money,
Translated from *Boileau*'s Translation,
And quote *Quotation* on *Quotation.*

    At *Wills* you hear a Poem read,
Where *Battus* from the Table-head,
265   Reclining on his Elbow-chair,
Gives Judgment with decisive Air.

To him the Tribe of circling Wits,
As to an Oracle submits.
He gives Directions to the Town,
270   To cry it up, or run it down.
(Like *Courtiers*, when they send a Note,
Instructing *Members* how to Vote.)
He sets the Stamp of Bad and Good,
Tho' not a Word be understood.
275   Your Lesson learnt, you'll be secure
To get the Name of *Conoisseur*.
And when your Merits once are known,
Procure Disciples of your own.

    For Poets (you can never want 'em,
280   Spread thro' *Augusta Trinobantum*)
Computing by their Pecks of Coals,
Amount to just Nine thousand Souls.
These o'er their proper Districts govern,
Of Wit and Humour, Judges sov'reign.
285   In ev'ry Street a City-bard
Rules, like an Alderman his Ward.
His indisputed Rights extend
Thro' all the Lane, from End to End.
The Neighbours round admire his *Shrewdness*,
290   For songs of *Loyalty* and *Lewdness*.
Out-done by none in Rhyming well,
Altho' he never learnt to spell.

    Two bordering Wits contend for Glory;
And one is *Whig*, and one is *Tory*.
295   And this, for Epicks claims the Bays,
And that, for Elegiack Lays.
Some famed for Numbers soft and smooth,
By Lovers spoke in *Punch*'s Booth.
And some as justly Fame extols
300   For lofty Lines in *Smithfield* Drols.
Bavius in *Wapping* gains Renown,
And *Mævius* reigns o'er *Kentish-Town*:
Tigellius plac'd in *Phœbus*' Car,
From *Ludgate* shines to *Temple-bar*.
305   Harmonius *Cibber* entertains
The Court with annual Birth-day Strains;
Whence *Gay* was banish'd in Disgrace,
Where *Pope* will never show his Face;
Where *Young* must torture his Invention,
310   To flatter *Knaves*, or lose his *Pension*.

    But these are not a thousandth Part
Of Jobbers in the Poets Art,

Attending each his proper Station,
And all in due Subordination;
315 Thro' ev'ry Alley to be found,
In Garrets high, or under Ground:
And when they join their *Pericranies*,
Out skips a *Book of Miscellanies*.

Hobbes clearly proves that ev'ry Creature
320 Lives in a State of War by Nature.
The Greater for the Smaller watch,
But meddle seldom with their Match.
A Whale of moderate Size will draw
A Shole of Herrings down his Maw.
325 A Fox with Geese his Belly crams;
A Wolf destroys a thousand Lambs.
But search among the rhiming Race,
The Brave are worried by the Base.
If, on *Parnassus*' Top you sit,
330 You rarely bite, are always bit:
Each Poet of inferior Size
On you shall rail and criticize;
And strive to tear you Limb from Limb,
While others do as much for him.
335 The Vermin only teaze and pinch
Their Foes superior by an Inch.
So, Nat'ralists observe, a Flea
Hath smaller Fleas that on him prey,
And these have smaller yet to bite 'em,
340 And so proceed *ad infinitum*:
Thus ev'ry Poet in his Kind,
Is bit by him that comes behind;
Who, tho' too little to be seen,
Can teaze, and gall, and give the Spleen;
345 Call Dunces, Fools, and Sons of Whores,
Lay *Grubstreet* at each others Doors:
Extol the *Greek* and *Roman* Masters,
And curse our modern Poetasters.
Complain, as many an ancient Bard did,
350 How Genius is no more rewarded;
How wrong a Taste prevails among us;
How much our Ancestors out-sung us;
Can personate an awkward Scorn
For those who are not Poets born:
355 And all their Brother Dunces lash,
Who crowd the Press with hourly Trash.

O, *Grubstreet*! how do I bemoan thee,
Whose graceless Children scorn to own thee!

This filial Piety forgot,
360 Deny their Country like a Scot:
Tho' by their Idiom and Grimace
They soon betray their native Place:
Yet *thou* hast greater Cause to be
Asham'd of them, than they of thee.
365 Degenerate from their ancient Brood,
Since first the Court allow'd them Food.

    Remains a Difficulty still,
To purchase Fame by writing ill:
From *Flecknoe* down to *Howard*'s Time,
370 How few have reach'd the *low Sublime*?
For when our high-born *Howard* dy'd,
Blackmore alone his Place supply'd:
And least a Chasm should intervene,
When Death had finish'd *Blackmore*'s Reign,
375 The *leaden Crown* devolv'd to thee,
Great Poet of the *Hollow-Tree*.
But, oh, how unsecure thy Throne!
Ten thousand Bards thy Right disown:
They plot to turn in factious Zeal,
380 *Duncenia* to a Common-Weal;
And with rebellious Arms pretend
An equal Priv'lege to *descend*.

    In Bulk there are not more Degrees,
From *Elephants* to *Mites* in Cheese,
385 Than what a curious Eye may trace
In Creatures of the rhiming Race.
From bad to worse, and worse they fall,
But, who can reach to Worst of all?
For, tho' in Nature Depth and Height
390 Are equally held infinite,
In Poetry the Height we know;
'Tis only infinite below.
For Instance: When you rashly think,
No Rhymer can like *Welsted* sink.
395 His Merits ballanc'd you shall find,
The Laureat leaves him far behind.
Concannen, more aspiring Bard,
Climbs downwards, deeper by a Yard:
Smart JEMMY MOOR with Vigor drops,
400 The Rest pursue as thick as Hops:
With Heads to Points the Gulph they enter,
Linkt perpendicular to the Centre:
And as their Heels elated rise,
Their Heads attempt the nether Skies.

405   O, what Indignity and Shame
To prostitute the Muse's Name,
By flatt'ring Kings whom Heaven design'd
The Plague and Scourges of Mankind.
Bred up in Ignorance and Sloth,
410 And ev'ry Vice that nurses both.

Fair *Britain* in thy Monarch blest,
Whose Virtues bear the strictest Test;
Whom never *Faction* cou'd bespatter,
Nor *Minister*, nor *Poet* flatter.
415 What Justice in rewarding Merit?
What Magnanimity of Spirit?
What Lineaments divine we trace
Thro' all his Figure, Mien and Face;
Tho' Peace with Olive bind his Hands,
420 Confest the conqu'ring Hero stands.
Hydaspes, *Indus*, and the *Ganges*,
Dread from his Hand impending Changes.
From him the *Tartar*, and *Chinese*,
Short by the Knees intreat for Peace.
425 The *Consort* of his Throne and Bed,
A perfect Goddess born and bred.
Appointed sov'reign Judge to sit
On Learning, Eloquence and Wit.
Our eldest Hope, divine *Iülus*,
430 (Late, very late, O, may he rule us.)
What early Manhood has he shown,
Before his downy Beard was grown!
Then think, what Wonders will be done
By going on as he begun;
435 An Heir for *Britain* to secure
As long as Sun and Moon endure.

The Remnant of the royal Blood,
Comes pouring on me like a Flood.
Bright Goddesses, in Number five;
440 Duke *William*, sweetest Prince alive.

Now sing the *Minister* of *State*,
Who shines alone, without a Mate.
Observe with what majestick Port
This *Atlas* stands to prop the Court:
445 Intent the Publick Debts to pay,
Like prudent *Fabius* by *Delay*.
Thou great Vicegerent of the King,
Thy Praises ev'ry Muse shall sing.
In all Affairs thou sole Director,
450 Of Wit and Learning chief Protector;

Tho' small the Time thou hast to spare,
The Church is thy peculiar Care.
Of pious Prelates what a Stock
You chuse to rule the Sable-flock.
455 You raise the Honour of the Peerage,
Proud to attend you at the Steerage.
You dignify the noble Race,
Content yourself with humbler Place.
Now Learning, Valour, Virtue, Sense,
460 To Titles give the sole Pretence.
St George beheld thee with Delight,
Vouchsafe to be an azure Knight,
When on thy Breast and Sides *Herculean*,
He fixt the *Star* and *String Cerulean*.

465 Say, Poet, in what other Nation,
Shone ever such a Constellation.
Attend ye *Popes*, and *Youngs*, and *Gays*,
And tune your Harps, and strow your Bays.
Your Panegyricks here provide,
470 You cannot err on Flatt'ry's Side.
Above the Stars exalt your Stile,
You still are low ten thousand Mile.
On *Lewis* all his Bards bestow'd,
Of Incense many a thousand Load;
475 But *Europe* mortify'd his Pride,
And swore the fawning Rascals ly'd:
Yet what the World refus'd to *Lewis*,
Apply'd to George exactly true is:
Exactly true! Invidious Poet!
480 'Tis fifty thousand Times below it.

Translate me now some Lines, if you can,
From *Virgil, Martial, Ovid, Lucan*;
They could all Pow'r in Heaven divide,
And do no Wrong to either Side:
485 They teach you how to split a Hair,
Give George and *Jove* an equal Share.
Yet, why should we be lac'd so straight;
I'll give my Monarch Butter-weight.
And Reason good; for many a Year
490 Jove never intermeddl'd here:
Nor, tho' his Priests be duly paid,
Did ever we *desire* his Aid:
We now can better do without him,
Since *Woolston* gave us Arms to rout him.

*** *Cætera desiderantur* ***

Samuel Johnson (1709–84)

Johnson was the son of a bookseller in Lichfield. After attending a local school he went to Pembroke College, Oxford, in 1728. His extreme poverty, however, may have led to his premature departure. He tried teaching and writing, but for many years he was little more than a literary hack, mainly on *The Gentleman's Magazine*. His work at this time included poetry, biography (the *Life of Savage*) and a tragedy, *Irene* (1749). In the same year he also published the second of his imitations of the Roman satirist, Juvenal, *The Vanity of Human Wishes*. Its predecessor, *London*, appeared in 1738. In the 1750s he wrote largely for his periodicals, *The Rambler*, *The Adventurer* and *The Idler* and in the middle of that decade issued his great *Dictionary of the English Language* (1755). This period concluded with his novel, *Rasselas* (1759). He received a government pension in 1762 and three years later completed his edition of Shakespeare. During this time also he met his biographer, Boswell, but it was not until ten years later that they made their famous tour of the Highlands and the Hebrides. Johnson's last great work was his *Lives of the English Poets* (1779–81). His latter years were marked by his increasing celebrity, his fame as a conversationalist and his friendship with eminent social figures of the period.

ON A LADY'S PRESENTING A SPRIG OF MYRTLE TO A GENTLEMAN

What Fears, what Terrors does thy Gift create!
Ambiguous Emblem of uncertain Fate!
The Myrtle, Ensign of supreme Command,
(Consign'd by *Venus* to *Melissa*'s Hand)
5   Not less capricious than a reigning Fair,
Oft favors, oft rejects the Lover's Care.
In Myrtle Groves oft sings the happy Swain,
In Myrtle Shades despairing Ghosts complain;
The Myrtle crowns the happy Lovers Heads,
10   Th'unhappy Lovers Graves the Myrtle spreads;
Oh! then the Meaning of thy Gift impart,
And cure the throbbings of an anxious Heart;
Soon must this Bough, as you shall fix his Doom,
Adorn *Philander*'s Head, or grace his Tomb.

[65]

TO MISS HICKMAN PLAYING ON THE SPINET

Bright Stella, form'd for universal Reign,
Too well You know to keep the Slaves You gain.
When in Your Eyes resistless Lightnings play,
Aw'd into Love, our conquer'd hearts obey,
5   And yield, reluctant, to despotick Sway.
But when your Musick sooths the raging pain,
We bid propitious Heav'n prolong your reign,
We bless the Tyrant, and we hug the Chain.

When old Timotheus struck the vocal String,
10   Ambitious Fury fir'd the Grecian King:
Unbounded Projects lab'ring in his Mind,
He pants for room, in one poor World confin'd.
Thus wak'd to rage by Musick's dreadfull Pow'r,
He bids the Sword destroy, the Flame devour.
15   Had Stella's gentle touches mov'd the Lyre,
Soon had the Monarch felt a nobler fire,
No more delighted with destructive War,
Ambitious only now to please the Fair,
Resign'd his Thirst of Empire to her Charms,
20   And found a Thousand Worlds in Stella's Arms.

LONDON: A POEM
IN IMITATION OF THE THIRD SATIRE OF JUVENAL

—— —— *Quis ineptæ*
Tam patiens urbis, tam ferreus ut teneat se?
JUV.

Tho' Grief and Fondness in my breast rebel,
When injur'd THALES bids the Town farewell,
Yet still my calmer Thoughts his Choice commend,
I praise the Hermit, but regret the Friend,
5   Resolv'd at length, from Vice and LONDON far,
To breathe in distant Fields a purer Air,
And, fix'd on CAMBRIA's solitary Shore,
Give to St David one *true Briton* more.
    For who would leave, unbrib'd, *Hibernia*'s Land,

10   Or change the rocks of *Scotland* for the *Strand*?
     There none are swept by sudden Fate away,
     But all whom Hunger spares, with Age decay:
     Here Malice, Rapine, Accident, conspire,
     And now a Rabble rages, now a Fire;
15   Their Ambush here relentless Ruffians lay,
     And here the fell Attorney prowls for Prey;
     Here falling Houses thunder on your Head,
     And here the female Atheist talks you dead.
       While THALES waits the Wherry that contains
20   Of dissipated Wealth the small Remains,
     On *Thames's Banks*, in silent Thought we stood,
     Where GREENWICH smiles upon the silver Flood:
     Struck with the seat that gave ELIZA birth,
     We kneel, and kiss the consecrated Earth;
25   In pleasing Dreams the blissful Age renew,
     And call BRITANNIA's Glories back to view;
     Behold her Cross triumphant on the Main,
     The Guard of Commerce, and the Dread of *Spain*,
     Ere Masquerades debauch'd, Excise oppress'd,
30   Or *English* honour grew a standing Jest.
       A transient Calm the happy Scenes bestow,
     And for a moment lull the Sense of Woe.
     At length awaking, with contemptuous Frown,
     Indignant THALES eyes the neighb'ring Town.
35   Since Worth, he cries, in these degen'rate Days,
     Wants ev'n the cheap Reward of empty Praise;
     In those curst Walls, devote to Vice and Gain,
     Since unrewarded Science toils in vain;
     Since Hope but sooths to double my Distress,
40   And ev'ry Moment leaves my Little less;
     While yet my steady Steps no Staff sustains,
     And Life still vig'rous revels in my Veins;
     Grant me, kind Heaven, to find some happier Place,
     Where Honesty and Sense are no Disgrace;
45   Some pleasing Bank where verdant Osiers play,
     Some peaceful Vale with Nature's Paintings gay;
     Where once the harrass'd Briton found Repose,
     And safe in Poverty defy'd his Foes;
     Some secret Cell, ye Pow'rs, indulgent give.
50   Let —— live here, for —— has learn'd to live.
     Here let those reign, whom Pensions can incite
     To vote a Patriot black, a Courtier white;
     Explain their Country's dear-bought Rights away,
     And plead for Pirates in the Face of Day;
55   With slavish Tenets taint our poison'd Youth,
     And lend a Lye the Confidence of Truth.
       Let such raise Palaces, and Manors buy,

Collect a Tax, or farm a Lottery,
With warbling Eunuchs fill a licens'd Stage,
60 And lull to Servitude a thoughtless Age.
   Heroes, proceed! what bounds your Pride shall hold?
What Check restrain your Thirst of Pow'r and Gold?
Behold rebellious Virtue quite o'erthrown,
Behold our Fame, our Wealth, our Lives your own.
65   To such, a groaning Nation's spoils are giv'n,
When publick Crimes inflame the Wrath of Heav'n:
But what, my Friend, what Hope remains for me,
Who start at Theft, and blush at Perjury?
Who scarce forbear, tho' BRITAIN's Court he sing,
70 To pluck a titled Poet's borrow'd Wing;
A Statesman's Logic unconvinc'd can hear,
And dare to slumber o'er the *Gazeteer*;
Despise a Fool in half his Pension drest,
And strive in vain to laugh at *Clodio*'s jest.
75   Others with softer Smiles, and subtler Art,
Can sap the Principles, or taint the Heart;
With more Address a Lover's Note convey,
Or bribe a Virgin's Innocence away.
Well may they rise, while I, whose rustic Tongue
80 Ne'er knew to puzzle Right, or varnish Wrong,
Spurn'd as a Begger, dreaded as a Spy,
Live unregarded, unlamented die.
   For what but social Guilt the Friend endears?
Who shares *Orgilio*'s Crimes, his Fortune shares.
85 But thou, should tempting Villainy present
All *Marlb'rough* hoarded, or all *Villiers* spent,
Turn from the glitt'ring Bribe thy scornful Eye,
Nor sell for Gold, what Gold could never buy,
The peaceful Slumber, self-approving Day,
90 Unsullied Fame, and Conscience ever gay.
   The cheated Nation's happy Fav'rites, see!
Mark whom the Great caress, who frown on me!
LONDON! the needy Villain's gen'ral Home,
The Common Sewer of *Paris* and of *Rome*;
95 With eager Thirst, by Folly or by Fate,
Sucks in the Dregs of each corrupted State.
Forgive my Transports on a Theme like this,
I cannot bear a *French* Metropolis.
   Illustrious EDWARD! from the Realms of Day,
100 The Land of Heroes and of Saints survey;
Nor hope the *British* Lineaments to trace,
The rustic Grandeur, or the surly Grace,
But lost in thoughtless Ease, and empty Show,
Behold the Warrior dwindled to a Beau;
105 Sense, Freedom, Piety, refin'd away,

Of France the Mimic, and of Spain the Prey.
  All that at home no more can beg or steal,
Or like a Gibbet better than a Wheel;
Hiss'd from the Stage, or hooted from the Court,
110 Their Air, their Dress, their Politicks import;
Obsequious, artful, voluble and gay,
On *Britain*'s fond Credulity they prey.
No gainful Trade their Industry can 'scape,
They sing, they dance, clean Shoes, or cure a Clap;
115 All Sciences a fasting Monsieur knows,
And bid him go to Hell, to Hell he goes.
  Ah! what avails it, that, from Slav'ry far,
I drew the Breath of Life in *English* air;
Was early taught a *Briton*'s right to prize,
120 And lisp the Tale of HENRY's Victories;
If the gull'd Conqueror receives the Chain,
And Flattery prevails when Arms are vain.
  Studious to please, and ready to submit,
The supple *Gaul* was born a Parasite:
125 Still to his Int'rest true, where'er he goes
Wit, Brav'ry, Worth, his lavish Tongue bestows;
In ev'ry Face a Thousand Graces shine,
From ev'ry Tongue flows Harmony divine.
These Arts in vain our rugged Natives try,
130 Strain out with fault'ring Diffidence a lie,
And get a Kick for aukward Flattery.
  Besides, with Justice, this discerning Age
Admires their wond'rous Talents for the Stage:
Well may they venture on the Mimic's Art,
135 Who play from Morn to Night a borrow'd Part;
Practis'd their Master's Notions to embrace,
Repeat his Maxims, and reflect his Face;
With ev'ry wild Absurdity comply,
And view each Object with another's Eye;
140 To shake with Laughter ere the Jest they hear,
To pour at Will the counterfeited Tear,
And as their Patron hints the Cold or Heat,
To shake in Dog-days, in *December* sweat.
  How, when Competitors like these contend,
145 Can surly Virtue hope to fix a Friend?
Slaves that with serious Impudence beguile,
And lye without a Blush, without a Smile;
Exalt each Trifle, ev'ry Vice adore,
Your Taste in Snuff, your Judgment in a Whore;
150 Can *Balbo*'s Eloquence applaud, and swear
He gropes his Breeches with a Monarch's air.
  For Arts like these preferr'd, admir'd, carest,
They first invade your Table, then your Breast;

Explore your Secrets with insidious Art,
155 Watch the weak Hour, and ransack all the Heart;
Then soon your ill-plac'd Confidence repay,
Commence your Lords, and govern or betray.
    By Numbers here from Shame or Censure free,
All Crimes are safe, but hated Poverty.
160 This, only this, the rigid Law persues,
This, only this, provokes the snarling Muse;
The sober Trader at a Tatter'd Cloak,
Wakes from his Dream, and labours for a Joke;
With brisker Air the silken Courtiers gaze,
165 And turn the varied Taunt a thousand Ways.
Of all the Griefs that harrass the Distrest,
Sure the most bitter is a scornful Jest;
Fate never wounds more deep the gen'rous Heart,
Than when a Blockhead's Insult points the Dart.
170   Has Heaven reserv'd, in Pity to the Poor,
No pathless Waste, or undiscover'd Shore;
No secret Island in the boundless Main?
No peaceful Desart yet unclaim'd by Spain?
Quick let us rise, the happy Seats explore,
175 And bear Oppression's Insolence no more.
This mournful Truth is ev'ry where confest,
SLOW RISES WORTH, BY POVERTY DEPREST:
But here more slow, where all are Slaves to Gold,
Where Looks are Merchandise, and Smiles are sold;
180 Where won by Bribes, by Flatteries implor'd,
The Groom retails the Favours of his Lord.
    But hark! th'affrighted Croud's tumultuous Cries
Roll thro' the Streets, and thunder to the Skies;
Rais'd from some pleasing Dream of Wealth and Pow'r,
185 Some pompous Palace, or some blissful Bow'r,
Aghast you start, and scarce with asking Sight
Sustain th'approaching Fire's tremendous Light;
Swift from pursuing Horrors take your Way,
And leave your little ALL to Flames a prey;
190 Then thro' the World a wretched Vagrant roam,
For where can starving Merit find a Home?
In vain your mournful Narrative disclose,
While all neglect, and most insult your Woes.
    Should Heaven's just Bolts *Orgilio*'s Wealth confound
195 And spread his flaming Palace on the Ground,
Swift o'er the Land the dismal Rumour flies,
And publick Mournings pacify the Skies;
The Laureat Tribe in servile Verse relate,
How Virtue wars with persecuting Fate;
200 With well-feign'd Gratitude the pension'd Band
Refund the Plunder of the begger'd Land.

See! while he builds, the gaudy Vassals come,
And crowd with sudden Wealth the rising Dome;
The Price of Boroughs and of Souls restore,
205 And raise his Treasures higher than before.
Now bless'd with all the Baubles of the Great,
The polish'd Marble, and the shining Plate,
Orgilio sees the golden Pile aspire,
And hopes from angry Heav'n another Fire.
210 Could'st thou resign the Park and Play content,
For the fair Banks of *Severn* or of *Trent*;
There might'st thou find some elegant Retreat,
Some hireling Senator's deserted Seat;
And stretch thy Prospects o'er the smiling Land,
215 For less than rent the Dungeons of the *Strand*;
There prune thy Walks, support thy drooping Flow'rs,
Direct thy Rivulets, and twine thy Bow'rs;
And, while thy grounds a cheap Repast afford,
Despite the Dainties of a venal Lord:
220 There ev'ry Bush with Nature's Musick rings,
There ev'ry Breeze bears Health upon its Wings;
On all thy Hours Security shall smile,
And bless thine Evening Walk and Morning Toil.
Prepare for Death, if here at Night you roam,
225 And sign your Will before you sup from Home.
Some fiery Fop, with new Commission vain,
Who sleeps on Brambles till he kills his Man;
Some frolick Drunkard, reeling from a Feast,
Provokes a Broil, and stabs you for a Jest.
230 Yet ev'n these Heroes, mischievously gay,
Lords of the Street, and Terrors of the Way;
Flush'd as they are with Folly, Youth and Wine,
Their prudent Insults to the Poor confine;
Afar they mark the Flambeau's bright Approach,
235 And shun the shining Train, and golden Coach.
In vain, these Dangers past, your Doors you close,
And hope the balmy Blessing of Repose:
Cruel with Guilt, and daring with Despair,
The midnight Murd'rer bursts the faithless Bar;
240 Invades the sacred Hour of silent Rest,
And leaves, unseen, a Dagger in your Breast.
Scarce can our Fields, such Crowds at *Tyburn* die,
With Hemp the Gallows and the Fleet supply.
Propose your Schemes, ye Senatorian Band,
245 Whose *Ways and Means* support the sinking Land;
Lest Ropes be wanting in the tempting Spring,
To rig another Convoy for the K—g.
A single Jail, in ALFRED's golden Reign,
Could half the Nation's Criminals contain;

250 Fair Justice then, without Constraint ador'd,
    Held high the steady Scale, but sheath'd the Sword;
    No Spies were paid, no *Special Juries* known,
    Blest Age! but ah! how diff'rent from our own!
       Much could I add,—but see the Boat at hand,
255 The Tide retiring, calls me from the Land:
    Farewel!—When Youth, and Health, and Fortune spent,
    Thou fly'st for Refuge to the Wilds of *Kent*;
    And tir'd like me with Follies and with Crimes,
    In angry Numbers warn'st succeeding Times;
260 Then shall thy Friend, nor thou refuse his Aid,
    Still Foe to Vice, forsake his *Cambrian* Shade;
    In Virtue's Cause once more exert his Rage,
    Thy Satire point, and animate thy Page.

TO POSTERITY

    Whene'er this Stone, now hid beneath the Lake,
    The Horse shall trample, or the Plough shall break,
    Then, O my Country! shalt thou groan distrest,
    Grief swell thine Eyes, and Terror chill thy Breast.
5   Thy Streets with Violence of Woe shall sound,
    Loud as the Billows bursting on the Ground.
    Then thro' thy Fields shall scarlet Reptiles stray,
    And Rapine and Pollution mark their Way.
    Their hungry Swarms the peaceful Vale shall fright
10 Still fierce to threaten, still afraid to fight;
    The teeming Year's whole Product shall devour,
    Insatiate pluck the Fruit, and crop the Flow'r:
    Shall glutton on the industrious Peasants Spoil,
    Rob without Fear, and fatten without Toil.
15 Then o'er the World shall Discord stretch her Wings,
    Kings change their Laws, and Kingdoms change their Kings.
    The Bear enrag'd th'affrighted Moon shall dread;
    The Lilies o'er the Vales triumphant spread;
    Nor shall the Lyon, wont of old to reign
20 Despotic o'er the desolated Plain,
    Henceforth th'inviolable Bloom invade,
    Or dare to murmur in the flow'ry Glade;
    His tortur'd Sons shall die before his Face,
    While he lies melting in a lewd Embrace;
25 And, yet more strange! his Veins a Horse shall drain,
    Nor shall the passive Coward once complain.

PROLOGUE TO GARRICK'S 'LETHE'

Prodigious Madness of the writing Race!
Ardent of Fame, yet fearless of Disgrace.
　　Without a boding Tear, or anxious Sigh,
The Bard obdurate sees his Brother die.
5　Deaf to the Critick, Sullen to the Friend,
Not One takes Warning, by another's End.
　　Oft has our Bard in this disastrous Year,
Beheld the Tragic Heroes taught to fear.
Oft has he seen the indignant Orange fly,
10　And heard th'ill Omen'd Catcall's direful Cry.
Yet dares to venture on the dangerous Stage,
And weakly hopes to 'scape the Critick's Rage.
　　This Night he hopes to shew that Farce may charm,
Tho' no lewd Hint the mantling Virgin warm,
15　That useful Truth with Humour may unite,
That Mirth may mend, and Innocence delight.

A TRANSLATION OF THE LATIN EPITAPH ON SIR THOMAS HANMER

Thou, who survey'st these walls with curious eye,
Pause at this tomb—where *Hanmer*'s ashes lie.
His various worth, thro' varied life attend,
And learn his virtues, while thou mourn'st his end.
5　His force of genius burn'd in early youth,
With thirst of knowledge, and with love of truth;
His learning, join'd with each endearing art,
Charm'd ev'ry ear, and gain'd on ev'ry heart;
Thus early wise, th'endanger'd realm to aid,
10　His country call'd him from the studious shade;
In life's first bloom his publick toils began,
At once commenc'd the senator and man.
In bus'ness dextrous, weighty in debate,
Thrice ten long years he labour'd for the state;
15　In ev'ry speech persuasive wisdom flow'd,
In ev'ry act, refulgent virtue glow'd;
Suspended faction ceas'd from rage and strife,
To hear his eloquence, and praise his life.

Resistless merit fix'd the senate's choice,
20 Who hail'd him Speaker, with united voice.
Illustrious age! how bright thy glories shone,
When *Hanmer* fill'd the chair, and *Ann* the throne!
Then—when dark arts obscur'd each fierce debate,
When mutual frauds perplex'd the maze of state,
25 The moderator firmly mild appear'd,
Beheld with love, with veneration heard.
This task perform'd, he sought no gainful post,
Nor wish'd to glitter at his country's cost;
Strict, on the right he fix'd his stedfast eye,
30 With temp'rate zeal, and wise anxiety;
Nor e'er from virtue's path was lur'd aside,
To pluck the flow'rs of pleasure, or of pride.
Her gifts despis'd, corruption blush'd and fled,
And fame persu'd him, where conviction led:
35 Age call'd, at length, his active mind to rest,
With honour sated, and with cares oppress'd;
To letter'd ease retir'd, and honest mirth,
To rural grandeur, and domestick worth,
Delighted still to please mankind, or mend,
40 The patriot's fire yet sparkled in the friend.
Calm conscience then his former life survey'd,
And recollected toils endear'd the shade;
Till nature call'd him to the gen'ral doom,
And virtue's sorrow dignify'd his tomb.

TO MISS ——

ON HER GIVING THE AUTHOR A GOLD AND SILK NET-WORK
PURSE OF HER OWN WEAVING

Tho' gold and silk their charms unite,
To make thy curious web delight,
In vain the vary'd work would shine,
If wrought by any hand but thine;
5 Thy hand, that knows the subtler art,
To weave those nets that catch the heart;
Spread out by me, the roving coin
Thy nets may catch, but not confine;
Nor can I hope, thy silken chain
10 The glitt'ring vagrants shall restrain.
Why, *Sylvia*, was it then decreed,
The heart, once caught, should ne'er be freed?

TO MISS ——
ON HER PLAYING UPON THE HARPSICHORD IN A ROOM
HUNG WITH SOME FLOWER-PIECES OF HER OWN PAINTING

When *Stella* strikes the tuneful string
In scenes of imitated Spring,
Where Beauty lavishes her pow'rs
On beds of never-fading flow'rs;
5   And pleasure propagates around
Each charm of modulated sound;
Ah! think not, in the dang'rous hour,
The nymph fictitious as the flow'r;
But shun, rash youth, the gay alcove,
10   Nor tempt the snares of wily love.
    When Charms thus press on ev'ry Sense,
What Thought of Flight, or of Defence?
Deceitful Hope, and vain Desire,
Forever flutter o'er her lyre;
15   Delighting, as the youth draws nigh,
To point the glances of her eye;
And forming with unerring art,
New chains to hold the captive-heart.
    But on those regions of delight,
20   Might Truth intrude, with daring Flight,
Could *Stella*, sprightly, fair and young,
One moment hear the moral song,
Instruction with her flow'rs might spring,
And Wisdom warble from her string.
25   Mark, when from thousand mingled dyes
Thou see'st one pleasing form arise;
How active light, and thoughtful shade,
In greater scenes each other aid;
Mark, when the diff'rent notes agree
30   In friendly contrariety;
How passion's well-accorded strife
Gives all the harmony of life:
Thy pictures shall thy conduct frame,
Consistent still, though not the same;
35   Thy musick teach the nobler art,
To tune the regulated heart.

STELLA IN MOURNING

When, lately *Stella*'s form display'd
The beauties of the gay brocade,
The nymphs, who found their pow'r decline,
Proclaim'd her, not so fair as fine.
5   'Fate! snatch away the bright disguise,
And let the goddess trust her eyes.'
Thus blindly pray'd the fretful fair,
And fate malicious heard the pray'r.
But brighten'd by the sable dress,
10   As virtue rises in distress,
Since *Stella* still extends her reign,
Ah! how shall envy sooth her pain?
     Th'adoring youth, and envious fair,
Henceforth shall form one common pray'r,
15   And Love and Hate alike implore
The skies, that *Stella* mourn no more.

THE WINTER'S WALK

Behold my fair, where-e'er we rove,
   What dreary prospects round us rise,
The naked hills, the leafless grove,
   The hoary ground, the frowning skies.

5   Nor only through the wasted plain,
   Stern winter, is thy force confest,
Still wider spreads thy horrid reign,
   I feel thy pow'r usurp my breast.

Enliv'ning hope, and fond desire,
10   Resign the heart to spleen and care,
Scarce frighted love maintains his fire,
   And rapture saddens to despair.

In groundless hope, and causeless fear,
   Unhappy man! behold thy doom,
15   Still changing with the changeful year,
   The slave of sunshine and of gloom.

Tir'd with vain joys, and false alarms,
  With mental and corporeal strife,
Snatch me, my *Stella*, to thy arms,
20   And hide me from the sight of life.

AN ODE

Stern winter now, by spring repress'd,
  Forbears the long-continu'd strife,
And nature, on her naked breast,
  Delights to catch the gales of life.

5 Now, o'er the rural kingdom roves
  Soft Pleasure with her laughing train,
Love warbles in the vocal groves,
  And vegetation paints the plain.

Unhappy! whom to beds of pain
10   Arthritic tyranny consigns,
Whom smiling nature courts in vain,
  Tho' rapture sings, and beauty shines.

Yet, tho' my limbs disease invades,
  Her wings Imagination tries,
15 And bears me to the peaceful shades,
  Where —'s humble turrets rise.

Here stop, my soul, thy rapid flight,
  Nor from the pleasing groves depart,
Where first great nature charm'd my sight,
20   Where wisdom first inform'd my heart.

Here, let me, thro' the vales, pursue
  A guide, a father, and a friend;
Once more great nature's work review,
  Once more on wisdom's voice attend.

25 From false caresses, causeless strife,
  Wild hope, vain fear, alike remov'd,
Here let me learn the use of life,
  Then best enjoy'd, when most improv'd.

Teach me, thou venerable bow'r,
   Cool meditation's quiet seat,
30
The gen'rous scorn of venal pow'r,
   The silent grandeur of retreat.

When Pride, by guilt, to greatness climbs,
   Or raging factions rush to war,
35
Here let me learn to shun the crimes
   I can't prevent, and will not share.

But, lest I fall by subtler foes,
   Bright wisdom teach me *Curio*'s art,
The swelling passions to compose,
40
   And quell the rebels of the heart.

TO LYCE, AN ELDERLY LADY

Ye nymphs whom starry rays invest,
   By flatt'ring poets giv'n;
Who shine, by lavish lovers drest,
   In all the pomp of heav'n;

5
Engross not all the beams on high,
   Which gild a lover's lays,
But as your sister of the sky,
   Let *Lyce* share the praise.

Her silver locks display the moon,
10
   Her brows a cloudy show,
Striped rainbows round her eyes are seen,
   And show'rs from either flow.

Her teeth the night with darkness dyes,
   She's starr'd with pimples o'er,
15
Her tongue like nimble lightning plies,
   And can with thunder roar.

But some *Zelinda* while I sing
   Denies my *Lyce* shines,
And all the pens of *Cupid*'s wing
20
   Attack my gentle lines.

Yet spite of fair *Zelinda*'s eye,
  And all her bards express,
My *Lyce* makes as good a sky,
  And I but flatter less.

PROLOGUE SPOKEN BY MR GARRICK AT THE OPENING OF THE THEATRE IN DRURY-LANE, 1747

When Learning's Triumph o'er her barb'rous Foes
First rear'd the Stage, immortal Shakespear rose;
Each Change of many-colour'd Life he drew,
Exhausted Worlds, and then imagin'd new:
5   Existence saw him spurn her bounded Reign,
And panting Time toil'd after him in vain:
His pow'rful Strokes presiding Truth impress'd,
And unresisted Passion storm'd the Breast.
  Then Johnson came, instructed from the School,
10   To please in Method, and invent by Rule;
His studious Patience, and laborious Art,
By regular Approach essay'd the Heart;
Cold Approbation gave the ling'ring Bays,
For those who durst not censure, scarce cou'd praise.
15   A Mortal born he met the general Doom,
But left, like *Egypt*'s Kings, a lasting Tomb.
  The Wits of *Charles* found easier Ways to Fame,
Nor wish'd for Johnson's Art, or Shakespear's Flame;
Themselves they studied, as they felt, they writ,
20   Intrigue was Plot, Obscenity was Wit.
Vice always found a sympathetick Friend;
They pleas'd their Age, and did not aim to mend.
Yet Bards like these aspir'd to lasting Praise,
And proudly hop'd to pimp in future Days.
25   Their Cause was gen'ral, their Supports were strong,
Their Slaves were willing, and their Reign was long;
Till Shame regain'd the Post that Sense betray'd,
And Virtue call'd Oblivion to her Aid.
  Then crush'd by Rules, and weaken'd as refin'd,
30   For Years the Pow'r of Tragedy declin'd;
From Bard, to Bard, the frigid Caution crept,
Till Declamation roar'd, while Passion slept.
Yet still did Virtue deign the Stage to tread,
Philosophy remain'd, though Nature fled.

35   But forc'd at length her antient Reign to quit,
        She saw great *Faustus* lay the Ghost of Wit:
        Exulting Folly hail'd the joyful Day,
        And Pantomime, and Song, confirm'd her Sway.
            But who the coming Changes can presage,
40   And mark the future Periods of the Stage?—
        Perhaps if Skill could distant Times explore,
        New *Behns*, new *Durfeys*, yet remain in Store.
        Perhaps, where *Lear* has rav'd, and *Hamlet* dy'd,
        On flying Cars new Sorcerers may ride.
45   Perhaps, for who can guess th'Effects of Chance?
        Here *Hunt* may box, or *Mahomet* may dance.
            Hard is his lot, that here by Fortune plac'd,
        Must watch the wild Vicissitudes of Taste;
        With ev'ry Meteor of Caprice must play,
50   And chase the new-blown Bubbles of the Day.
        Ah! let not Censure term our Fate our Choice,
        The Stage but echoes back the publick Voice.
        The Drama's Laws the Drama's Patrons give,
        For we that live to please, must please to live.
55   Then prompt no more the Follies you decry,
        As Tyrants doom their Tools of Guilt to die;
        'Tis yours this Night to bid the Reign commence
        Of rescu'd Nature, and reviving Sense;
        To chase the Charms of Sound, the Pomp of Show,
60   For useful Mirth, and salutary Woe;
        Bid scenic Virtue form the rising Age,
        And Truth diffuse her Radiance from the Stage.

THE VANITY OF HUMAN WISHES
THE TENTH SATIRE OF JUVENAL, IMITATED

        Let Observation with extensive View,
        Survey Mankind, from *China* to *Peru*;
        Remark each anxious Toil, each eager Strife,
        And watch the busy Scenes of crouded Life;
5   Then say how Hope and Fear, Desire and Hate,
        O'erspread with Snares the clouded Maze of Fate,
        Where wav'ring Man, betray'd by vent'rous Pride,
        To tread the dreary Paths without a Guide;
        As treach'rous Phantoms in the Mist delude,
10   Shuns fancied Ills, or chases airy Good.

How rarely Reason guides the stubborn Choice,
Rules the bold Hand, or prompts the suppliant Voice,
How Nations sink, by darling Schemes oppress'd,
When Vengeance listens to the Fool's Request.
15 Fate wings with ev'ry Wish th' afflictive Dart,
Each Gift of Nature, and each Grace of Art,
With fatal Heat impetuous Courage glows,
With fatal Sweetness Elocution flows,
Impeachment stops the Speaker's pow'rful Breath,
20 And restless Fire precipitates on Death.
   But scarce observ'd the Knowing and the Bold,
Fall in the gen'ral Massacre of Gold;
Wide-wasting Pest! that rages unconfin'd,
And crouds with Crimes the Records of Mankind,
25 For Gold his Sword the Hireling Ruffian draws,
For Gold the hireling Judge distorts the Laws;
Wealth heap'd on Wealth, nor Truth nor Safety buys,
The Dangers gather as the Treasures rise.
   Let Hist'ry tell where rival Kings command,
30 And dubious Title shakes the madded Land,
When Statutes glean the Refuse of the Sword,
How much more safe the Vassal than the Lord,
Low sculks the Hind beneath the Rage of Pow'r,
And leaves the wealthy Traytor in the *Tow'r*,
35 Untouch'd his Cottage, and his Slumbers sound,
Tho' Confiscation's Vulturs hover round.
   The needy Traveller, serene and gay,
Walks the wild Heath, and sings his Toil away.
Does Envy seize thee? crush th' upbraiding Joy,
40 Increase his Riches and his Peace destroy,
Now Fears in dire Vicissitude invade,
The rustling Brake alarms, and quiv'ring Shade,
Nor Light nor Darkness bring his Pain Relief,
One shews the Plunder, and one hides the Thief.
45 Yet still one gen'ral Cry the Skies assails,
And Gain and Grandeur load the tainted Gales;
Few know the toiling Statesman's Fear or Care,
Th' insidious Rival and the gaping Heir.
   Once more, *Democritus*, arise on Earth,
50 With chearful Wisdom and instructive Mirth,
See motly Life in modern Trappings dress'd,
And feed with varied Fools th' eternal Jest:
Thou who couldst laugh where Want enchain'd Caprice,
Toil crush'd Conceit, and Man was of a Piece;
55 Where Wealth unlov'd without a Mourner dy'd;
And scarce a Sycophant was fed by Pride;
Where ne'er was known the Form of mock Debate,
Or seen a new-made Mayor's unwieldy State;

Where Change of Fav'rites made no Change of Laws,
60 And Senates heard before they judg'd a Cause;
How wouldst thou shake at *Britain*'s modish Tribe,
Dart the quick Taunt, and edge the piercing Gibe?
Attentive Truth and Nature to descry,
And pierce each Scene with Philosophic Eye.
65 To thee were solemn Toys or empty Shew,
The Robes of Pleasure and the Veils of Woe:
All aid the Farce, and all thy Mirth maintain,
Whose Joys are causeless, or whose Griefs are vain.
    Such was the Scorn that fill'd the Sage's Mind,
70 Renew'd at ev'ry Glance on Humankind;
How just that Scorn ere yet thy Voice declare,
Search every State, and canvass ev'ry Pray'r.
    Unnumber'd Suppliants croud Preferment's Gate,
Athirst for Wealth, and burning to be great;
75 Delusive Fortune hears th' incessant Call,
They mount, they shine, evaporate, and fall.
On ev'ry Stage the Foes of Peace attend,
Hate dogs their Flight, and Insult mocks their End.
Love ends with Hope, the sinking Statesman's Door
80 Pours in the Morning Worshiper no more;
For growing Names the weekly Scribbler lies,
To growing Wealth the Dedicator flies,
From every Room descends the painted Face,
That hung the bright *Palladium* of the Place,
85 And smoak'd in Kitchens, or in Auctions sold,
To better Features yields the Frame of Gold;
For now no more we trace in ev'ry Line
Heroic Worth, Benevolence Divine:
The Form distorted justifies the Fall,
90 And Detestation rids th' indignant Wall.
    But will not *Britain* hear the last Appeal,
Sign her Foes Doom, or guard her Fav'rites Zeal;
Through Freedom's Sons no more Remonstrance rings,
Degrading Nobles and controuling Kings;
95 Our supple Tribes repress their Patriot Throats,
And ask no Questions but the Price of Votes;
With Weekly Libels and Septennial Ale,
Their Wish is full to riot and to rail.
    In full-blown Dignity, see *Wolsey* stand,
100 Law in his Voice, and Fortune in his Hand:
To him the Church, the Realm, their Pow'rs consign,
Thro' him the Rays of regal Bounty shine,
Turn'd by his Nod the Stream of Honour flows,
His Smile alone Security bestows:
105 Still to new Heights his restless Wishes tow'r,
Claim leads to Claim, and Pow'r advances Pow'r;

Till Conquest unresisted ceas'd to please,
And Rights submitted, left him none to seize.
At length his Sov'reign frowns—the Train of State
110 Mark the keen Glance, and watch the Sign to hate;
Where-e'er he turns he meets a Stranger's Eye,
His Suppliants scorn him, and his Followers fly;
Now drops at once the Pride of aweful State,
The golden Canopy, the glitt'ring Plate,
115 The regal Palace, the luxurious Board,
The liv'ried Army, and the menial Lord.
With Age, with Cares, with Maladies oppress'd,
He seeks the Refuge of Monastic Rest.
Grief aids Disease, remember'd Folly stings,
120 And his last Sighs reproach the Faith of Kings.
  Speak thou, whose Thoughts at humble Peace repine,
Shall *Wolsey*'s Wealth, with *Wolsey*'s End be thine?
Or liv'st thou now, with safer Pride content,
The wisest Justice on the Banks of *Trent*?
125 For why did *Wolsey* near the Steeps of Fate,
On weak Foundations raise th' enormous Weight?
Why but to sink beneath Misfortune's Blow,
With louder Ruin to the Gulphs below?
  What gave great *Villiers* to th' Assassin's Knife,
130 And fix'd Disease on *Harley*'s closing Life?
What murder'd *Wentworth*, and what exil'd *Hyde*,
By Kings protected, and to Kings ally'd?
What but their Wish indulg'd in Courts to shine,
And Pow'r too great to keep or to resign?
135 When first the College Rolls receive his Name,
The young Enthusiast quits his Ease for Fame;
Through all his Veins the Fever of Renown
Burns from the strong Contagion of the Gown;
O'er *Bodley*'s Dome his future Labours spread,
140 And *Bacon*'s Mansion trembles o'er his Head.
Are these thy Views? proceed, illustrious Youth,
And Virtue guard thee to the Throne of Truth!
Yet should thy Soul indulge the gen'rous Heat,
Till captive Science yields her last Retreat;
145 Should Reason guide thee with her brightest Ray,
And pour on misty Doubt resistless Day;
Should no false Kindness lure to loose Delight,
Nor Praise relax, nor Difficulty fright;
Should tempting Novelty thy Cell refrain,
150 And Sloth effuse her opiate Fumes in vain;
Should Beauty blunt on Fops her fatal Dart,
Nor claim the Triumph of a letter'd Heart;
Should no Disease thy torpid Veins invade,
Nor Melancholy's Phantoms haunt thy Shade;

155 Yet hope not Life from Grief or Danger free,
    Nor think the Doom of Man revers'd for thee:
    Deign on the passing World to turn thine Eyes,
    And pause awhile from Letters, to be wise;
    There mark what Ills the Scholar's Life assail,
160 Toil, Envy, Want, the Patron, and the Jail.
    See Nations slowly wise, and meanly just,
    To buried Merit raise the tardy Bust.
    If Dreams yet flatter, once again attend,
    Hear *Lydiat*'s life, and *Galileo*'s end.
165   Nor deem, when Learning her last Prize bestows
    The glitt'ring Eminence exempt from Foes;
    See when the Vulgar 'scape, despis'd or aw'd,
    Rebellion's vengeful Talons seize on *Laud*.
    From meaner Minds, tho' smaller Fines content
170 The plunder'd Palace or sequester'd Rent;
    Mark'd out by dangerous Parts he meets the Shock,
    And fatal Learning leads him to the Block:
    Around his Tomb let Art and Genius weep,
    But hear his Death, ye Blockheads, hear and sleep.
175   The festal Blazes, the triumphal Show,
    The ravish'd Standard, and the captive Foe,
    The Senate's Thanks, the Gazette's pompous Tale,
    With Force resistless o'er the Brave prevail.
    Such Bribes the rapid *Greek* o'er *Asia* whirl'd,
180 For such the steady *Romans* shook the World;
    For such in distant Lands the *Britons* shine,
    And stain with Blood the *Danube* or the *Rhine*;
    This Pow'r has Praise, that Virtue scarce can warm,
    Till Fame supplies the universal Charm.
185 Yet Reason frowns on War's unequal Game,
    Where wasted Nations raise a single Name,
    And mortgag'd States their Grandsires Wreaths regret,
    From Age to Age in everlasting Debt;
    Wreaths which at last the dear-bought Right convey
190 To rust on Medals, or on Stones decay.
       On what Foundation stands the Warrior's Pride,
    How just his Hopes let *Swedish Charles* decide;
    A Frame of Adamant, a Soul of Fire,
    No Dangers fright him, and no Labours tire;
195 O'er Love, o'er Fear extends his wide Domain,
    Unconquer'd Lord of Pleasure and of Pain;
    No Joys to him pacific Scepters yield,
    War sounds the Trump, he rushes to the Field;
    Behold surrounding Kings their Pow'rs combine,
200 And One capitulate, and One resign;
    Peace courts his Hand, but spreads her Charms in vain;
    'Think Nothing gain'd,' he cries, 'till nought remain,

On *Moscow*'s Walls till *Gothic* Standards fly,
And All be mine beneath the Polar Sky.'
205 The March begins in Military State,
And Nations on his Eye suspended wait;
Stern Famine guards the solitary Coast,
And Winter barricades the Realms of Frost;
He comes, nor Want nor Cold his Course delay;—
210 Hide, blushing Glory, hide *Pultowa*'s Day:
The vanquish'd Hero leaves his broken Bands,
And shews his Miseries in distant Lands;
Condemn'd a needy Supplicant to wait,
While Ladies interpose, and Slaves debate.
215 But did not Chance at length her Error mend?
Did no subverted Empire mark his End?
Did rival Monarchs give the fatal Wound?
Or hostile Millions press him to the Ground?
His Fall was destin'd to a barren Strand,
220 A petty Fortress, and a dubious Hand;
He left the Name, at which the World grew pale,
To point a Moral, or adorn a Tale.
    All Times their Scenes of pompous Woes afford,
From *Persia*'s Tyrant to *Bavaria*'s Lord.
225 In gay Hostility, and barb'rous Pride,
With half Mankind embattled at his Side,
Great *Xerxes* comes to seize the certain Prey,
And starves exhausted Regions in his Way;
Attendant Flatt'ry counts his Myriads o'er,
230 Till counted Myriads sooth his Pride no more;
Fresh Praise is try'd till Madness fires his Mind,
The Waves he lashes, and enchains the Wind;
New Pow'rs are claim'd, new Pow'rs are still bestow'd,
Till rude Resistance lops the spreading God;
235 The daring *Greeks* deride the Martial Shew,
And heap their Vallies with the gaudy Foe;
Th' insulted Sea with humbler Thoughts he gains,
A single Skiff to speed his Flight remains;
Th' incumber'd Oar scarce leaves the dreaded Coast
240 Through purple Billows and a floating Host.
    The bold *Bavarian*, in a luckless Hour,
Tries the dread Summits of *Cesarean* Pow'r,
With unexpected Legions bursts away,
And sees defenceless Realms receive his Sway;
245 Short Sway! fair *Austria* spreads her mournful Charms,
The Queen, the Beauty, sets the World in Arms;
From Hill to Hill the Beacons rousing Blaze
Spreads wide the Hope of Plunder and of Praise;
The fierce *Croatian*, and the wild *Hussar*,
250 With all the Sons of Ravage croud the War;

The baffled Prince in Honour's flatt'ring Bloom
Of hasty Greatness finds the fatal Doom,
His Foes Derision, and his Subjects Blame,
And steals to Death from Anguish and from **Shame.**
255　Enlarge my Life with Multitude of Days,
In Health, in Sickness, thus the Suppliant prays;
Hides from himself his State, and shuns to know,
That Life protracted is protracted Woe.
Time hovers o'er, impatient to destroy,
260　And shuts up all the Passages of Joy:
In vain their Gifts the bounteous Seasons pour,
The Fruit Autumnal, and the Vernal Flow'r,
With listless Eyes the Dotard views the Store,
He views, and wonders that they please no more;
265　Now pall the tastless Meats, and joyless Wines,
And Luxury with Sighs her Slave resigns.
Approach, ye Minstrels, try the soothing Strain,
Diffuse the tuneful Lenitives of Pain:
No Sounds alas would touch th' impervious Ear,
270　Though dancing Mountains witness'd *Orpheus* near;
Nor Lute nor Lyre his feeble Pow'rs attend,
Nor sweeter Musick of a virtuous Friend,
But everlasting Dictates croud his Tongue,
Perversely grave, or positively wrong.
275　The still returning Tale, and ling'ring Jest,
Perplex the fawning Niece and pamper'd Guest,
While growing Hopes scarce awe the gath'ring **Sneer,**
And scarce a Legacy can bribe to hear;
The watchful Guests still hint the last Offence,
280　The Daughter's Petulance, the Son's Expence,
Improve his heady Rage with treach'rous Skill,
And mould his Passions till they make his Will.
　　Unnumber'd Maladies his Joints invade,
Lay Siege to Life and press the dire Blockade;
285　But unextinguish'd Av'rice still remains,
And dreaded Losses aggravate his Pains;
He turns, with anxious Heart and cripled Hands,
His Bonds of Debt, and Mortgages of Lands;
Or views his Coffers with suspicious Eyes,
290　Unlocks his Gold, and counts it till he dies.
　　But grant, the Virtues of a temp'rate Prime
Bless with an Age exempt from Scorn or Crime;
An Age that melts with unperceiv'd Decay,
And glides in modest Innocence away;
295　Whose peaceful Day Benevolence endears,
Whose Night congratulating Conscience cheers;
The gen'ral Fav'rite as the gen'ral Friend:
Such Age there is, and who shall wish its End?

Yet ev'n on this her Load Misfortune flings,
300 To press the weary Minutes flagging Wings:
New Sorrow rises as the Day returns,
A Sister sickens, or a Daughter mourns.
Now Kindred Merit fills the sable Bier,
Now lacerated Friendship claims a Tear.

305 Year chases Year, Decay pursues Decay,
Still drops some Joy from with'ring Life away;
New Forms arise, and diff'rent Views engage,
Superfluous lags the Vet'ran on the Stage,
Till pitying Nature signs the last Release,
310 And bids afflicted Worth retire to Peace.
        But few there are whom Hours like these await,
Who set unclouded in the Gulphs of Fate.
From *Lydia*'s Monarch should the Search descend,
By *Solon* caution'd to regard his End,
315 In Life's last Scene what Prodigies surprise,
Fears of the Brave, and Follies of the Wise?
From *Marlb'rough*'s Eyes the Streams of Dotage flow,
And *Swift* expires a Driv'ler and a Show.
        The teeming Mother, anxious for her Race,
320 Begs for each Birth the Fortune of a Face:
Yet *Vane* could tell what Ills from Beauty spring;
And *Sedley* curs'd the Form that pleas'd a King.
Ye Nymphs of rosy Lips and radiant Eyes,
Whom Pleasure keeps too busy to be wise,
325 Whom Joys with soft Varieties invite,
By Day the Frolick, and the Dance by Night,
Who frown with Vanity, who smile with Art,
And ask the latest Fashion of the Heart,
What Care, what Rules your heedless Charms shall save,
330 Each Nymph your Rival, and each Youth your Slave?
Against your Fame with Fondness Hate combines,
The Rival batters, and the Lover mines.
With distant Voice neglected Virtue calls,
Less heard and less, the faint Remonstrance falls;
335 Tir'd with Contempt, she quits the slipp'ry Reign,
And Pride and Prudence take her Seat in vain.
In croud at once, where none the Pass defend,
The harmless Freedom, and the private Friend.
The Guardians yield, by Force superior ply'd;
340 To Int'rest, Prudence; and to Flatt'ry, Pride.
Here Beauty falls betray'd, despis'd, distress'd,
And hissing Infamy proclaims the rest.
        Where then shall Hope and Fear their Objects find?
Must dull Suspence corrupt the stagnant Mind?
345 Must helpless Man, in Ignorance sedate,
Roll darkling down the Torrent of his Fate?

     Must no Dislike alarm, no Wishes rise,
     Nor Cries invoke the Mercies of the Skies?
     Enquirer, cease, Petitions yet remain,
350 Which Heav'n may hear, nor deem Religion vain.
     Still raise for Good the supplicating Voice,
     But leave to Heav'n the Measure and the Choice.
     Safe in his Pow'r, whose Eyes discern afar
     The secret Ambush of a specious Pray'r.
355 Implore his Aid, in his Decisions rest,
     Secure whate'er he gives, he gives the best.
     Yet when the Sense of sacred Presence fires,
     And Strong Devotion to the Skies aspires,
     Pour forth thy Fervours for a healthful Mind,
360 Obedient Passions, and a Will resign'd;
     For Love, which scarce collective Man can fill;
     For Patience sov'reign o'er transmuted Ill;
     For Faith, that panting for a happier Seat,
     Counts Death kind Nature's Signal of Retreat:
365 These Goods for Man the Laws of Heav'n ordain,
     These Goods he grants, who grants the Pow'r to gain;
     With these celestial Wisdom calms the Mind,
     And makes the Happiness she does not find.

A NEW PROLOGUE SPOKEN AT THE REPRESENTATION OF *COMUS*

     Ye patriot Crouds, who burn for *England*'s Fame,
     Ye Nymphs, whose Bosoms beat at Milton's Name,
     Whose gen'rous Zeal, unbought by flatt'ring Rhimes,
     Shames the mean Pensions of *Augustan* Times;
5   Immortal Patrons of succeeding Days,
     Attend this Prelude of perpetual Praise!
     Let Wit, condemn'd the feeble War to wage
     With close Malevolence, or public Rage;
     Let Study, worn with Virtue's fruitless Lore,
10 Behold this Theatre, and grieve no more.
     This Night, distinguish'd by your Smile, shall tell,
     That never Briton can in vain excel;
     The slighted Arts Futurity shall trust,
     And rising Ages hasten to be just.
15   At length our mighty Bard's victorious Lays
     Fill the loud Voice of universal Praise,

And baffled Spite, with hopeless Anguish dumb,
Yields to Renown the Centuries to come.
With ardent Haste, each Candidate of Fame
20   Ambitious catches at his tow'ring Name:
He sees, and pitying sees, vain Wealth bestow
Those pageant Honours which he scorn'd below:
While Crowds aloft the laureat Bust behold,
Or trace his Form on circulating Gold,
25   Unknown, unheeded, long his Offspring lay,
And Want hung threat'ning o'er her slow Decay.
What tho' she shine with no Miltonian Fire,
No fav'ring Muse her morning Dreams inspire;
Yet softer Claims the melting Heart engage,
30   Her Youth laborious, and her blameless Age:
Hers the mild Merits of domestic Life,
The patient Suff'rer, and the faithful Wife.
Thus grac'd with humble Virtue's native Charms
Her Grandsire leaves her in *Britannia*'s Arms,
35   Secure with Peace, with Competence, to dwell,
While tutelary Nations guard her Cell.
Yours is the Charge, ye Fair, ye Wise, ye Brave!
'Tis yours to crown Desert—beyond the Grave!

THE ANT

From Proverbs, chap. vi. ver.

Turn on the prudent Ant, thy heedful eyes,
Observe her labours, Sluggard, and be wise.
No stern command, no monitory voice
Prescribes her duties, or directs her choice,
5   Yet timely provident, she hastes away
To snatch the blessings of the plenteous day;
When fruitful summer loads the teeming plain,
She gleans the harvest, and she stores the grain.
    How long shall sloth usurp thy useless hours,
10   Dissolve thy vigour, and enchain thy powers?
While artful shades thy downy couch enclose,
And soft solicitation courts repose,
Amidst the drousy charms of dull delight,
Year chases year, with unremitted flight,
15   Till want, now following fraudulent and slow,
Shall spring to seize thee like an ambush'd foe.

PROLOGUE TO 'THE GOOD NATUR'D MAN'

Prest by the load of life, the weary mind
Surveys the general toil of human kind;
With cool submission joins the labouring train,
And social sorrow loses half its pain:
5   Our anxious Bard, without complaint, may share
This bustling season's epidemic care.
Like Cæsar's pilot, dignified by fate,
Tost in one common storm with all the great;
Distrest alike, the statesman and the wit,
10   When one a borough courts, and one the pit.
The busy candidates for power and fame,
Have hopes, and fears, and wishes, just the same;
Disabled both to combat, or to fly,
Must hear all taunts, and hear without reply.
15   Uncheck'd on both, loud rabbles vent their rage,
As mongrels bay the lion in a cage.
Th'offended burgess hoards his angry tale,
For that blest year when all that vote may rail;
Their schemes of spite the poet's foes dismiss,
20   Till that glad night when all that hate may hiss.
This day the powder'd curls and golden coat,
Says swelling Crispin, begg'd a cobbler's vote.
This night our wit, the pert apprentice cries,
Lies at my feet, I hiss him, and he dies.
25   The great, 'tis true, can charm th'electing tribe;
The bard may supplicate, but cannot bribe.
Yet judg'd by those, whose voices ne'er were sold,
He feels no want of ill persuading gold;
But confident of praise, if praise be due,
30   Trusts without fear, to merit, and to you.

[EPITAPH ON WILLIAM HOGARTH]

The Hand of Art here torpid lies
    That wav'd th'essential Form of Grace,
Here death has clos'd the curious eyes
    That saw the manners in the face.

5   If Genius warm thee, Reader, stay,
    If Merit touch thee, shed a tear,
Be Vice and Dulness far away
    Great Hogarth's honour'd Dust is here.

[TO MRS THRALE ON HER THIRTY FIFTH BIRTHDAY]

    Oft in Danger yet alive
    We are come to Thirty five;
    Long may better Years arrive,
    Better Years than Thirty five;
5   Could Philosophers contrive
    Life to stop at Thirty five,
    Time his Hours should never drive
    O'er the Bounds of Thirty five:
    High to soar and deep to dive
10   Nature gives at Thirty five;
    Ladies—stock and tend your Hive,
    Trifle not at Thirty five:
    For howe'er we boast and strive,
    Life declines from Thirty five;
15   He that ever hopes to thrive
    Must begin by Thirty five;
And those who wisely wish to wive,
Must look on *Thrale* at Thirty five.

[LINES ON THOMAS WARTON'S POEMS]

I

    Wheresoe'er I turn my View,
    All is strange, yet nothing new;
    Endless Labour all along,
    Endless Labour to be wrong;
5   Phrase that Time has flung away,
    Uncouth Words in Disarray:
    Trickt in Antique Ruff and Bonnet,
    Ode and Elegy and Sonnet.

2

Hermit hoar, in solemn cell,
   Wearing out life's evening gray;
Smite thy bosom, sage, and tell,
   Where is bliss? and which the way?

5   Thus I spoke; and speaking sigh'd;
   —Scarce repress'd the starting tear;—
When the smiling sage reply'd—
   —Come, my lad, and drink some beer.

PROLOGUE TO 'A WORD TO THE WISE'

This night presents a play, which publick rage,
Or right, or wrong, once hooted from the stage;
From zeal or malice now no more we dread,
For English vengeance *wars not with the dead.*
5   A generous foe regards, with pitying eye,
The man whom fate has laid, where all must lye.
To wit, reviving from its author's dust,
Be kind, ye judges, or at least be just:
Let no resentful petulance invade
10   Th'oblivious grave's inviolable shade.
Let one great payment every claim appease,
And him who cannot hurt, allow to please;
To please by scenes unconscious of offence,
By harmless merriment, or useful sense.
15   Where aught of bright, or fair, the piece displays,
Approve it only—'tis too late to praise.
If want of skill, or want of care appear,
Forbear to hiss—the Poet cannot hear.
By all, like him, must praise and blame be found;
20   At best, a fleeting gleam, or empty sound.
Yet then shall calm reflection bless the night,
When liberal pity dignify'd delight;
When pleasure fired her torch at Virtue's flame,
And mirth was bounty with a humbler name.

[ANACREON, ODE IX]

Lovely Courier of the sky
Whence or whither dost thou fly?
Scatt'ring, as thy Pinions play,
Liquid Fragrance all the way:
5   Is it Business? is it Love?
Tell me, Tell me, gentle Dove.

'Soft Anacreon's Vows I bear,
Vows to Myrtale the fair;
Grac'd with all that charms the heart,
10   Blushing Nature, smiling Art.
Venus, courted with an Ode,
On the Bard her Dove bestow'd,
Vested with a Master's Right
Now Anacreon rules my Flight.
15   His the Letters which you see,
Weighty Charge consign'd to me:
Think not yet my Service hard,
Joyless Task without Reward;
Smiling at my Master's Gates,
20   Freedom my Return awaits,
But the Liberal Grant in vain
Tempts me to be wild again;
Can a prudent Dove decline
Blissful Bondage such as mine?
25   Over Hills and Fields to roam,
Fortune's Guest, without a home,
Under Leaves to hide one's head,
Slightly shelter'd, coarsely fed?
Now my better Lot bestows
30   Sweet Repast, and soft Repose:
Now the generous Bowl I sip
As it leaves Anacreon's Lip,
Void of Care, and free from dread
From his Fingers snatch his Bread,
35   Then with luscious Plenty gay
Round his Chamber dance and play,
Or from Wine as Courage springs,
O'er his Face extend my Wings;
And when Feast and Frolick tire,
40   Drop asleep upon his Lyre.

This is all;—be quick and go,
More than all thou canst not know;
Let me now my Pinions ply,
I have chatter'd like a Pye.'

A SHORT SONG OF CONGRATULATION

Long-expected one and twenty
Ling'ring year at last is flown,
Pomp and Pleasure, Pride and Plenty
Great Sir John, are all your own.

5   Loosen'd from the Minor's tether,
Free to mortgage or to sell,
Wild as wind, and light as feather
Bid the slaves of thrift farewel.

Call the Bettys, Kates, and Jennys
10   Ev'ry name that laughs at Care,
Lavish of your Grandsire's guineas,
Show the Spirit of an heir.

All that prey on vice and folly
Joy to see their quarry fly,
15   Here the Gamester light and jolly,
There the Lender grave and sly.

Wealth, Sir John, was made to wander,
Let it wander as it will;
See the Jocky, see the Pander,
20   Bid them come, and take their fill.

When the bonny Blade carouses,
Pockets full, and Spirits high,
What are acres? what are houses?
Only dirt, or wet or dry.

25   If the Guardian or the Mother
Tell the woes of wilful waste,
Scorn their counsel and their pother,
You can hang or drown at last.

ON THE DEATH OF DR ROBERT LEVET

Condemn'd to hope's delusive mine,
  As on we toil from day to day,
By sudden blasts, or slow decline,
  Our social comforts drop away.

5   Well tried through many a varying year,
  See LEVET to the grave descend;
Officious, innocent, sincere,
  Of ev'ry friendless name the friend.

Yet still he fills affection's eye,
10   Obscurely wise, and coarsely kind;
Nor, letter'd arrogance, deny
  Thy praise to merit unrefin'd.

When fainting nature call'd for aid,
  And hov'ring death prepar'd the blow,
15   His vig'rous remedy display'd
  The power of art without the show.

In misery's darkest caverns known,
  His useful care was ever nigh,
Where hopeless anguish pour'd his groan,
20   And lonely want retir'd to die.

No summons mock'd by chill delay,
  No petty gain disdain'd by pride,
The modest wants of ev'ry day
  The toil of ev'ry day supplied.

25   His virtues walk'd their narrow round,
  Nor made a pause, nor left a void;
And sure th'Eternal Master found
  The single talent well employ'd.

The busy day, the peaceful night,
30   Unfelt, uncounted, glided by;
His frame was firm, his powers were bright,
  Tho' now his eightieth year was nigh.

Then with no throbbing fiery pain,
  No cold gradations of decay,
35   Death broke at once the vital chain,
  And free'd his soul the nearest way.

TRANSLATION OF HORACE 'ODES' BOOK IV.
VII

The snow dissolv'd no more is seen,
The fields, and woods, behold, are green,
The changing year renews the plain,
The rivers know their banks again,
5　The spritely Nymph and naked Grace
The mazy dance together trace.
The changing year's successive plan
Proclaims mortality to Man.
Rough Winter's blasts to Spring give way,
10　Spring yields to Summer's sovereign ray,
Then Summer sinks in Autumn's reign,
And Winter chills the World again.
Her losses soon the Moon supplies,
But wretched Man, when once he lies
15　Where Priam and his sons are laid,
Is nought but Ashes and a Shade.
Who knows if Jove who counts our Score
Will toss us in a morning more?
What with your friend you nobly share
20　At least you rescue from your heir.
Not you, Torquatus, boast of Rome,
When Minos once has fix'd your doom,
Or Eloquence, or splendid birth
Or Virtue shall replace on earth.
25　Hyppolytus unjustly slain
Diana calls to life in vain,
Nor can the might of Theseus rend
The chains of hell that hold his friend.

Oliver Goldsmith (1729–74)

Like Swift, Goldsmith was an Irishman and, like him also, he went to Trinity College, Dublin. He considered clerical, legal and medical careers, but finally settled in 1755 for travelling around Europe. Like Johnson, he sought a living as a literary hack, supplemented by work as a doctor. He became a member of Dr Johnson's literary circle, but both here and in other social groups Goldsmith seems to have been regarded as somewhat of a butt and a buffoon. His work covers not only poetry, but also essays, plays (*She Stoops to Conquer* and *The Good Natured Man*) and a novel (*The Vicar of Wakefield*).

[PROLOGUE OF LABERIUS]

Necessitas cujus cursus transversi impetum, &c.

What! no way left to shun th' inglorious stage,
And save from infamy my sinking age.
Scarce half alive, oppress'd with many a year,
What in the name of dotage drives me here?
5   A time there was, when glory was my guide,
Nor force nor fraud could turn my steps aside,
Unaw'd by pow'r and unappal'd by fear,
With honest thrift I held my honour dear,
But this vile hour disperses all my store,
10   And all my hoard of honour is no more.
For ah! too partial to my life's decline,
Caesar persuades, submission must be mine,
Him I obey, whom heaven itself obeys,
Hopeless of pleasing, yet inclin'd to please.
15   Here then at once, I welcome every shame,
And cancel at threescore a life of fame;
No more my titles shall my children tell,
The old buffoon will fit my name as well;
This day beyond its term my fate extends,
20   For life is ended when our honour ends.

Oliver Goldsmith

THE GIFT
TO IRIS, IN BOW-STREET, COVENT-GARDEN

Say, cruel Iris, pretty rake,
    Dear mercenary beauty,
What annual offering shall I make,
    Expressive of my duty.

5   My heart, a victim to thine eyes,
    Should I at once deliver,
Say, would the angry fair one prize
    The gift, who slights the giver.

A bill, a jewel, watch, or toy,
10   My rivals give——and let 'em.
If gems, or gold, impart a joy,
    I'll give them——when I get 'em.

I'll give——but not the full-blown rose,
    Or rose-bud more in fashion;
15   Such short-liv'd offerings but disclose
    A transitory passion.

I'll give thee something yet unpaid,
    No less sincere, than civil:
I'll give thee——Ah! too charming maid;
20   I'll give thee——To the Devil.

A SONNET

Weeping, murmuring, complaining,
    Lost to every gay delight;
MYRA, too sincere for feigning,
    Fears th' approaching bridal night.

5   Yet, why this killing soft dejection?
    Why dim thy beauty with a tear?
Had MYRA followed my direction,
    She long had wanted cause to fear.

AN ELEGY
ON THAT GLORY OF HER SEX MRS MARY BLAIZE

Good people all, with one accord,
    Lament for Madam BLAIZE,
Who never wanted a good word——
    From those who spoke her praise.

5   The needy seldom pass'd her door,
    And always found her kind;
She freely lent to all the poor,——
    Who left a pledge behind.

She strove the neighbourhood to please,
10   With manners wond'rous winning,
And never follow'd wicked ways,——
    Unless when she was sinning.

At church, in silks and sattins new,
    With hoop of monstrous size,
15   She never slumber'd in her pew,——
    But when she shut her eyes.

Her love was sought, I do aver,
    By twenty beaus and more;
The king himself has follow'd her,——
20   *When she has walk'd before.*

But now her wealth and finery fled,
    Her hangers-on cut short all;
The doctors found, when she was dead,——
    Her last disorder mortal.

25   Let us lament, in sorrow sore,
    For Kent-Street well may say,
That had she liv'd a twelve-month more,——
    She had not dy'd to-day.

THE DOUBLE TRANSFORMATION: A TALE

Secluded from domestic strife
Jack Book-worm led a college life;
A fellowship at twenty five
Made him the happiest man alive,
5   He drank his glass, and crack'd his joke,
And Freshmen wonder'd as he spoke:
   Such pleasures unallay'd with care,
Could any accident impair?
Could Cupid's shaft at length transfix
10   Our swain arriv'd at thirty six?
O had the archer ne'er come down
To ravage in a country town!
Or Flavia been content to stop,
At triumphs in a Fleet-street shop.
15   O had her eyes forgot to blaze!
Or Jack had wanted eyes to gaze:
O—but let exclamation cease,
Her presence banish'd all his peace.
So with decorum all things carried,
20   Miss frown'd, and blush'd, and then was—married.
   Need we expose to vulgar sight,
The raptures of the bridal night?
Need we intrude on hallow'd ground,
Or draw the curtains clos'd around:
25   Let it suffice, that each had charms,
He clasp'd a goddess in his arms;
And tho' she felt his usage rough,
Yet in a man 'twas well enough.
   The honey-moon like lightening flew,
30   The second brought its transports too.
A third, a fourth were not amiss,
The fifth was friendship mix'd with bliss:
But when a twelvemonth pass'd away
Jack found his goddess made of clay:
35   Found half the charms that deck'd her face,
Arose from powder, shreds or lace;
But still the worst remain'd behind,
That very face had rob'd her mind.
   Skill'd in no other arts was she,
40   But dressing, patching, repartee;
And just as humour rose or fell,
By turns a slattern or a belle:

'Tis true she dress'd with modern grace,
Half naked at a ball or race;
45   But when at home, at board or bed,
Five greasy nightcaps wrap'd her head:
Could so much beauty condescend,
To be a dull domestic friend?
Could any courtain lectures bring,
50   To decency so fine a thing?
In short by night 'twas fits or fretting,
By day 'twas gadding or coquetting.
Fond to be seen she kept a bevy,
Of powder'd coxcombs at her levy;
55   The squire and captain took their stations,
And twenty other near relations;
Jack suck'd his pipe and often broke
A sigh in suffocating smoke;
While all their hours were pass'd between
60   Insulting repartee or spleen:
     Thus as her faults each day were known,
He thinks her features coarser grown;
He fancies every vice she shews,
Or thins her lips, or points her nose:
65   Whenever rage or envy rise,
How wide her mouth, how wild her eyes!
He knows not how, but so it is,
Her face is grown a knowing phyz;
And tho' her fops are wondrous civil,
70   He thinks her ugly as the Devil.
     Now to perplex the ravell'd nooze,
As each a different way pursues,
While sullen or loquacious strife,
Promis'd to hold them on for life,
75   That dire disease whose ruthless power
Withers the beauty's transient flower:
Lo! the small pox with horrid glare,
Levell'd its terrors at the fair;
And rifling every youthful grace,
80   Left but the remnant of a face.
     The glass grown hateful to her sight,
Reflected now a perfect fright:
Each former art she vainly tries
To bring back lustre to her eyes.
85   In vain she tries her pastes and creams,
To smooth her skin, or hide its seams;
Her country beaux and city cousins,
Lovers no more; flew off by dozens:
The squire himself was seen to yield,
90   And even the captain quit the field.

Poor Madam now condemn'd to hack
The rest of life with anxious Jack,
Perceiving others fairly flown
Attempted pleasing him alone.
95   Jack soon was dazzl'd to behold
Her present face surpass the old;
With modesty her cheeks are dy'd,
Humility displaces pride;
For tawdry finery is seen,
100   A person ever neatly clean:
No more presuming on her sway
She learns good nature every day,
Serenely gay, and strict in duty,
Jack finds his wife a perfect beauty.

[DESCRIPTION OF AN AUTHOR'S BED-CHAMBER]

Where the Red Lion flaring o'er the way,
Invites each passing stranger that can pay;
Where Calvert's butt, and Parson's black champaign,
Regale the drabs and bloods of Drury-lane;
5   There in a lonely room, from bailiffs snug,
The muse found Scroggen stretch'd beneath a rug,
A window patch'd with paper lent a ray,
That dimly shew'd the state in which he lay;
The sanded floor that grits beneath the tread:
10   The humid wall with paltry pictures spread:
The royal game of goose was there in view,
And the twelve rules the royal martyr drew;
The seasons fram'd with listing found a place,
And brave prince William shew'd his lamp-black face:
15   The morn was cold, he views with keen desire
The rusty grate unconscious of a fire:
With beer and milk arrears the frieze was scor'd,
And five crack'd tea cups dress'd the chimney board.
A night-cap deck'd his brows instead of bay,
20   A cap by night—a stocking all the day!

ON SEEING MRS **** PERFORM IN THE CHARACTER OF ****

To you bright fair the nine address their lays,
And tune my feeble voice to sing thy praise.
The heart-felt power of every charm divine,
Who can withstand their all-commanding shine?
5   See how she moves along with every grace
While soul-brought tears steal down each shining face.
She speaks, 'tis rapture all and nameless bliss,
Ye gods what transport e'er compar'd to this,
As when in Paphian groves the queen of love,
10   With fond complaint address'd the listening Jove,
'Twas joy, and endless blisses all around,
And rocks forgot their hardness at the sound.
Then first, at last even Jove was taken in,
And felt her charms, without disguise, within.

ON THE DEATH OF THE RIGHT HONOURABLE ****

Ye muses, pour the pitying tear
For Pollio snatch'd away:
O had he liv'd another year!
——*He had not dy'd to-day.*

5   O, were he born to bless mankind,
In virtuous times of yore,
Heroes themselves had fallen behind!
——*Whene'er he went before.*

How sad the groves and plains appear,
10   And sympathetic sheep:
Even pitying hills would drop a tear!
——*If hills could learn to weep.*

His bounty in exalted strain
Each bard might well display:
15   Since none implor'd relief in vain!
——*That went reliev'd away.*

And hark! I hear the tuneful throng
   His obsequies forbid.
He still shall live, shall live as long
20   ——*As ever dead man did.*

AN ELEGY ON THE DEATH OF
A MAD DOG

Good people all, of every sort,
   Give ear unto my song;
And if you find it wond'rous short,
   It cannot hold you long.

5   In Isling town there was a man,
   Of whom the world might say,
That still a godly race he ran,
   Whene'er he went to pray.

A kind and gentle heart he had,
10   To comfort friends and foes;
The naked every day he clad,
   When he put on his cloaths.

And in that town a dog was found,
   As many dogs there be,
15   Both mungrel, puppy, whelp, and hound,
   And curs of low degree.

This dog and man at first were friends;
   But when a pique began,
The dog, to gain some private ends,
20   Went mad and bit the man.

Around from all the neighbouring streets,
   The wondering neighbours ran,
And swore the dog had lost his wits,
   To bite so good a man.

25   The wound it seem'd both sore and sad,
   To every christian eye;
And while they swore the dog was mad,
   They swore the man would die.

But soon a wonder came to light,
    That shew'd the rogues they lied,
The man recovered of the bite,
    The dog it was that dy'd.

30

SONG FROM *THE VICAR OF WAKEFIELD*

When lovely woman stoops to folly,
    And finds too late that men betray,
What charm can sooth her melancholy,
    What art can wash her guilt away?

The only art her guilt to cover,
    To hide her shame from every eye,
To give repentance to her lover,
    And wring his bosom——is to die.

5

EDWIN AND ANGELINA: A BALLAD

Turn, gentle hermit of the dale,
    And guide my lonely way,
To where yon taper cheers the vale,
    With hospitable ray.

For here forlorn and lost I tread,
    With fainting steps and slow;
Where wilds immeasurably spread,
    Seem lengthening as I go.

5

'Forbear, my son,' the hermit cries,
    'To tempt the dangerous gloom;
For yonder faithless phantom flies
    To lure thee to thy doom.

10

'Here to the houseless child of want,
    My door is open still;
And tho' my portion is but scant,
    I give it with good will.

15

'Then turn to-night, and freely share
  Whate'er my cell bestows;
My rushy couch, and frugal fare,
20   My blessing and repose.

'No flocks, that range the valley free,
  To slaughter I condemn:
Taught by that power that pities me,
  I learn to pity them.

25   'But from the mountain's grassy side,
  A guiltless feast I bring;
A scrip with herbs and fruits supply'd,
  And water from the spring.

'Then, pilgrim, turn, thy cares forego;
30   All earth-born cares are wrong:
"Man wants but little here below,
  Nor wants that little long."'

Soft as the dew from heav'n descends,
  His gentle accents fell:
35   The modest stranger lowly bends,
  And follows to the cell.

Far in a wilderness obscure
  The lonely mansion lay;
A refuge to the neighbouring poor,
40   And strangers led astray.

No stores beneath its humble thatch
  Requir'd a master's care;
The wicket op'ning with a latch,
  Receiv'd the harmless pair.

45   And now when busy crowds retire
  To take their evening rest,
The hermit trimm'd his little fire,
  And chear'd his pensive guest:

And spread his vegetable store,
50   And gayly prest, and smil'd;
And, skill'd in legendary lore,
  The lingering hours beguil'd.

Around in sympathetic mirth
  Its tricks the kitten tries,
55   The cricket chirrups in the hearth;
  The crackling faggot flies.

But nothing could a charm impart
 To sooth the stranger's woe;
For grief was heavy at his heart,
60 And tears began to flow.

His rising cares the hermit spy'd,
 With answering care opprest;
'And whence, unhappy youth,' he cry'd,
 'The sorrows of thy breast?

65 'From better habitations spurn'd,
 Reluctant dost thou rove;
Or grieve for friendship unreturn'd,
 Or unregarded love?

'Alas! the joys that fortune brings,
70 Are trifling and decay;
And those who prize the paltry things,
 More trifling still than they.

'And what is friendship but a name,
 A charm that lulls to sleep;
75 A shade that follows wealth or fame,
 But leaves the wretch to weep?

'And love has still an emptier sound,
 The modern fair one's jest:
On earth unseen, or only found
80 To warm the turtle's nest.

'For shame fond youth thy sorrows hush,
 And spurn the sex,' he said:
But while he spoke, a rising blush
 His love-lorn guest betray'd.

85 Surpriz'd he sees new beauties rise,
 Swift mantling to the view;
Like colours o'er the morning skies,
 As bright, as transient too.

The bashful look, the rising breast,
90 Alternate spread alarms:
The lovely stranger stands confest
 A maid in all her charms.

'And, ah, forgive a stranger rude,
 A wretch forlorn,' she cry'd;
95 'Whose feet unhallowed thus intrude
 Where heaven and you reside.

'But let a maid thy pity share,
    Whom love has taught to stray;
Who seeks for rest, but finds despair
100   Companion of her way.

'My father liv'd beside the Tyne,
    A wealthy Lord was he;
And all his wealth was mark'd as mine,
    He had but only me.

105 'To win me from his tender arms,
    Unnumber'd suitors came;
Who prais'd me for imputed charms,
    And felt or feign'd a flame.

'Each hour a mercenary crowd,
110   With richest proffers strove:
Among the rest young EDWIN bow'd,
    But never talk'd of love.

'In humble simplest habit clad,
    No wealth nor power had he;
115 Wisdom and worth were all he had,
    But these were all to me.

'The blossom opening to the day,
    The dews of heaven refin'd,
Could nought of purity display,
120   To emulate his mind.

'The dew, the blossom on the tree,
    With charms inconstant shine;
Their charms were his, but woe to me,
    Their constancy was mine.

125 'For still I try'd each fickle art,
    Importunate and vain;
And while his passion touch'd my heart,
    I triumph'd in his pain.

'Till quite dejected with my scorn,
130   He left me to my pride;
And sought a solitude forlorn,
    In secret where he died.

'But mine the sorrow, mine the fault,
    And well my life shall pay;
135 I'll seek the solitude he sought,
    And stretch me where he lay.

'And there forlorn despairing hid,
   I'll lay me down and die:
'Twas so for me that EDWIN did,
140   And so for him will I.'

'Forbid it, heaven!' the hermit cry'd,
   And clasp'd her to his breast:
The wondering fair one turn'd to chide,
   'Twas EDWIN's self that prest.

145   'Turn, ANGELINA, ever dear,
   My charmer, turn to see,
Thy own, thy long-lost EDWIN here,
   Restor'd to love and thee.

'Thus let me hold thee to my heart,
150   And ev'ry care resign:
And shall we never, never part,
   My life—my all that's mine.

'No, never, from this hour to part,
   We'll live and love so true;
155 The sigh that rends thy constant heart,
   Shall break thy EDWIN's too.'

THE CAPTIVITY
AN ORATORIO

Act I Scene I

Israelites sitting on the Banks of the Euphrates

1st Prophet

Recitative

   Ye Captive tribes that hourly work and weep
Where flows Euphrates murmuring to the deep,
Suspend a while the task, the tear suspend,
And turn to God your father and your friend:
5   Insulted, chain'd, and all the world a foe,
Our God alone is all we boast below.

Oliver Goldsmith

Chorus of Israelites

Our God is all we boast below:
To him we turn our eyes,
And every added weight of woe
10   Shall make our homage rise;

And tho' no temple richly drest
Nor sacrifice is here,
Wee'l make his temple in our breast
And offer up a tear.

2^d Prophet

Recitative

15   That strain once more, it bids remembrance rise,
And calls my long lost country to mine eyes.
Ye fields of Sharon, drest in flowery pride,
Ye Plains where Jordan rolls its glassy tide,
Ye hills of Lebanon with cedars crown'd,
20   Ye Gilead groves that fling perfumes around:
These hills how sweet, those plains how wondrous fair,
But sweeter still when heaven was with us there.

Air

O memory thou fond deceiver,
Still importunate and vain,
25   To former joys recurring ever,
And turning all the past to pain:

Hence deceiver most distressing,
Seek the happy and the free,
They who want each other blessing
30   Ever want a friend in thee.

1st Prophet

Recitative

Yet, why repine? What tho' by bonds confin'd?
Should bonds enslave the vigour of the mind?
Have we not cause for triumph when we see
Ourselves alone from idol worship free?

35   Are not this very day those rites begun
      Where prostrate folly hails the rising sun?
      Do not our tyrant Lords this day ordain
      For superstition's rites and mirth profane?
      And should we mourn? Should coward virtue fly
40   When impious folly rears her front on high?
      No, rather let us triumph still the more
      And as our fortune sinks our wishes soar.

                          Air

      The triumphs that on vice attend
      Shall ever in confusion end;
45   The good man suffers but to gain
      And every virtue springs from pain.

      As Aromatic plants bestow
      No spicy fragrance while they grow,
      But crush'd or trodden to the ground
50   Diffuse their balmy sweets around.

                    2^d Prophet

                      Recitative

      But hush, my sons, our tyrant Lords are near;
      The sound of barbarous mirth offends mine ear.
      Triumphant music floats along the vale:
      Near, nearer still, it gathers on the gale;
55   The growing note their near approach declares:
      Desist my sons, nor mix the strain with theirs.

              Enter Chaldean Priests attended

                     1st Priest

                          Air

      Come on, my companions, the triumph display:
      Let rapture the minutes employ,
      The sun calls us out on this festival day,
60   And our monarch partakes of our Joy.

      Like the sun our great monarch all pleasure supplies;
      Both similar blessings bestow:
      The sun with his splendour illumines the skies,
      And our Monarch enlivens below.

Oliver Goldsmith

Chaldean Woman

Air

65   Haste, ye sprightly sons of pleasure,
Love presents its brightest treasure,
Leave all other sports for me.

Chaldean Attendant

Or rather, loves delights despising,
Haste to raptures ever rising,
70   Wine shall bless the brave and free.

2ᵈ Priest

Wine and beauty thus inviting,
Each to different joys exciting,
Whither shall my choice encline?

1ˢᵗ Priest

I'll waste no longer thought in chusing,
75   But, neither love nor wine refusing,
I'll make them both together mine.

Recitative

But whence, when joy should brighten o'er the land,
This sullen gloom in Judah's Captive band?
Ye sons of Judah, why the lute unstrung,
80   Or why those harps on yonder willows hung?
Come, leave your griefs, and Join our warbling Choir:
For who like you can wake the sleeping lyre?

2ᵈ Prophet

Bow'd down with Chains, the scorn of all mankind,
To Want, to toil, and every ill consign'd;
85   Is this a time to bid us raise the strain
And mix in rites that heaven regards with pain?
No, never; may this hand forget each art
That speeds the powers of music to the heart,
Ere I forget the land that gave me birth,
90   Or Join with sounds profane its sacred mirth.

1ˢᵗ Priest

Insulting slaves, if gentler methods fail,
The whips and angry tortures shall prevail.

Exeunt Chaldeans.

1ˢᵗ Prophet

Why, let them come, one good remains to cheer:
We fear the Lord, and know no other fear.

Chorus

95   Can whips or tortures hurt the mind
On God's supporting breast reclin'd?
Stand fast and let our tyrants see
That fortitude is Victory.

End of the first Act

Act II

Scene as Before

Chorus of Israelites

O Peace of mind, thou lovely guest,
100   Thou softest soother of the breast,
Dispense thy balmy store;
Wing all our thoughts to reach the skies,
Till earth, diminish'd to our eyes,
Shall vanish as we soar.

1ˢᵗ Priest

Recitative

105   No more, too long has justice been delay'd,
The king's commands must fully be obey'd;
Compliance with his will your peace secures:
Praise but our Gods, and every good is yours.

But if, rebellious to his high command,
110   You spurn the favours offer'd from his hand,
Think timely, think what ills remain behind:
Reflect, nor tempt to rage the royal mind.

2ᵈ Priest

Air

Fierce is the whirlwind howling
O'er Afric's sandy plain
115   And Fierce the tempest rolling
Along the furrow'd main.

But storms that fly
To rend the sky,
Every ill presaging,
120   Less dreadful shew
To worlds below
Than angry monarchs raging.

Israelitish Woman

Recitative

Ah me! what angry terrors round us grow,
How shrinks my soul to meet the threaten'd blow;
125   Ye Prophets, skill'd in heaven's eternal truth,
Forgive my sexe's fears, forgive my youth,
If shrinking thus when frowning power appears
I wish for life, and yield me to my fears.
Let us one hour, one little hour, obey;
130   Tomorrows tears may wash our stains away.

Air

To the last moment of his breath
On hope the wretch relies,
And even the pang preceding death
Bids Expectation rise.

135   Hope like the gleaming taper's light
Adorns and cheers our way,
And still, as darker grows the night,
Emits a brighter ray.

2^d Priest

Recitative

Why this delay? at length for joy prepare;
140   I read your looks, and see compliance there.
Come raise the strain and grasp the full ton'd lyre:
The time, the theme, the place and all conspire.

Chaldean Woman

Air

See the ruddy morning smiling,
Hear the grove to bliss beguiling;
145   Zephyrs through the valley playing,
Streams along the meadow straying.

1st Priest

While these a constant revel keep,
Shall reason only bid me weep?
Hence, intruder! wee'l pursue
150   Nature, a better guide than you.

2^d Priest

Air

Every moment as it flows
Some peculiar pleasure owes:
Then let us, providently wise,
Seize the Debtor as it flies.

155   Think not to morrow can repay
The pleasures that we lose to day;
To morrow's most unbounded store
Can but pay its proper score.

1st Priest

Recitative

But Hush, see, foremost of the Captive Choir,
160   The Master Prophet Grasps his full ton'd lyre.

Mark where he sits with executing art,
Feels for each tone, and speeds it to the heart.
See, inspiration fills his rising form,
Awful as clouds that nurse the growing storm,
165   And now his voice, accordant to the string,
Prepares our monarch's victories to sing.

1st Prophet

Air

From North, from South, from East, from West,
Conspiring foes shall come;
Tremble, thou vice polluted breast;
170   Blasphemers, all be dumb.

The tempest gathers all around,
On Babylon it lies;
Down with her, down, down to the ground,
She sinks, she groans, she dies.

2d Prophet

175   Down with her, Lord, to lick the dust,
Ere yonder setting sun;
Serve her as she hath servd the just.
'Tis fixt, it shall be done.

1st Priest

Recitative

Enough. When slaves thus insolent presume,
180   The king himself shall judge and fix their doom.
Short-sighted wretches, have not you, and all
Beheld our power in Zedekiah's fall?
To yonder gloomy dungeon turn your eyes;
See where dethron'd your captive monarch lies,
185   Deprived of sight, and rankling in his chain,
He calls on death to terminate his pain.
Yet know ye slaves, that still remain behind
More Pondrous chains and dungeons more confind.

Chorus

Arise, all potent ruler, rise
190   And vindicate the peoples cause;
Till every tongue in every land
Shall offer up unfain'd applause.

End of the 2ᵈ Act

Act III

Scene as before

1ˢᵗ Priest

Recitative

Yes, my Companions, heaven's decrees are past,
And our fixt Empire shall for ever last,
195   In vain the madning prophet threatens woe,
In vain rebellion aims her secret blow;
Still shall our fame and growing power be spread,
And still our vengeance crush the guilty head.

Air

Coeval with man
200   Our Empire Began,
And never shall fall
Till ruin shakes all;
With the ruin of all
Shall Babylon fall.

2ᵈ Prophet

Recitative

205   Tis thus that pride triumphant rears the head:
A little while and all her power is fled.
But ha! what means yon sadly plaintive train,
That this way slowly bends along the plain:
And now, methinks, a pallid coarse they bear
210   To yonder bank, and rest the body there.
Alas, too well mine eyes observant trace
The last remains of Judah's royal race:
Our monarch falls and now our fears are ore.
The Wretched Zedekiah is no more.

Air

215   Ye wretches who, by fortune's hate,
In want and sorrow groan,
Come ponder his severer fate,
And learn to bless your own.

Ye sons, from fortune's lap supply'd,
220   A while the bliss suspend;
Like yours his life began in pride,
Like his your lives may end.

2^d Prophet

Behold his squalid coarse with sorrow worn,
His wretched limbs with pondrous fetters torn;
225   Those eyeless orbs that shock with ghastly glare,
Those ill becoming robes and matted hair.
And shall not heaven for this its terrors shew,
And deal its angry vengeance on the foe?
How long, how long, Almighty lord of all,
230   Shall wrath vindictive threaten ere it fall?

Israelitish Woman

Air

As panting flies the hunted hind,
Where brooks refreshing stray,
And rivers through the valley wind,
That stop the hunters way:
235   Thus we, O Lord, alike distresst,
For streams of mercy Long;
Those streams which chear the sore opprest,
And overwhelm the strong.

1st Prophet

Recitative

But whence that shout? Good heavens! amazement all!
240   See yonder tower just nodding to the fall:
See where an army covers all the ground,
Saps the strong wall, and pours destruction round.

The ruin smokes, destruction pours along;
How low the great, how feeble are the strong!
245 The foe prevails, the lofty walls recline:
O God of hosts the victory is thine!

Chorus of Israelites

Down with her, Lord, to lick the dust;
Let vengeance be begun:
Serve her as she hath servd the just,
250 And let thy will be done.

1st Priest

All, All is lost. The Syrian army fails;
Cyrus, the conqueror of the world, prevails.
Save us, O Lord, to thee tho' Late we pray,
And give repentance but an hour's delay.

2d Priest

Air

255 Thrice happy, who, in happy hour,
To heaven their praise bestow,
And own his all consuming power,
Before they feel the blow.

1st Prophet

Recitative

Now, Now's our time. Ye wretches bold and blind,
260 Brave but to God, and Cowards to Mankind;
Too late you seek that power unsought before:
Your wealth, your pride, your empire are no more.

Air

O Lucifer, thou son of morn,
Alike of heaven and man the foe,
265 Heaven, men, and all
Now press thy fall,
And sink thee lowest of the low.

2ᵈ Priest

O Babylon, how art thou fallen,
Thy fall more dreadful from delay!
270   Thy streets forelorn
To wilds shall turn,
Where toads shall pant and vultures prey.

1ˢᵗ Prophet

Recitative

Such be her fate. But listen, from afar
The Clarion's note proclaims the finish'd war!
275   Cyrus, our Great restorer, is at hand,
And this way leads his formidable band.
Now give your songs of Sion to the wind,
And hail the benefactor of mankind;
He comes pursuant to divine decree,
280   To Chain the strong and set the captive free.

Chorus of Youths

Rise to raptures past expressing,
Sweeter from remember'd woes;
Cyrus comes, our wrongs redressing,
Comes to give the world repose.

Chorus of Virgins

285   Cyrus comes, the world redressing,
Love and pleasure in his train,
Comes to heighten every blessing,
Comes to soften every pain.

Chorus of Youths and Virgins

Hail to him with mercy reigning,
290   Skilld in every peaceful art,
Who from bonds our limbs unchaining,
Only binds the willing heart.

Last Chorus

But Chief to thee, our God, our father, friend,
Let praise be given to all eternity;
295   O thou, without beginning, without end,
Let us, and all, begin, and end in thee.

Finis

THE TRAVELLER
OR
A PROSPECT OF SOCIETY

Remote, unfriended, melancholy, slow,
Or by the lazy Scheld, or wandering Po;
Or onward, where the rude Carinthian boor
Against the houseless stranger shuts the door;
5   Or where Campania's plain forsaken lies,
A weary waste expanding to the skies:
Where'er I roam, whatever realms to see,
My heart untravell'd fondly turns to thee;
Still to my brother turns, with ceaseless pain,
10   And drags at each remove a lengthening chain.

Eternal blessings crown my earliest friend,
And round his dwelling guardian saints attend;
Blest be that spot, where chearful guests retire
To pause from toil, and trim their evening fire;
15   Blest that abode, where want and pain repair,
And every stranger finds a ready chair;
Blest be those feasts with simple plenty crown'd,
Where all the ruddy family around
Laugh at the jests or pranks that never fail,
20   Or sigh with pity at some mournful tale,
Or press the bashful stranger to his food,
And learn the luxury of doing good.

But me, not destin'd such delights to share,
My prime of life in wand'ring spent and care:
25   Impell'd, with steps unceasing, to pursue
Some fleeting good, that mocks me with the view;

That, like the circle bounding earth and skies,
Allures from far, yet, as I follow, flies;
My fortune leads to traverse realms alone,
30   And find no spot of all the world my own.

Even now, where Alpine solitudes ascend,
I sit me down a pensive hour to spend;
And, plac'd on high above the storm's career,
Look downward where an hundred realms appear;
35   Lakes, forests, cities, plains extending wide,
The pomp of kings, the shepherd's humbler pride.

When thus Creation's charms around combine,
Amidst the store, should thankless pride repine?
Say, should the philosophic mind disdain
40   That good, which makes each humbler bosom vain?
Let school-taught pride dissemble all it can,
These little things are great to little man;
And wiser he, whose sympathetic mind
Exults in all the good of all mankind.
45   Ye glittering towns, with wealth and splendour crown'd,
Ye fields, where summer spreads profusion round,
Ye lakes, whose vessels catch the busy gale,
Ye bending swains, that dress the flow'ry vale,
For me your tributary stores combine;
50   Creation's heir, the world, the world is mine.

As some lone miser visiting his store,
Bends at his treasure, counts, recounts it o'er;
Hoards after hoards his rising raptures fill,
Yet still he sighs, for hoards are wanting still:
55   Thus to my breast alternate passions rise,
Pleas'd with each good that heaven to man supplies:
Yet oft a sigh prevails, and sorrows fall,
To see the hoard of human bliss so small;
And oft I wish, amidst the scene, to find
60   Some spot to real happiness consign'd,
Where my worn soul, each wand'ring hope at rest,
May gather bliss to see my fellows blest.

But where to find that happiest spot below,
Who can direct, when all pretend to know?
65   The shudd'ring tenant of the frigid zone
Boldly proclaims that happiest spot his own,
Extols the treasures of his stormy seas,
And his long nights of revelry and ease;
The naked Negro, panting at the line,
70   Boasts of his golden sands and palmy wine,

Basks in the glare, or stems the tepid wave,
And thanks his Gods for all the good they gave,
Such is the patriot's boast, where'er we roam,
His first best country ever is at home.

75   And yet, perhaps, if countries we compare,
And estimate the blessings which they share;
Though patriots flatter, still shall wisdom find
An equal portion dealt to all mankind,
As different good, by Art or Nature given,
80   To different nations makes their blessings even.

Nature, a mother kind alike to all,
Still grants her bliss at Labour's earnest call;
With food as well the peasant is supply'd
On Idra's cliffs as Arno's shelvy side;
85   And though the rocky crested summits frown,
These rocks, by custom, turn to beds of down.
From Art more various are the blessings sent;
Wealth, commerce, honour, liberty, content:
Yet these each other's power so strong contest,
90   That either seems destructive of the rest.
Where wealth and freedom reign contentment fails,
And honour sinks where commerce long prevails.
Hence every state, to one lov'd blessing prone,
Conforms and models life to that alone.
95   Each to the favourite happiness attends,
And spurns the plan that aims at other ends;
'Till, carried to excess in each domain,
This favourite good begets peculiar pain.

But let us try these truths with closer eyes,
100   And trace them through the prospect as it lies:
Here for a while my proper cares resign'd,
Here let me sit in sorrow for mankind,
Like yon neglected shrub, at random cast,
That shades the steeps, and sighs at every blast.

105   Far to the right, where Appennine ascends,
Bright as the summer, Italy extends;
Its uplands sloping deck the mountain's side,
Woods over woods, in gay theatric pride;
While oft some temple's mould'ring tops between,
110   With venerable grandeur mark the scene.

Could Nature's bounty satisfy the breast,
The sons of Italy were surely blest.
Whatever fruits in different climes are found,
That proudly rise or humbly court the ground,

115 Whatever blooms in torrid tracts appear,
     Whose bright succession decks the varied year;
     Whatever sweets salute the northern sky
     With vernal lives that blossom but to die;
     These here disporting, own the kindred soil,
120 Nor ask luxuriance from the planter's toil;
     While sea-born gales their gelid wings expand
     To winnow fragrance round the smiling land.

     But small the bliss that sense alone bestows,
     And sensual bliss is all the nation knows.
125 In florid beauty groves and fields appear,
     Man seems the only growth that dwindles here.
     Contrasted faults through all his manners reign,
     Though poor, luxurious, though submissive, vain,
     Though grave, yet trifling, zealous, yet untrue,
130 And even in penance planning sins anew.
     All evils here contaminate the mind,
     That opulence departed leaves behind;
     For wealth was theirs, nor far remov'd the date,
     When commerce proudly flourish'd through the state:
135 At her command the palace learnt to rise,
     Again the long-fall'n column sought the skies;
     The canvass glow'd beyond even Nature warm,
     The pregnant quarry teem'd with human form.
     Till, more unsteady than the southern gale,
140 Commerce on other shores display'd her sail;
     While nought remain'd of all that riches gave,
     But towns unman'd, and lords without a slave:
     And late the nation found, with fruitless skill,
     Its former strength was but plethoric ill.

145 Yet, still the loss of wealth is here supplied
     By arts, the splendid wrecks of former pride;
     From these the feeble heart and long fall'n mind
     An easy compensation seem to find.
     Here may be seen, in bloodless pomp array'd,
150 The paste-board triumph and the cavalcade;
     Processions form'd for piety and love,
     A mistress or a saint in every grove.
     By sports like these are all their cares beguil'd,
     The sports of children satisfy the child;
155 Each nobler aim represt by long controul,
     Now sinks at last, or feebly mans the soul;
     While low delights, succeeding fast behind,
     In happier meanness occupy the mind:
     As in those domes, where Caesars once bore sway,
160 Defac'd by time and tottering in decay,

There in the ruin, heedless of the dead,
The shelter-seeking peasant builds his shed,
And, wond'ring man could want the larger pile,
Exults, and owns his cottage with a smile.

165   My soul turn from them, turn we to survey
Where rougher climes a nobler race display,
Where the bleak Swiss their stormy mansions tread,
And force a churlish soil for scanty bread;
No product here the barren hills afford,
170 But man and steel, the soldier and his sword.
No vernal blooms their torpid rocks array,
But winter lingering chills the laps of May;
No Zephyr fondly sues the mountain's breast,
But meteors glare, and stormy glooms invest.
175 Yet still, even here, content can spread a charm,
Redress the clime, and all its rage disarm.
Though poor the peasant's hut, his feasts though small,
He sees his little lot, the lot of all;
Sees no contiguous palace rear its head
180 To shame the meanness of his humble shed;
No costly lord the sumptuous banquet deal
To make him loath his vegetable meal;
But calm, and bred in ignorance and toil,
Each wish contracting, fits him to the soil.
185 Chearful at morn he wakes from short repose,
Breasts the keen air, and carrols as he goes;
With patient angle trolls the finny deep,
Or drives his vent'rous plow-share to the steep;
Or seeks the den where snow tracks mark the way,
190 And drags the struggling savage into day.
At night returning, every labour sped,
He sits him down the monarch of a shed;
Smiles by his chearful fire, and round surveys
His childrens looks, that brighten at the blaze:
195 While his lov'd partner, boastful of her hoard,
Displays her cleanly platter on the board;
And haply too some pilgrim, thither led,
With many a tale repays the nightly bed.

    Thus every good his native wilds impart,
200 Imprints the patriot passion on his heart,
And even those ills, that round his mansion rise,
Enhance the bliss his scanty fund supplies.
Dear is that shed to which his soul conforms,
And dear that hill which lifts him to the storms;
205 And as a child, when scaring sounds molest,
Clings close and closer to the mother's breast;

So the loud torrent, and the whirlwind's roar,
But bind him to his native mountains more.

Such are the charms to barren states assign'd;
210   Their wants but few, their wishes all confin'd.
Yet let them only share the praises due,
If few their wants, their pleasures are but few;
For every want, that stimulates the breast,
Becomes a source of pleasure when redrest.
215   Whence from such lands each pleasing science flies,
That first excites desire, and then supplies;
Unknown to them, when sensual pleasures cloy,
To fill the languid pause with finer joy;
Unknown those powers that raise the soul to flame,
220   Catch every nerve, and vibrate through the frame.
Their level life is but a smould'ring fire,
Unquench'd by want, unfann'd by strong desire;
Unfit for raptures, or, if raptures cheer
On some high festival of once a year,
225   In wild excess the vulgar breast takes fire,
Till, buried in debauch, the bliss expire.

But not their joys alone thus coarsly flow:
Their morals, like their pleasures, are but low.
For, as refinement stops, from sire to son
230   Unalter'd, unimprov'd their manners run,
And love's and friendship's finely pointed dart
Fall blunted from each indurated heart.
Some sterner virtues o'er the mountain's breast
May sit, like falcons cow'ring on the nest;
235   But all the gentler morals, such as play
Through life's more cultur'd walks, and charm the way,
These far dispers'd, on timorous pinions fly,
To sport and flutter in a kinder sky.

To kinder skies, where gentler manners reign,
240   I turn; and France displays her bright domain.
Gay sprightly land of mirth and social ease,
Pleas'd with thyself, whom all the world can please,
How often have I led thy sportive choir,
With tuneless pipe, beside the murmuring Loire?
245   Where shading elms along the margin grew,
And freshen'd from the wave the Zephyr flew;
And haply, tho' my harsh touch faltering still,
But mock'd all tune, and marr'd the dancer's skill;
Yet would the village praise my wond'rous power,
250   And dance, forgetful of the noon-tide hour.

Alike all ages. Dames of ancient days
Have led their children through the mirthful maze,
And the gay grandsire, skill'd in gestic lore,
Has frisk'd beneath the burthen of threescore.

255 So blest a life these thoughtless realms display,
Thus idly busy rolls their world away:
Theirs are those arts that mind to mind endear,
For honour forms the social temper here.
Honour, that praise which real merit gains,
260 Or even imaginary worth obtains,
Here passes current; paid from hand to hand,
It shifts in splendid traffic round the land:
From courts, to camps, to cottages it strays,
And all are taught an avarice of praise;
265 They please, are pleas'd, they give to get esteem,
Till, seeming blest, they grow to what they seem.

But while this softer art their bliss supplies,
It gives their follies also room to rise;
For praise too dearly lov'd, or warmly sought,
270 Enfeebles all internal strength of thought,
And the weak soul, within itself unblest,
Leans for all pleasure on another's breast.
Hence ostentation here, with tawdry art,
Pants for the vulgar praise which fools impart;
275 Here vanity assumes her pert grimace,
And trims her robes of frize with copper lace,
Here beggar pride defrauds her daily cheer,
To boast one splendid banquet once a year;
The mind still turns where shifting fashion draws,
280 Nor weighs the solid worth of self applause.

To men of other minds my fancy flies,
Embosom'd in the deep where Holland lies,
Methinks her patient sons before me stand,
Where the broad ocean leans against the land,
285 And, sedulous to stop the coming tide,
Lift the tall rampire's artificial pride.
Onward methinks, and diligently slow
The firm connected bulwark seems to grow;
Spreads its long arms amidst the watry roar,
290 Scoops out an empire, and usurps the shore.
While the pent ocean rising o'er the pile,
Sees an amphibious world beneath him smile:
The slow canal, the yellow blossom'd vale,
The willow tufted bank, the gliding sail,
295 The crowded mart, the cultivated plain,
A new creation rescu'd from his reign.

Thus, while around, the wave-subjected soil
Impels the native to repeated toil,
Industrious habits in each bosom reign,
300   And industry begets a love of gain.
Hence all the good from opulence that springs,
With all those ills superfluous treasure brings,
Are here display'd. Their much-lov'd wealth imparts
Convenience, plenty, elegance, and arts;
305   But view them closer, craft and fraud appear,
Even liberty itself is barter'd here.
At gold's superior charms all freedom flies,
The needy sell it, and the rich man buys:
A land of tyrants, and a den of slaves,
310   Here wretches seek dishonourable graves,
And calmly bent, to servitude conform,
Dull as their lakes that slumber in the storm.

Heavens! how unlike their Belgic fires of old!
Rough, poor, content, ungovernably bold;
315   War in each breast, and freedom on each brow;
How much unlike the sons of Britain now!

Fir'd at the sound, my genius spreads her wing,
And flies where Britain courts the western spring;
Where lawns extend that scorn Arcadian pride,
320   And brighter streams than fam'd Hydaspis glide.
There all around the gentlest breezes stray,
There gentle music melts on every spray;
Creation's mildest charms are there combin'd,
Extremes are only in the master's mind;
325   Stern o'er each bosom reason holds her state.
With daring aims, irregularly great,
Pride in their port, defiance in their eye,
I see the lords of human kind pass by,
Intent on high designs, a thoughtful band,
330   By forms unfashion'd, fresh from Nature's hand;
Fierce in their native hardiness of soul,
True to imagin'd right, above controul,
While even the peasant boasts these rights to scan,
And learns to venerate himself as man.

335   Thine, Freedom, thine the blessings pictur'd here,
Thine are those charms that dazzle and endear;
Too blest indeed, were such without alloy,
But foster'd even by Freedom ills annoy:
That independence Britons prize too high,
340   Keeps man from man, and breaks the social tie;
The self-dependent lordlings stand alone,
All claims that bind and sweeten life unknown;

Here by the bonds of nature feebly held,
Minds combat minds, repelling and repell'd;
345 Ferments arise, imprison'd factions roar,
Represt ambition struggles round her shore,
Till over-wrought, the general system feels
Its motions stopt, or phrenzy fire the wheels.

Nor this the worst. As nature's ties decay,
350 As duty, love, and honour fail to sway,
Fictitious bonds, the bonds of wealth and law,
Still gather strength, and force unwilling awe.
Hence all obedience bows to these alone,
And talent sinks, and merit weeps unknown;
355 Till Time may come, when, stript of all her charms,
The land of scholars, and the nurse of arms;
Where noble stems transmit the patriot flame,
Where kings have toil'd, and poets wrote for fame;
One sink of level avarice shall lie,
360 And scholars, soldiers, kings unhonor'd die.

Yet think not, thus when Freedom's ills I state,
I mean to flatter kings, or court the great;
Ye powers of truth that bid my soul aspire,
Far from my bosom drive the low desire;
365 And thou fair freedom, taught alike to feel
The rabble's rage, and tyrant's angry steel;
Thou transitory flower, alike undone
By proud contempt, or favour's fostering sun,
Still may thy blooms the changeful clime endure,
370 I only would repress them to secure;
For just experience tells in every soil,
That those who think must govern those that toil,
And all that freedom's highest aims can reach,
Is but to lay proportion'd loads on each.
375 Hence, should one order disproportion'd grow,
Its double weight must ruin all below.
O then how blind to all that truth requires,
Who think it freedom when a part aspires!
Calm is my soul, nor apt to rise in arms,
380 Except when fast approaching danger warms:
But when contending chiefs blockade the throne,
Contracting regal power to stretch their own,
When I behold a factious band agree
To call it freedom, when themselves are free;
385 Each wanton judge new penal statutes draw,
Laws grind the poor, and rich men rule the law;
The wealth of climes, where savage nations roam,
Pillag'd from slaves, to purchase slaves at home;

Fear, pity, justice, indignation start,
390 Tear off reserve, and bare my swelling heart;
'Till half a patriot, half a coward grown.
I fly from petty tyrants to the throne.

Yes, brother, curse with me that baleful hour,
When first ambition struck at regal power;
395 And thus, polluting honour in its source,
Gave wealth to sway the mind with double force.
Have we not seen, round Britain's peopled shore,
Her useful sons exchang'd for useless ore?
Seen all her triumphs but destruction haste,
400 Like flaring tapers brightening as they waste;
Seen opulence, her grandeur to maintain,
Lead stern depopulation in her train,
And over fields, where scatter'd hamlets rose,
In barren solitary pomp repose?
405 Have we not seen, at pleasure's lordly call,
The smiling long-frequented village fall;
Beheld the duteous son, the sire decay'd,
The modest matron, and the blushing maid,
Forc'd from their homes, a melancholy train,
410 To traverse climes beyond the western main;
Where wild Oswego spreads her swamps around,
And Niagara stuns with thund'ring sound?

Even now, perhaps, as there some pilgrim strays
Through tangled forests, and through dangerous ways;
415 Where beasts with man divided empire claim,
And the brown Indian marks with murderous aim;
There, while above the giddy tempest flies,
And all around distressful yells arise,
The pensive exile, bending with his woe,
420 To stop too fearful, and too faint to go,
Casts a long look where England's glories shine,
And bids his bosom sympathize with mine.

Vain, very vain, my weary search to find
That bliss which only centres in the mind:
425 Why have I stray'd, from pleasure and repose,
To seek a good each government bestows?
In every government, though terrors reign,
Though tyrant kings, or tyrant laws restrain,
How small, of all that human hearts endure,
430 That part which laws or kings can cause or cure.
Still to ourselves in every place consign'd,
Our own felicity we make or find:
With secret course, which no loud storms annoy,
Glides the smooth current of domestic joy.

435 The lifted ax, the agonizing wheel,
Luke's iron crown, and Damien's bed of steel,
To men remote from power but rarely known,
Leave reason, faith and conscience all our own.

A NEW SIMILE
IN THE MANNER OF SWIFT

Long had I sought in vain to find
A likeness for the scribbling kind;
The modern scribbling kind, who write,
In wit, and sense, and nature's spite:
5 'Till reading, I forget what day on,
A chapter out of Took's Pantheon;
I think I met with something there,
To suit my purpose to a hair;
But let us not proceed too furious,
10 First please to turn to God Mercurius;
You'll find him pictured at full length
In book the second, page the tenth:
The stress of all my proofs on him I lay,
And now proceed we to our simile.

15 Imprimis, pray observe his hat
Wings upon either side——mark that.
Well! what is it from thence we gather?
Why these denote a brain of feather.
A brain of feather! very right,
20 With wit that's flighty, learning light;
Such as to modern bard's decreed:
A just comparison,—proceed.

In the next place, his feet peruse,
Wings grow again from both his shoes;
25 Design'd no doubt, their part to bear,
And waft his godship through the air;
And here my simile unites,
For in a modern poet's flights,
I'm sure it may be justly said,
30 His feet are useful as his head.

Lastly, vouchsafe t' observe his hand,
Fill'd with a snake incircled wand;
By classic authors, term'd caducis,
And highly fam'd for several uses.

35   To wit—most wond'rously endu'd,
        No poppy water half so good;
        For let folks only get a touch,
        It's soporific virtue's such,
        Tho' ne'er so much awake before,
40   That quickly they begin to snore.
        Add too, what certain writers tell,
        With this he drives men's souls to hell.

            Now to apply, begin we then;
        His wand's a modern author's pen;
45   The serpents round about it twin'd,
        Denote him of the reptile kind;
        Denote the rage with which he writes,
        His frothy slaver, venom'd bites;
        An equal semblance still to keep,
50   Alike too, both conduce to sleep,
        This diff'rence only, as the God,
        Drove souls to Tart'rus with his rod;
        With his goosequill the scribbing elf,
        Instead of others, damns himself.

55   And here my simile almost tript,
        Yet grant a word by way of postscript,
        Moreover, Merc'ry had a failing:
        Well! what of that? out with it—stealing;
        In which all modern bards agree,
60   Being each as great a thief as he:
        But ev'n this deities' existence,
        Shall lend my simile assistance.
        Our modern bards! why what a pox
        Are they but senseless stones and blocks?

VERSES IN REPLY TO AN INVITATION TO
DINNER AT DR BAKER'S

            Your mandate I got,
        You may all go to pot;
        Had your senses been right,
        You'd have sent before night;
5   As I hope to be saved,
        I put off being shaved;
        For I could not make bold,
        While the matter was cold,

To meddle in suds,
10 Or to put on my duds;
So tell Horneck and Nesbitt,
And Baker and his bit,
And Kauffman beside,
And the Jessamy bride,
15 With the rest of the crew,
The Reynoldses two,
Little Comedy's face,
And the Captain in lace.
(By the bye you may tell him,
20 I have something to sell him;
Of use I insist,
When he comes to enlist.
Your worships must know
That a few days ago,
25 An order went out,
For the foot guards so stout
To wear tails in high taste,
Twelve inches at least:
Now I've got him a scale
30 To measure each tail,
To lengthen a short tail,
And a long one to curtail.)—
       Yet how can I when vext,
Thus stray from my text?
35 Tell each other to rue
Your Devonshire crew,
For sending so late
To one of my state.
But 'tis Reynolds's way
40 From wisdom to stray,
And Angelica's whim
To be frolick like him,
But, alas! your good worships, how could they be wiser,
When both have been spoil'd in to-day's Advertiser?

[EPILOGUE TO *THE SISTER: A COMEDY*]

What! five long acts—and all to make us wiser!
Our authoress sure has wanted an adviser.
Had she consulted *me*, she should have made
Her moral play a speaking masquerade,
5 Warm'd up each bustling scene, and in her rage
Have emptied all the Green-room on the stage.

My life on't, this had kept her play from sinking,
Have pleas'd our eyes, and sav'd the pain of thinking.
Well, since she thus has shewn her want of skill,
10   What if I give a masquerade? I will.
But how! ay, there's the rub! (*pausing*) I've got my cue:
The world's a masquerade! the masquers, you, you, you.
                              [*To Boxes, Pit, Gallery*
Lud! what a groupe the motley scene discloses!
False wits, false wives, false virgins, and false spouses:
15   Statesmen with bridles on; and, close beside 'em,
Patriots, in party colour'd suits that ride 'em.
There Hebes, turn'd of fifty, try once more,
To raise a flame in Cupids of threescore.
These, in their turn, with appetites as keen,
20   Deserting fifty, fasten on fifteen.
Miss, not yet full fifteen, with fire uncommon,
Flings down her sampler, and takes up the woman:
The little urchin smiles, and spreads her lure,
And tries to kill ere she's got power to cure.
25   Thus 'tis with all—Their chief and constant care
Is to seem every thing—but what they are.
Yon broad, bold, angry spark, I fix my eye on,
Who seems t' have robb'd his vizor from the lion,
Who frowns, and talks, and swears, with round parade,
30   Looking, as who should say, *Damme! who's afraid!*   [*mimicking.*
Strip but his vizor off, and sure I am,
You'll find his lionship a very lamb.
Yon politician, famous in debate,
Perhaps to vulgar eyes bestrides the state;
35   Yet, when he deigns his real shape t' assume,
He turns old woman, and bestrides a broom.
Yon patriot too, who presses on your sight,
And seems to every gazer all in white;
If with a bribe his candour you attack,
40   He bows, turns round, and whip—the man's a black!
Yon critic too—but whither do I run?
If I proceed, our bard will be undone!
Well then, a truce, since she requests it too;
Do you spare her, and I'll for once spare you.

THE DESERTED VILLAGE

Sweet AUBURN, loveliest village of the plain,
Where health and plenty cheared the labouring swain,

Where smiling spring its earliest visit paid,
And parting summer's lingering blooms delayed,
5 Dear lovely bowers of innocence and ease,
Seats of my youth, when every sport could please,
How often have I loitered o'er thy green,
Where humble happiness endeared each scene;
How often have I paused on every charm,
10 The sheltered cot, the cultivated farm,
The never failing brook, the busy mill,
The decent church that topt the neighbouring hill,
The hawthorn bush, with seats beneath the shade,
For talking age and whispering lovers made.
15 How often have I blest the coming day,
When toil remitting lent its turn to play,
And all the village train from labour free
Led up their sports beneath the spreading tree,
While many a pastime circled in the shade,
20 The young contending as the old surveyed;
And many a gambol frolicked o'er the ground,
And slights of art and feats of strength went round.
And still as each repeated pleasure tired,
Succeeding sports the mirthful band inspired;
25 The dancing pair that simply sought renown
By holding out to tire each other down,
The swain mistrustless of his smutted face,
While secret laughter tittered round the place,
The bashful virgin's side-long looks of love,
30 The matron's glance that would those looks reprove.
These were thy charms, sweet village; sports like these,
With sweet succession, taught even toil to please;
These round thy bowers their chearful influence shed,
These were thy charms—But all these charms are fled.

35 Sweet smiling village, loveliest of the lawn,
Thy sports are fled, and all thy charms withdrawn;
Amidst thy bowers the tyrant's hand is seen,
And desolation saddens all thy green:
One only master grasps the whole domain,
40 And half a tillage stints thy smiling plain;
No more thy glassy brook reflects the day,
But choaked with sedges, works its weedy way.
Along thy glades, a solitary guest,
The hollow sounding bittern guards its nest;
45 Amidst thy desert walks the lapwing flies,
And tires their ecchoes with unvaried cries.
Sunk are thy bowers in shapeless ruin all,
And the long grass o'ertops the mouldering wall,

And trembling, shrinking from the spoiler's hand,
50   Far, far away thy children leave the land.

Ill fares the land, to hastening ills a prey,
Where wealth accumulates, and men decay;
Princes and lords may flourish, or may fade;
A breath can make them, as a breath has made,
55   But a bold peasantry, their country's pride,
When once destroyed, can never be supplied.

A time there was, ere England's griefs began,
When every rood of ground maintained its man;
For him light labour spread her wholesome store,
60   Just gave what life required, but gave no more.
His best companions, innocence and health;
And his best riches, ignorance of wealth.

But times are altered; trade's unfeeling train
Usurp the land and dispossess the swain;
65   Along the lawn, where scattered hamlets rose,
Unwieldy wealth, and cumbrous pomp repose;
And every want to oppulence allied,
And every pang that folly pays to pride.
These gentle hours that plenty bade to bloom,
70   Those calm desires that asked but little room,
Those healthful sports that graced the peaceful scene,
Lived in each look, and brightened all the green;
These far departing seek a kinder shore,
And rural mirth and manners are no more.

75   Sweet AUBURN! parent of the blissful hour,
Thy glades forlorn confess the tyrant's power,
Here as I take my solitary rounds,
Amidst thy tangling walks, and ruined grounds,
And, many a year elapsed, return to view
80   Where once the cottage stood, the hawthorn grew,
Remembrance wakes with all her busy train,
Swells at my breast, and turns the past to pain.

In all my wanderings round this world of care,
In all my griefs—and GOD has given my share—
85   I still had hopes my latest hours to crown,
Amidst these humble bowers to lay me down:
To husband out life's taper at the close,
And keep the flame from wasting by repose.
I still had hopes, for pride attends us still,
90   Amidst the swains to shew my book-learned skill,

Around my fire an evening groupe to draw,
And tell of all I felt, and all I saw;
And, as an hare whom hounds and horns pursue,
Pants to the place from whence at first she flew,
95 I still had hopes, my long vexations past,
Here to return—and die at home at last.

O blest retirement, friend to life's decline,
Retreats from care that never must be mine,
Now happy he who crowns in shades like these,
100 A youth of labour with an age of ease;
Who quits a world where strong temptations try,
And, since 'tis hard to combat, learns to fly.
For him no wretches, born to work and weep,
Explore the mine, or tempt the dangerous deep;
105 No surly porter stands in guilty state
To spurn imploring famine from the gate,
But on he moves to meet his latter end,
Angels around befriending virtue's friend;
Bends to the grave with unperceived decay,
110 While resignation gently slopes the way;
And all his prospects brightening to the last,
His Heaven commences ere the world be past!

Sweet was the sound when oft at evening's close,
Up yonder hill the village murmur rose;
115 There as I past with careless steps and slow,
The mingling notes came softened from below;
The swain responsive as the milk-maid sung,
The sober herd that lowed to meet their young;
The noisy geese that gabbled o'er the pool,
120 The playful children just let loose from school;
The watch-dog's voice that bayed the whispering wind,
And the loud laugh that spoke the vacant mind,
These all in sweet confusion sought the shade,
And filled each pause the nightingale had made.
125 But now the sounds of population fail,
No chearful murmurs fluctuate in the gale,
No busy steps the grass-grown foot-way tread,
For all the bloomy flush of life is fled.
All but yon widowed, solitary thing
130 That feebly bends beside the plashy spring;
She, wretched matron, forced, in age, for bread,
To strip the brook with mantling cresses spread,
To pick her wintry faggot from the thorn,
To seek her nightly shed, and weep till morn;
135 She only left of all the harmless train,
The sad historian of the pensive plain.

Near yonder copse, where once the garden smil'd,
And still where many a garden flower grows wild;
There, where a few torn shrubs the place disclose,
140   The village preacher's modest mansion rose.
A man he was, to all the country dear,
And passing rich with forty pounds a year;
Remote from towns he ran his godly race,
Nor ere had changed, nor wish'd to change his place;
145   Unpractised he to fawn, or seek for power,
By doctrines fashioned to the varying hour;
Far other aims his heart had learned to prize,
More skilled to raise the wretched than to rise.
His house was known to all the vagrant train,
150   He chid their wanderings, but relieved their pain;
The long remembered beggar was his guest,
Whose beard descending swept his aged breast;
The ruined spendthrift, now no longer proud,
Claimed kindred there, and had his claims allowed;
155   The broken soldier, kindly bade to stay,
Sate by his fire, and talked the night away;
Wept o'er his wounds, or tales of sorrow done,
Shouldered his crutch, and shewed how fields were won.
Pleased with his guests, the good man learned to glow,
160   And quite forgot their vices in their woe;
Careless their merits, or their faults to scan,
His pity gave ere charity began.

Thus to relieve the wretched was his pride,
And even his failings leaned to Virtue's side;
165   But in his duty prompt at every call,
He watched and wept, he prayed and felt, for all.
And, as a bird each fond endearment tries,
To tempt its new fledged offspring to the skies;
He tried each art, reproved each dull delay,
170   Allured to brighter worlds, and led the way.

Beside the bed where parting life was layed,
And sorrow, guilt, and pain, by turns dismayed,
The reverend champion stood. At his control,
Despair and anguish fled the struggling soul;
175   Comfort came down the trembling wretch to raise,
And his last faultering accents whispered praise.

At church, with meek and unaffected grace,
His looks adorned the venerable place;
Truth from his lips prevailed with double sway,
180   And fools, who came to scoff, remained to pray.

The service past, around the pious man,
With steady zeal each honest rustic ran;
Even children followed with endearing wile,
And plucked his gown, to share the good man's smile.
185 His ready smile a parent's warmth exprest,
Their welfare pleased him, and their cares distrest;
To them his heart, his love, his griefs were given,
But all his serious thoughts had rest in Heaven.
As some tall cliff that lifts its awful form,
190 Swells from the vale, and midway leaves the storm,
Tho' round its breast the rolling clouds are spread,
Eternal sunshine settles on its head.

Beside yon straggling fence that skirts the way,
With blossomed furze unprofitably gay,
195 There, in his noisy mansion, skill'd to rule,
The village master taught his little school;
A man severe he was, and stern to view,
I knew him well, and every truant knew;
Well had the boding tremblers learned to trace
200 The day's disasters in his morning face;
Full well they laugh'd with counterfeited glee,
At all his jokes, for many a joke had he;
Full well the busy whisper circling round,
Conveyed the dismal tidings when he frowned;
205 Yet he was kind, or if severe in aught,
The love he bore to learning was in fault;
The village all declared how much he knew;
'Twas certain he could write, and cypher too;
Lands he could measure, terms and tides presage,
210 And even the story ran that he could gauge.
In arguing too, the parson owned his skill,
For e'en tho' vanquished, he could argue still;
While words of learned length, and thundering sound,
Amazed the gazing rustics ranged around,
215 And still they gazed, and still the wonder grew,
That one small head could carry all he knew.

But past is all his fame. The very spot
Where many a time he triumphed, is forgot.
Near yonder thorn, that lifts its head on high,
220 Where once the sign-post caught the passing eye,
Low lies that house where nut-brown draughts inspired,
Where grey-beard mirth and smiling toil retired,
Where village statesmen talked with looks profound,
And news much older than their ale went round.
225 Imagination fondly stoops to trace
The parlour splendours of that festive place;

The white-washed wall, the nicely sanded floor,
The varnished clock that clicked behind the door;
The chest contrived a double debt to pay,
230   A bed by night, a chest of drawers by day;
The pictures placed for ornament and use,
The twelve good rules, the royal game of goose;
The hearth, except when winter chill'd the day,
With aspen boughs, and flowers, and fennel gay,
235   While broken tea-cups, wisely kept for shew,
Ranged o'er the chimney, glistened in a row.

Vain transitory splendours! Could not all
Reprieve the tottering mansion from its fall!
Obscure it sinks, nor shall it more impart
240   An hour's importance to the poor man's heart;
Thither no more the peasant shall repair
To sweet oblivion of his daily care;
No more the farmer's news, the barber's tale,
No more the wood-man's ballad shall prevail;
245   No more the smith his dusky brow shall clear,
Relax his ponderous strength, and lean to hear;
The host himself no longer shall be found
Careful to see the mantling bliss go round;
Nor the coy maid, half willing to be prest,
250   Shall kiss the cup to pass it to the rest.

Yes! let the rich deride, the proud disdain,
These simple blessings of the lowly train,
To me more dear, congenial to my heart,
One native charm, than all the gloss of art;
255   Spontaneous joys, where Nature has its play,
The soul adopts, and owns their first born sway,
Lightly they frolic o'er the vacant mind,
Unenvied, unmolested, unconfined.
But the long pomp, the midnight masquerade,
260   With all the freaks of wanton wealth arrayed,
In these, ere triflers half their wish obtain,
The toiling pleasure sickens into pain;
And, even while fashion's brightest arts decoy,
The heart distrusting asks, if this be joy.

265   Ye friends to truth, ye statesmen who survey
The rich man's joys encrease, the poor's decay,
'Tis yours to judge, how wide the limits stand
Between a splendid and an happy land.
Proud swells the tide with loads of freighted ore,
270   And shouting Folly hails them from her shore;

Hoards, even beyond the miser's wish abound,
And rich men flock from all the world around.
Yet count our gains. This wealth is but a name
That leaves our useful products still the same.
275 Not so the loss. The man of wealth and pride,
Takes up a space that many poor supplied;
Space for his lake, his park's extended bounds,
Space for his horses, equipage, and hounds;
The robe that wraps his limbs in silken sloth,
280 Has robbed the neighbouring fields of half their growth;
His seat, where solitary sports are seen,
Indignant spurns the cottage from the green;
Around the world each needful product flies,
For all the luxuries the world supplies.
285 While thus the land adorned for pleasure all
In barren splendour feebly waits the fall.

As some fair female unadorned and plain,
Secure to please while youth confirms her reign,
Slights every borrowed charm that dress supplies,
290 Nor shares with art the triumph of her eyes.
But when those charms are past, for charms are frail,
When time advances, and when lovers fail,
She then shines forth sollicitous to bless,
In all the glaring impotence of dress.
295 Thus fares the land, by luxury betrayed,
In nature's simplest charms at first arrayed,
But verging to decline, its splendours rise,
Its vistas strike, its palaces surprize;
While scourged by famine from the smiling land,
300 The mournful peasant leads his humble band;
And while he sinks without one arm to save,
The country blooms—a garden, and a grave.

Where then, ah, where shall poverty reside,
To scape the pressure of contiguous pride?
305 If to some common's fenceless limits strayed,
He drives his flock to pick the scanty blade,
Those fenceless fields the sons of wealth divide,
And even the bare-worn common is denied.

If to the city sped—What waits him there?
310 To see profusion that he must not share;
To see ten thousand baneful arts combined
To pamper luxury, and thin mankind;
To see those joys the sons of pleasure know,
Extorted from his fellow-creature's woe.

315   Here, while the courtier glitters in brocade,
      There the pale artist plies the sickly trade;
      Here, while the proud their long drawn pomps display,
      There the black gibbet glooms beside the way.
      The dome where pleasure holds her midnight reign,
320   Here richly deckt admits the gorgeous train,
      Tumultuous grandeur crowds the blazing square,
      The rattling chariots clash, the torches glare;
      Sure scenes like these no troubles ere annoy!
      Sure these denote one universal joy!
325   Are these thy serious thoughts?—Ah, turn thine eyes
      Where the poor houseless shivering female lies.
      She once, perhaps, in village plenty blest,
      Has wept at tales of innocence distrest;
      Her modest looks the cottage might adorn,
330   Sweet as the primrose peeps beneath the thorn;
      Now lost to all; her friends, her virtue fled,
      Near her betrayer's door she lays her head,
      And pinch'd with cold, and shrinking from the shower,
      With heavy heart deplores that luckless hour,
335   When idly first, ambitious of the town,
      She left her wheel and robes of country brown.

      Do thine, sweet AUBURN, thine, the lovliest train,
      Do thy fair tribes participate her pain?
      Even now, perhaps, by cold and hunger led,
340   At proud men's doors they ask a little bread!

      Ah, no. To distant climes, a dreary scene,
      Where half the convex world intrudes between,
      Through torrid tracts with fainting steps they go,
      Where wild Altama murmurs to their woe.
345   Far different there from all that charm'd before,
      The various terrors of that horrid shore.
      Those blazing suns that dart a downward ray,
      And fiercely shed intolerable day;
      Those matted woods where birds forget to sing,
350   But silent bats in drowsy clusters cling,
      Those poisonous fields with rank luxuriance crowned
      Where the dark scorpion gathers death around;
      Where at each step the stranger fears to wake
      The rattling terrors of the vengeful snake;
355   Where crouching tigers wait their hapless prey,
      And savage men more murderous still than they;
      While oft in whirls the mad tornado flies,
      Mingling the ravaged landscape with the skies.
      Far different these from every former scene,
360   The cooling brook, the grassy vested green,

The breezy covert of the warbling grove,
That only sheltered thefts of harmless love.

Good Heaven! what sorrows gloom'd that parting day,
That called them from their native walks away;
365   When the poor exiles, every pleasure past,
Hung round their bowers, and fondly looked their last,
And took a long farewell, and wished in vain
For seats like these beyond the western main;
And shuddering still to face the distant deep,
370   Returned and wept, and still returned to weep.
The good old sire, the first prepared to go
To new found worlds, and wept for others woe.
But for himself, in conscious virtue brave,
He only wished for worlds beyond the grave,
375   His lovely daughter, lovelier in her tears,
The fond companion of his helpless years,
Silent went next, neglectful of her charms,
And left a lover's for a father's arms.
With louder plaints the mother spoke her woes,
380   And blest the cot where every pleasure rose;
And kist her thoughtless babes with many a tear,
And claspt them close in sorrow doubly dear;
Whilst her fond husband strove to lend relief
In all the silent manliness of grief.

385   O luxury! Thou curst by heaven's decree,
How ill exchanged are things like these for thee!
How do thy potions with insidious joy,
Diffuse their pleasures only to destroy!
Kingdoms by thee, to sickly greatness grown,
390   Boast of a florid vigour not their own.
At every draught more large and large they grow,
A bloated mass of rank unwieldy woe;
Till sapped their strength, and every part unsound,
Down, down they sink, and spread a ruin round.

395   Even now the devastation is begun,
And half the business of destruction done;
Even now, methinks, as pondering here I stand,
I see the rural virtues leave the land.
Down where yon anchoring vessel spreads the sail
400   That idly waiting flaps with every gale,
Downward they move, a melancholy band,
Pass from the shore, and darken all the strand.
Contented toil, and hospitable care,
And kind connubial tenderness, are there;

405 And piety with wishes placed above,
    And steady loyalty, and faithful love.
    And thou, sweet Poetry, thou loveliest maid,
    Still first to fly where sensual joys invade;
    Unfit in these degenerate times of shame,
410 To catch the heart, or strike for honest fame;
    Dear charming nymph, neglected and decried,
    My shame in crowds, my solitary pride,
    Thou source of all my bliss, and all my woe,
    That found'st me poor at first, and keep'st me so;
415 Thou guide by which the nobler arts excell,
    Thou nurse of every virtue, fare thee well.
    Farewell, and O where'er thy voice be tried,
    On Torno's cliffs, or Pambamarca's side,
    Whether where equinoctial fervours glow,
420 Or winter wraps the polar world in snow,
    Still let thy voice prevailing over time,
    Redress the rigours of the inclement clime;
    Aid slighted truth, with thy persuasive strain
    Teach erring man to spurn the rage of gain;
425 Teach him that states of native strength possest,
    Tho' very poor, may still be very blest;
    That trade's proud empire hastes to swift decay,
    As ocean sweeps the labour's mole away;
    While self dependent power can time defy,
430 As rocks resist the billows and the sky.

THE HAUNCH OF VENISON
A POETICAL EPISTLE TO LORD CLARE

  Thanks, my Lord, for your Venison for finer or fatter
  Never rang'd in a forest, or smoak'd on a platter;
  The Haunch was a picture for Painters to study,
  The fat was so white, and the lean was so ruddy.
5 Tho' my stomach was sharp I could scarce help regretting,
  To spoil such a delicate picture by eating;
  I had thoughts, in my Chambers, to place it in view,
  To be shewn to my Friends as a piece of *Virtu*;
  As in some *Irish* houses, where things are so so,
10 One Gammon of Bacon hangs up for a show:
  But for eating a Rasher of what they take pride in,
  They'd as soon think of eating the Pan it is fry'd in.

But hold—let me pause—Don't I hear you pronounce,
This tale of the Bacon a damnable Bounce?
15   Well, suppose it a Bounce, sure a Poet may try,
By a Bounce now and then, to get Courage to fly:
But, my Lord, it's no bounce: I protest in my Turn,
It's a truth—and your Lordship may ask Mr *Burn*.
    To go on with my Tale—as I gaz'd on the Haunch,
20   I thought of a Friend that was trusty and staunch;
So I cut it, and sent it to *Reynolds* undrest,
To paint it, or eat it, just as he lik'd best.
Of the Neck and the Breast I had next to dispose;
'Twas a Neck and a Breast that might rival *M[on]r[o]es*
25   But in parting with these I was puzzled again,
With the how, and the who, and the where, and the when.
There's *H[owar]d* and *C[ole]y* and *H[awo]rth* and *H[i]ff*,
I think they love Venison—I know they love Beef.
There's my Countryman *H[i]gg[i]ns*—Oh! let him alone,
30   For making a Blunder, or picking a Bone.
But hang it—to Poets who seldom can eat,
Your very good Mutton's a very good Treat;
Such Dainties to them! their Health it might hurt,
It's like sending them Ruffles, when wanting a Shirt.
35   While thus I debated, in Reveries center'd,
An Acquaintance, a Friend as he call'd himself, enter'd;
An under-bred, fine-spoken Fellow was he,
And he smil'd as he look'd at the Venison and me.
What have we got here? Why this is good eating!
40   Your own I suppose—or is it in Waiting?
Why whose should it be? cried I, with a Flounce,
I get these Things often;—but that was a Bounce:
Some Lords, my acquaintance, that settle the nation
Are pleas'd to be kind—but I hate ostentation.
45   If that be the case then, cried he, very gay,
I'm glad I have taken this House in my Way.
To-morrow you take a poor dinner with me;
No words—I insist on't—precisely at three:
We'll have *Johnson*, and *Burke*, all the Wits will be there,
50   My acquaintance is slight or I'd ask my *Lord Clare*.
And now that I think on't, as I am a sinner!
We wanted this Venison to make out the Dinner.
What say you—a pasty—it shall, and it must,
And my Wife, little Kitty, is famous for crust.
55   Here, Porter this venison with me to Mile-end;
No stirring—I beg—my dear friend—my dear friend!
Thus snatching his hat, he brusht off like the wind,
And the porter and eatables follow'd behind.
    Left alone to reflect, having emptied my shelf,
60   *And no body with me at sea but myself*;

Tho' I could not help thinking my gentleman hasty,
Yet *Johnson*, and *Burke*, and a good venison pasty,
Were things that I never dislik'd in my life,
Tho' clogged with a coxcomb, and *Kitty* his Wife.
65   So next Day in due splendor to make my approach,
I drove to his door in my own Hackney-Coach.
     When come to the place where we all were to dine,
(A chair lumber'd closet, just twelve feet by nine:)
My friend bade me welcome, but struck me quite dumb,
70   With tidings that *Johnson* and *Burke* could not come.
For I knew it, he cried, both eternally fail,
The one with his speeches, and t'other with *Thrale*;
But no matter, I'll warrant we'll make up the party,
With two full as clever, and ten times as hearty.
75   The one is a Scotchman, the other a Jew,
They both of them merry, and authors like you;
The one writes the *Snarler*, the other the *Scourge*;
Some think he writes *Cinna*—he owns to *Panurge*.
While thus he describ'd them by trade and by name,
80   They enter'd, and dinner was serv'd as they came.
     At the top a fried liver, and bacon were seen,
At the bottom was tripe, in a swinging tureen;
At the Sides there was spinnage and pudding made hot;
In the middle a place where the pasty—was not.
85   Now, my Lord, as for Tripe it's my utter aversion,
And your Bacon I hate like a *Turk* or a *Persian*;
So there I sat stuck, like a horse in a pound,
While the bacon and liver went merrily round:
But what vex'd me most was that d—'d *Scottish* Rogue,
90   With his long-winded speeches, his smiles and his brogue.
And Madam, quoth he, may this bit be my poison,
A prettier dinner I never set eyes on;
Pray a slice of your liver, tho' may I be curst,
But I've eat of your tripe, till I'm ready to burst.
95   The Tripe, quoth the *Jew*, with his chocolate cheek,
I could dine on this tripe seven days in the week:
I like these here dinners, so pretty and small;
But your Friend there, the Doctor, eats nothing at all.
O-Oh! quoth my Friend, he'll come on in a trice,
100   He's keeping a corner for something that's nice:
There's a Pasty—A Pasty! repeated the *Jew*;
I don't care, if I keep a corner for't too.
What the De'il, Mon, a Pasty! re-echoed the *Scot*;
Tho' splitting I'll still keep a corner for thot.
105   We'll all keep a corner, the Lady cried out;
We'll all keep a corner was echoed about.
While thus we resolv'd, and the Pasty delay'd,
With looks quite petrified, enter'd the Maid;

A visage so sad, and so pale with affright,
110   Wak'd *Priam* by drawing his curtains by night.
But we quickly found out, for who could mistake her?
That she came with some terrible news from the Baker:
And so it fell out, for that negligent sloven
Had shut out the Pasty on shutting his oven.
115   Sad Philomel thus—but let Similes drop—
And now that I think on't, the Story may stop.
To be plain, my good Lord, it's but labour misplac'd,
To send such good verses to one of your taste;
You've got an odd something—a kind of discerning—
120   A relish—a taste—sicken'd over by learning;
At least, it's your temper, as very well known,
That you think very slightly of all that's your own:
So, perhaps, in your habits of thinking amiss,
You may make a mistake, and think slightly of this.

[PROLOGUE TO *ZOBEIDE*]

In these bold times, when Learning's sons explore
The distant climate and the savage shore;
When wise *Astronomers* to *India* steer,
And quit for *Venus*, many a brighter here;
5   When *Botanists*, all cold to smiles and dimpling,
Forsake the fair, and patiently—go simpling;
While every bosom swells with wond'rous scenes,
Priests, cannibals, and hoity-toity queens:
Our bard into the general spirit enters,
10   And fits his little frigate for adventures:
With *Scythian* stores, and trinkets deeply laden,
He this way steers his course, in hopes of trading—
Yet ere he lands he'as ordered me before,
To make an observation on the shore.
15   Where are we driven? Our reck'ning sure is lost!
This seems a barren and a dangerous coast.
Lord what a sultry climate am I under!
Yon ill-foreboding cloud seems big with thunder.
                         (*to the Upper Gallery.*)
There Mangroves spread, and larger than I've seen 'em—
                                (*to the Pit.*)
20   Here trees of stately size—and monkies in 'em—
                           (*to the pidgeon holes.*)

Here ill-condition'd oranges abound—   (*to the Stage.*)
And apples (*taking up and tasting*) *bitter* apples strew the ground.
The place is uninhabited I fear;
I heard a hissing—there are serpents here!
25 O there the natives are—a savage race!
The men have tails, the women paint the face!
No doubt they're all barbarians—Yes, 'tis so,
I'll try to make palaver with them though;   (*makes signs*)
'Tis best however keeping at a distance.
30 Good Savages, our Captain craves assistance;
Our ship's well stor'd;—in yonder creek we've laid her,
His honour is no mercenary trader;
To make you finer is his sole endeavour;
He seeks no benefit, content with favour.
35 This is his first adventure, lend him aid,
Or you may chance to spoil a thriving trade.
His goods he hopes are prime, and brought from far,
Equally fit for gallantry and war.
What no reply to promises so ample?
40 I'd best step back—and order up a sample.

THRENODIA AUGUSTALIS

OVERTURE A SOLEMN DIRGE

AIR. TRIO.

Arise ye sons of worth, arise
And waken every note of woe,
When truth and virtue reach the skies,
'Tis ours to weep the want below.

CHORUS

5 *When truth and virtue reach the skies,*
'Tis ours to weep the want below.

MAN SPEAKER

The praise attending pomp and power,
The incense given to kings,

Are but the trappings of an hour,
10   Mere transitory things!
The base bestow them; but the good agree
To spurn the venal gifts as flattery.——
But when to pomp, and power, are join'd
An equal dignity of mind;
15   When titles are the smallest claim;
When wealth, and rank, and noble blood,
But aid the power of doing good,
Then all their trophies last—and flattery turns to fame!
    Blest spirit thou, whose fame just born to bloom,
20   Shall spread and flourish from the tomb,
How hast thou left mankind for heaven!
Even now reproach and faction mourn,
And, wondering how their rage was born,
Request to be forgiven!
25   Alas! they never had thy hate;
Unmoved in conscious rectitude
Thy towering mind self-centered stood,
Nor wanted Man's opinion to be great.
In vain, to charm thy ravished sight,
30   A thousand gifts would fortune send;
In vain, to drive thee from the right,
A thousand sorrows urged thy end:
Like some well-fashion'd arch thy patience stood,
And purchased strength from its encreasing load.
35   Pain met thee like a friend that set thee free,
Affliction still is virtue's opportunity!
Virtue, on herself relying,
Every passion hush'd to rest,
Loses every pain of dying
40   In the hopes of being blest.
Every added pang she suffers,
Some encreasing good bestows,
And every shock that malice offers,
Only rocks her to repose.

SONG, BY A MAN. *Affettuoso*

45   *Virtue, on herself relying,*
      Every passion hush'd to rest,
      Loses every pain of dying
      In the hopes of being blest.
      Every added Pang she suffers,
50   *Some encreasing good bestows,*
      Every shock that malice offers,
      Only rocks her to repose.

WOMAN SPEAKER

Yet ah! what terrors frown'd upon her fate,
Death with its formidable band,
55   Fever and pain, and pale consumptive care,
Determined took their stand.
Nor did the cruel ravagers design
To finish all their efforts at a blow;
But, mischievously slow,
60   They robbed the relic and defac'd the shrine.——
With unavailing grief,
Despairing of relief,
Her weeping children round,
Beheld each hour
65   Death's growing pow'r,
And trembled as he frown'd.
As helpless friends who view from shore
The labouring ship, and hear the tempest roar,
While winds and waves their wishes cross;
70   They stood while hope and comfort fail,
Not to assist, but to bewail
The inevitable loss.——
Relentless tyrant, at thy call
How do the good, the virtuous fall?
75   Truth, beauty, worth, and all that most engage,
But wake thy vengeance and provoke thy rage.

SONG, BY A MAN. *Basso. Staccato. Spirituoso*

When vice my dart and scythe supply,
How great a king of Terrors I!
If folly, fraud, your hearts engage,
80   *Tremble ye mortals at my rage.*

Fall, round me fall ye little things,
Ye statesmen, warriors, poets, kings,
If virtue fail her counsel sage
Tremble ye mortals at my rage.

MAN SPEAKER

85   Yet let that wisdom, urged by her example,
Teach us to estimate what all must suffer:
Let us prize death as the best gift of nature,
As a safe inn where weary travellers,

When they have journyed thro' a world of cares,
90 May put off life and be at rest for ever.
Groans, weeping friends, indeed, and gloomy sables
May oft distract us with their sad solemnity.
The preparation is the executioner.
Death, when unmasked, shews me a friendly face,
95 And is a terror only at a distance:
For as the line of life conducts me on
To death's great court, the prospect seems more fair;
'Tis nature's kind retreat, that's always open
To take us in when we have drain'd the cup
100 Of life, or worn our days to wretchedness.———
In that secure, serene retreat,
Where all the humble, all the great,
Promiscuously recline;
Where wildly huddled to the eye,
105 The beggar's pouch and prince's purple lie,
May every bliss be thine.
And ah! blest spirit, whereso'er thy flight,
Through rolling worlds, or fields of liquid light,
May cherubs welcome their expected guest,
110 May saints with songs receive thee to their rest,
May peace that claim'd while here thy warmest love,
May blissful endless peace be thine above.

SONG, BY A WOMAN. *Amoroso*

Lovely lasting peace below,
Comforter of every woe,
115 *Heavenly born, and bred on high,*
To crown the favourites of the sky:
Lovely lasting peace appear,
This world itself, if thou art here,
Is once again with Eden blest,
120 *And man contains it in his breast.*

WOMAN SPEAKER

Our vows are heard! Long, long to mortal eyes,
Her soul was fitting to its kindred skies:
Celestial-like her bounty fell,
Where modest want and patient sorrow dwell.
125 Want pass'd for merit at her door,
Unseen the modest were supplied,
Her constant pity fed the poor,
Then only poor, indeed, the day she died.

And Oh, for this! while sculpture decks thy shrine,
130   And art exhausts profusion round,
The tribute of a tear be mine,
A simple song, a sigh profound.
There faith shall come, a pilgrim grey,
To bless the tomb that wraps thy clay;
135   And calm religion shall repair
To dwell a weeping hermit there.
Truth, fortitude, and friendship shall agree
To blend their virtues while they think of thee.

AIR. CHORUS. *Pomposo*

Let us, let all the world agree,
140   *To profit by resembling thee.*

END OF THE FIRST PART

PART II

OVERTURE PASTORALE
MAN SPEAKER

Fast by that shore where Thames' translucent stream
Reflects new glories on his breast,
Where, splendid as the youthful poet's dream,
He forms a scene beyond Elysium blest;
145   Where sculptur'd elegance and native grace
Unite to stamp the beauties of the place;
While, sweetly blending, still are seen
The wavy lawn, the sloping green;
While novelty, with cautious cunning,
150   Through every maze of fancy running,
From China borrows aid to deck the scene.
There sorrowing by the river's glassy bed,
Forlorn, a rural band complain'd,
All whom AUGUSTA's bounty fed,
155   All whom her clemency sustain'd.
The good old sire, unconscious of decay,
The modest matron, clad in home-spun grey,
The military boy, the orphan'd maid,
The shatter'd veteran, now first dismay'd;
160   These sadly join beside the murmuring deep,
And as they view the towers of Kew,
Call on their mistress, now no more, and weep.

CHORUS. *Affettuoso. Largo*

> *Ye shady walks, ye waving greens,*
> *Ye nodding tow'rs, ye fairy scenes,*
165   *Let all your ecchoes now deplore,*
> *That She who form'd your beauties is no more.*

MAN SPEAKER

First of the train the patient rustic came,
Whose callous hand had form'd the scene,
Bending at once with sorrow and with age,
170   With many a tear, and many a sigh between,
And where, he cried, shall now my babes have bread,
Or how shall age support its feeble fire?
No lord will take me now, my vigour fled,
Nor can my strength perform what they require:
175   Each grudging master keeps the labourer bare,
A sleek and idle race is all their care.
My noble mistress thought not so!
Her bounty, like the morning dew,
Unseen, tho' constant, used to flow;
180   And as my strength decay'd, her bounty grew.

WOMAN SPEAKER

In decent dress, and coarsely clean,
The pious matron next was seen,
Clasp'd in her hand a godly book was borne,
By use and daily meditation worn:
185   That decent dress, this holy guide,
AUGUSTA's care had well supply'd.
And ah! she cries, all woe begone,
What now remains for me?
Oh! where shall weeping want repair
190   To ask for charity?
Too late in life for me to ask,
And shame prevents the deed,
And tardy, tardy are the times
To succour should I need.

195   But all my wants, before I spoke,
Were to my mistress known;
She still reliev'd, nor sought my praise,
Contented with her own.

But every day her name I'll bless,
200 My morning prayer, my evening song,
I'll praise her while my life shall last,
A life that cannot last me long.

SONG, BY A WOMAN

Each day, each hour, her name I'll bless,
My morning and my evening song,
205 *And when in death my vows shall cease,*
My children shall the note prolong.

MAN SPEAKER

The hardy veteran after struck the sight,
Scarr'd, mangl'd, maim'd in every part,
Lopp'd of his limbs in many a gallant fight,
210 In nought entire—except his heart:
Mute for a while, and sullenly distress'd,
At last the impetuous sorrow fir'd his breast.
Wild is the whirlwind rolling
O'er Afric's sandy plain,
215 And wild the tempest howling
Along the billow'd main:
But every danger felt before,
The raging deep, the whirlwind's roar,
Less dreadful struck me with dismay,
220 Than what I feel this fatal day.
Oh, let me fly a land that spurns the brave,
Oswego's dreary shores shall be my grave;
I'll seek that less inhospitable coast,
And lay my body where my limbs were lost.

SONG BY A MAN. *Basso. Spirituoso*

225 *Old Edward's sons, unknown to yield,*
Shall crowd from Cressy's laurell'd field
To do thy memory right:
For thine and Britain's wrongs they feel,
Again they snatch the gleamy steel,
230 *And wish th' avenging fight.*

WOMAN SPEAKER

In innocence and youth complaining,
Next appear'd a lovely maid,
Affliction o'er each feature reigning,
Kindly came in beauty's aid;
235 Every grace that grief dispenses,
Every glance that warms the soul,
In sweet succession charm'd the senses,
While pity harmoniz'd the whole.
The garland of beauty, 'tis thus she would say,
240 No more shall my crook or my temples adorn,
I'll not wear a garland, AUGUSTA's away,
I'll not wear a garland until she return:
But alas! that return I never shall see,
The ecchoes of Thames' shall my sorrows proclaim,
245 There promis'd a lover to come, but oh me!
'Twas death, 'twas the death of my mistress that came.
But ever, for ever, her image shall last,
I'll strip all the Spring of its earliest bloom;
On her grave shall the cowslip and primrose be cast,
250 And the new-blossom'd thorn shall whiten her tomb.

SONG BY A WOMAN. *Pastorale*

With garlands of beauty the queen of the May
No more will her crook or her temples adorn;
For who'd wear a garland when she is away,
When she is remov'd, and shall never return?

255 *On the grave of* AUGUSTA *these garlands be plac't,*
We'll rifle the Spring of its earliest bloom,
And there shall the cowslip and primrose be cast,
And the new-blossom'd thorn shall whiten her tomb.

CHORUS. *Altro Modo*

On the grave of AUGUSTA *this garland be plac't,*
260 *We'll rifle the Spring of its earliest bloom,*
And there shall the cowslip and primrose be cast,
And the tears of her country shall water her tomb.

[SONG FOR *SHE STOOPS TO CONQUER*]

Ah me, when shall I marry me?
Lovers are plenty but fail to relieve me;
He, fond youth, that could carry me,
Offers to love but means to deceive me.

5   But I will rally and combat the ruiner;
Not a look, not a smile shall my passion discover;
She that gives all to the false one pursuing her
Makes but a penitent, loses a lover.

[FIRST EPILOGUE INTENDED FOR
SHE STOOPS TO CONQUER]

*Enter Mrs Bulkley, who curtsies very low as beginning to speak. Then enter
Miss Catley, who stands full before her, and curtsies to the Audience.*

MRS BULKLEY
Hold, Ma'am, your pardon. What's your business here?
                    MISS CATLEY
The Epilogue.
                    MRS BULKLEY
          The Epilogue?
                    MISS CATLEY
                         Yes, the Epilogue, my dear.
                    MRS BULKLEY
Sure you mistake, Ma'am. The Epilogue, *I* bring it.
                    MISS CATLEY
Excuse me, Ma'am. The Author bid *me* sing it.
                    Recitative
5   Ye beaux and belles, that form this splendid ring,
Suspend your conversation while I sing.
                    MRS BULKLEY
Why sure the Girl's beside herself: an Epilogue of singing,
A hopeful end indeed to such a blest beginning.
Besides, a singer in a comic set!
10   Excuse me, Ma'am, I know the etiquette.
                    MISS CATLEY
What if we leave it to the House?

Mrs BULKLEY
The House!—Agreed.
Miss CATLEY
Agreed.
Mrs BULKLEY
And she, who's party's largest, shall proceed.
And first I hope, you'll readily agree
I've all the critics and the wits for me.
15 They, I am sure, will answer my commands,
Ye candid judging few, hold up your hands;
What, no return? I find too late, I fear,
That modern judges seldom enter here.
Miss CATLEY
I'm for a different set.—Old men, whose trade is
20 Still to gallant and dangle with the ladies.
Recitative
Who mump their passion, and who, grimly smiling,
Still thus address the fair with voice beguiling.

Air.—Cotillon

Turn, my fairest, turn, if ever
Strephon caught thy ravish'd eye.
25 Pity take on your swain so clever,
Who without your aid must die.
Yes, I shall die, hu, hu, hu, hu,
Yes, I must die, ho, ho, ho, ho.
Da Capo
Mrs BULKLEY
Let all the old pay homage to your merit:
30 Give me the young, the gay, the men of spirit.
Ye travelled tribe, ye macaroni train
Of French friseurs and nosegays justly vain,
Who take a trip to Paris once a year
To dress, and look like awkward Frenchmen here,
35 Lend me your hands.—O fatal news to tell,
Their hands are only lent to the Heinelle.
Miss CATLEY
Ay, take your travellers, travellers indeed!
Give me my bonny Scot, that travels from the Tweed.
Where are the Cheels? Ah! Ah, I well discern
40 The smiling looks of each bewitching bairne.
Air.—A bonny young lad is my Jockey
I'll sing to amuse you by night and by day,
And be unco merry when you are but gay;
When you with your bagpipes are ready to play,
My voice shall be ready to carol away
45 With Sandy, and Sawney, and Jockey,
With Sawney, and Jarvie, and Jockey.

Mrs BULKLEY

Ye Gamesters, who so eager in pursuit,
Make but of all your fortune one *va Toute:*
Ye Jockey tribe whose stock of words are few,
50 'I hold the odds.—Done, done, with you, with you.'
Ye Barristers, so fluent with grimace,
'My Lord,—your Lordship misconceives the case.'
Doctors, who cough and answer every misfortuner,
'I wish I'd been call'd in a little sooner.'
55 Assist my cause with hands and voices hearty,
Come end the contest here, and aid my party.

Air—Baleinamony

Miss CATLEY

Ye brave Irish lads, hark away to the crack,
Assist me, I pray, in this woful attack;
For sure I don't wrong you, you seldom are slack,
60 When the ladies are calling, to blush, and hang back.
      For you're always polite and attentive,
      Still to amuse us inventive,
      And death is your only preventive.
          Your hands and your voices for me.

Mrs BULKLEY

65 Well, Madam, what if, after all this sparring,
We both agree, like friends, to end our jarring?

Miss CATLEY

And that our friendship may remain unbroken,
What if we leave the Epilogue unspoken?

Mrs BULKLEY

Agreed.

Miss CATLEY

      Agreed.

Mrs BULKLEY

          And now with late repentance,
70 Un-epilogued the Poet waits his sentence.
Condemn the stubborn fool who can't submit
To thrive by flattery, though he starves by wit.

[*Exeunt.*

[SECOND REJECTED EPILOGUE TO
SHE STOOPS TO CONQUER]

There is a place,—so Ariosto sings,
A Treasury for lost and missing things.

Lost human Wits have Places there Assign'd them,
And they who lose their Senses, there may find them,
5 But where's this place, this Storehouse of the Age?
The Moon, says he: but I affirm the Stage.
At least in many things I think I see
His lunar and our Mimic World agree.
Both shine at night, for, but at Foote's alone,
10 We scarce exhibit till the Sun goes down.
Both, prone to change, no settled limits fix,
'Tis said the folks of both are lunaticks.
But in this paralell my best pretence is,
That mortals visit both to find their Senses.
15 To this strange spot, Rakes, Macaronis, Cits,
Come thronging to Collect their scatter'd Wits.
The gay Coquet, who ogles all the day,
Comes here by night, and goes a prude away.
The Gamester too, who eager in pursuit,
20 Makes but of all his fortune one *va toute*,
Whose Mind is barren, and whose words are few;
'I take the odds'—'Done, done, with you, and you,'
Comes here to saunter, having made his betts,
Finds his lost Senses out, and pays his Debts.
25 The Mohawk too—with angry phrases stor'd
As 'damme Sir', and 'Sir I wear a Sword':
Here lessoned for awhile, and hence retreating,
Goes out, affronts his man, and takes a beating.
Here come the Sons of Scandal and of News,
30 But find no Sense—for they had none to lose.
The poet too—comes hither to be wiser,
And so for once I'll be the Man's Adviser.
What could he hope in this lord loving Age,
Without a brace of lords upon the State,
35 In robes and stars, unless the bard adorn us,
You grow familiar, lose respect, and scorn us.
Then not one passion, fury, sentiment
Sure his poetick fire is wholly spent!
Oh how I love to hear applauses shower
40 On my fix'd Attitude of half an hour.

(Stands in an Attitude)

And then with whining, staring, struggling, slapping,
To force their feelings and provoke their clapping.
Hither the affected City Dame advancing,
Who sighs for Opera's, and doats on dancing,
45 Who hums a favourite Air, and spreading wide,
Swings round the room, the Heinele of Cheapside,
Taught by our Art her Ridicule to pause on
Quits *Che faro* and calls for Nancy Dawson.

Of all the tribe here wanting an Adviser
50 Our Author's the least likely to grow wiser,
Has he not seen how you your favours place
On Sentimental Queens, and Lords in lace?
Without a Star, a coronet or Garter,
How can the piece expect, or hope for Quarter?
55 No high-life scenes, no sentiment, the creature
Still stoops among the low to copy Nature.
Yes, he's far gone. And yet some pity mix
The English Laws forbid to punish Lunaticks.

EPILOGUE, SPOKEN BY MR LEE LEWES, IN THE CHARACTER OF HARLEQUIN, AT HIS BENEFIT

Hold! Prompter, hold! a word before your nonsense,
I'll speak a word or two to ease my conscience.
My pride forbids it ever shou'd be said,
My heels eclips'd the honours of my head,
5   That I found humour in a pyeball vest,
Or ever thought that jumping was a jest.

[Taking off his mask

Whence, and what art thou, visionary birth?
Nature disowns, and reason scorns thy mirth;
In thy black aspect ev'ry passion sleeps,
10   The joy that dimples, and the woe that weeps.
How hast thou fill'd the scene with all thy brood,
Of fools persuing, and of fools persu'd!
Whose ins and outs no ray of sense discloses,
Whose only plot it is to break our noses;
15   Whilst from below the trap-door daemons rise,
And from above the dangling deities;
And shall I mix in this unhallow'd crew?
May rosin'd lightning blast me if I do.
No—I will act, I'll vindicate the stage;
20   Shakespeare himself shall feel my tragic rage.
Off! off! vile trappings! a new passion reigns,
The mad'ning monarch revels in my veins.
Oh! for a Richard's voice to catch the theme:
Give me another horse! bind up my wounds!—
    soft—'twas but a dream.
25   Ay, it was a dream, for now there's no retreating:
If I cease Harlequin, I cease from eating.

'Twas thus that Aesop's Stag, a creature blameless,
Yet something vain, like one that shall be nameless,
Once on the margin of a fountain stood,
30 And cavil'd at his image in the flood.
'The deuce confound (he cries) these drumstick shanks,
They neither have my gratitude nor thanks;
They're perfectly disgraceful! Strike me dead!
But, for a head, yes, yes, I have a head.
35 How piercing is that eye! How sleek that brow!
My horns! I'm told horns are the fashion now.'
Whilst thus he spoke, astonish'd! to his view,
Near, and more near, the hounds and huntsmen drew.
Hoicks! hark forward! came thund'ring from behind,
40 He bounds aloft, outstrips the fleeting wind:
He quits the woods, and tries the beaten ways;
He starts, he pants, he takes the circling maze.
At length, his silly head, so priz'd before,
Is taught its former folly to deplore;
45 Whilst his strong limbs conspire to set him free,
And at one bound he saves himself, like me.

        [*Taking a jump through the stage door*

RETALIATION
A POEM

Of old, when Scarron his companions invited,
Each guest brought his dish, and the feast was united;
If our landlord supplies us with beef, and with fish,
Let each guest bring himself, and he brings the best dish:
5 Our Dean shall be venison, just fresh from the plains;
Our Burke shall be tongue, with a garnish of brains;
Our Will shall be wild fowl, of excellent flavour,
And Dick with his pepper, shall heighten their savour:
Our Cumberland's sweet-bread its place shall obtain,
10 And Douglass's pudding, substantial and plain:
Our Garrick's a sallad, for in him we see
Oil, vinegar, sugar, and saltness agree:
To make out the dinner, full certain I am,
That Ridge is anchovy, and Reynolds is lamb;
15 That Hickey's a capon, and by the same rule,
Magnanimous Goldsmith, a gooseberry fool:
At a dinner so various, at such a repast,
Who'd not be a glutton, and stick to the last:

Here, waiter, more wine, let me sit while I'm able,
20 'Till all my companions sink under the table;
Then with chaos and blunders encircling my head,
Let me ponder, and tell what I think of the dead.

Here lies the good Dean, re-united to earth,
Who mixt reason with pleasure, and wisdom with mirth:
25 If he had any faults, he has left us in doubt,
At least, in six weeks, I could not find 'em out;
Yet some have declar'd, and it can't be denied 'em,
That sly-boots was cursedly cunning to hide 'em.

Here lies our good Edmund, whose genius was such,
30 We scarcely can praise it, or blame it too much;
Who, born for the Universe, narrow'd his mind,
And to party gave up, what was meant for mankind.
Tho' fraught with all learning, kept straining his throat,
To persuade Tommy Townsend to lend him a vote;
35 Who, too deep for his hearers, still went on refining,
And thought of convincing, while they thought of dining;
Tho' equal to all things, for all things unfit,
Too nice for a statesman, too proud for a wit:
For a patriot too cool; for a drudge, disobedient,
40 And too fond of the *right* to pursue the *expedient*.
In short, 'twas his fate, unemploy'd, or in place, Sir,
To eat mutton cold, and cut blocks with a razor.

Here lies honest William, whose heart was a mint,
While the owner ne'er knew half the good that was in't;
45 The pupil of impulse, it forc'd him along,
His conduct still right, with his argument wrong;
Still aiming at honour, yet fearing to roam,
The coachman was tipsy, the chariot drove home;
Would you ask for his merits, alas! he had none,
50 What was good was spontaneous, his faults were his own.

Here lies honest Richard, whose fate I must sigh at,
Alas, that such frolic should now be so quiet!
What spirits were his, what wit and what whim,
Now breaking a jest, and now breaking a limb;
55 Now rangling and grumbling to keep up the ball,
Now teazing and vexing, yet laughing at all?
In short so provoking a Devil was Dick,
That we wish'd him full ten times a day at Old Nick,
But missing his mirth and agreeable vein,
60 As often we wish'd to have Dick back again.

Here Cumberland lies having acted his parts,
The Terence of England, the mender of hearts;

A flattering painter, who made it his care
To draw men as they ought to be, not as they are.
His gallants are all faultless, his women divine,
And comedy wonders at being so fine;
Like a tragedy queen he has dizen'd her out,
Or rather like tragedy giving a rout.
His fools have their follies so lost in a croud
Of virtues and feelings, that folly grows proud,
And coxcombs alike in their failings alone,
Adopting his portraits are pleas'd with their own.
Say, where has our poet this malady caught,
Or wherefore his characters thus without fault?
Say was it that vainly directing his view,
To find out mens virtues and finding them few,
Quite sick of pursuing each troublesome elf,
He grew lazy at last and drew from himself?

Here Douglas retires from his toils to relax,
The scourge of impostors, the terror of quacks:
Come all ye quack bards, and ye quacking divines,
Come and dance on the spot where your tyrant reclines,
When Satire and Censure encircl'd his throne,
I fear'd for your safety, I fear'd for my own;
But now he is gone, and we want a detector,
Our Dodds shall be pious, our Kenricks shall lecture;
Macpherson write bombast, and call it a style,
Our Townshend make speeches, and I shall compile;
New Lauders and Bowers the Tweed shall cross over,
No countryman living their tricks to discover;
Detection her taper shall quench to a spark,
And Scotchman meet Scotchman and cheat in the dark.

Here lies David Garrick, describe me who can,
An abridgment of all that was pleasant in man;
As an actor, confest without rival to shine,
As a wit, if not first, in the very first line,
Yet with talents like these, and an excellent heart,
The man had his failings, a dupe to his art;
Like an ill judging beauty, his colours he spread,
And beplaister'd, with rouge, his own natural red.
On the stage he was natural, simple, affecting,
'Twas only that, when he was off, he was acting:
With no reason on earth to go out of his way,
He turn'd and he varied full ten times a day;
Tho' secure of our hearts, yet confoundedly sick,
If they were not his own by finessing and trick,
He cast off his friends, as a huntsman his pack;
For he knew when he pleased he could whistle them back.

Of praise, a mere glutton, he swallowed what came,
110 And the puff of a dunce, he mistook it for fame;
'Till his relish grown callous, almost to disease,
Who pepper'd the highest, was surest to please.
But let us be candid, and speak out our mind,
If dunces applauded, he paid them in kind.
115 Ye Kenricks, ye Kellys, and Woodfalls so grave,
What a commerce was yours, while you got and you gave?
How did Grub-street re-echo the shouts that you rais'd,
While he was beroscius'd, and you were beprais'd?
But peace to his spirit, wherever it flies,
120 To act as an angel, and mix with the skies:
Those poets, who owe their best fame to his skill,
Shall still be his flatterers, go where he will.
Old Shakespeare receive him with praise and with love,
And Beaumonts and Bens be his Kellys above.

125   Here Hickey reclines, a most blunt, pleasant creature,
And slander itself must allow him good-nature:
He cherish'd his friend, and he relish'd a bumper;
Yet one fault he had, and that one was a thumper:
Perhaps you may ask if that man was a miser?
130 I answer, no, no, for he always was wiser;
Too courteous, perhaps, or obligingly flat;
His very worst foe can't accuse him of that.
Perhaps he confided in men as they go,
And so was too foolishly honest; ah, no.
135 Then what was his failing? come tell it, and burn ye,
He was, could he help it? a special attorney.

    Here Reynolds is laid, and to tell you my mind,
He has not left a better or wiser behind;
His pencil was striking, resistless and grand,
140 His manners were gentle, complying and bland;
Still born to improve us in every part,
His pencil our faces, his manners our heart:
To coxcombs averse, yet most civilly staring,
When they judged without skill he was still hard of hearing:
145 When they talk'd of their Raphaels, Corregios and stuff,
He shifted his trumpet, and only took snuff.

Thomas Gray (1716–71)

Gray was educated at Eton, where his friends included Horace Walpole and Richard West, whose death he commemorates in his sonnet, and at Peterhouse, Cambridge. He travelled on the Continent with Walpole, but was content mainly to live in Cambridge, removing to Pembroke in 1756 as a result of a practical joke on him. He was made Professor of History in 1768 but never lectured. An important friendship of his life was that with the minor poet and his biographer, William Mason. In later years he also became friendly with the much younger Charles de Bonstetten. Also at this time he undertook tours of Scotland and the Lake District, but his name will always be associated with Stoke Poges, the scene of his famous elegy and the place of his own burial.

ODE ON THE SPRING

Lo! where the rosy-bosom'd Hours,
Fair VENUS' train appear,
Disclose the long-expecting flowers,
And wake the purple year!
5   The Attic warbler pours her throat,
Responsive to the cuckow's note,
The untaught harmony of spring:
While whisp'ring pleasure as they fly,
Cool Zephyrs thro' the clear blue sky
10   Their gather'd fragrance fling.

Where'er the oak's thick branches stretch
A broader browner shade;
Where'er the rude and moss-grown beech
O'er-canopies the glade
15   Beside some water's rushy brink
With me the Muse shall sit, and think
(At ease reclin'd in rustic state)
How vain the ardour of the Crowd,
How low, how little are the Proud,
20   How indigent the Great!

[165]

Still is the toiling hand of Care:
The panting herds repose:
Yet hark, how thro' the peopled air
The busy murmur glows!
25   The insect youth are on the wing,
Eager to taste the honied spring,
And float amid the liquid noon:
Some lightly o'er the current skim,
Some shew their gayly-gilded trim
30   Quick-glancing to the sun.

To Contemplation's sober eye
Such is the race of Man:
And they that creep, and they that fly,
Shall end where they began.
35   Alike the Busy and the Gay
But flutter thro' life's little day,
In fortune's varying colours drest:
Brush'd by the hand of rough Mischance,
Or chill'd by age, their airy dance
40   They leave, in dust to rest.

Methinks I hear in accents low
The sportive kind reply:
Poor moralist! and what art thou?
A solitary fly!
45   Thy Joys no glittering female meets,
No hive hast thou of hoarded sweets,
No painted plumage to display:
On hasty wings thy youth is flown;
Thy sun is set, thy spring is gone——
50   We frolick, while 'tis May.

ODE ON A DISTANT PROSPECT OF
ETON COLLEGE

Ἄνθρωπος' ἱκανὴ πρόφασις εἰς τὸ δυστυχεῖν
MENANDER.

Ye distant spires, ye antique towers,
That crown the watry glade,
Where grateful Science still adores
Her HENRY's holy Shade;

And ye, that from the stately brow
Of WINDSOR's heights th' expanse below
Of grove, of lawn, of mead survey,
Whose turf, whose shade, whose flowers among
Wanders the hoary Thames along
His silver-winding way.

Ah happy hills, ah pleasing shade,
Ah fields belov'd in vain,
Where once my careless childhood stray'd,
A stranger yet to pain!
I feel the gales, that from ye blow,
A momentary bliss bestow,
As waving fresh their gladsome wing,
My weary soul they seem to sooth,
And, redolent of joy and youth,
To breathe a second spring.

Say, Father THAMES, for thou hast seen
Full many a sprightly race
Disporting on thy margent green
The paths of pleasure trace,
Who foremost now delight to cleave
With pliant arm thy glassy wave?
The captive linnet which enthrall?
What idle progeny succeed
To chase the rolling circle's speed,
Or urge the flying ball?

While some on earnest business bent
Their murm'ring labours ply
'Gainst graver hours, that bring constraint
To sweeten liberty:
Some bold adventurers disdain
The limits of their little reign,
And unknown regions dare descry:
Still as they run they look behind,
They hear a voice in every wind,
And snatch a fearful joy.

Gay hope is theirs by fancy fed,
Less pleasing when possest;
The tear forgot as soon as shed,
The sunshine of the breast:
Theirs buxom health of rosy hue,
Wild wit, invention ever-new,

And lively chear of vigour born;
The thoughtless day, the easy night,
The spirits pure, the slumbers light,
50   That fly th' approach of morn.

Alas, regardless of their doom,
The little victims play!
No sense have they of ills to come,
Nor care beyond to-day:
55   Yet see how all around 'em wait
The Ministers of human fate,
And black Misfortune's baleful train!
Ah, shew them where in ambush stand
To seize their prey the murth'rous band!
60   Ah, tell them, they are men!

These shall the fury Passions tear,
The vultures of the mind,
Disdainful Anger, pallid Fear,
And Shame that sculks behind;
65   Or pineing Love shall waste their youth,
Or Jealousy with rankling tooth,
That inly gnaws the secret heart,
And Envy wan, and faded Care,
Grim-visag'd comfortless Despair,
70   And Sorrow's piercing dart.

Ambition this shall tempt to rise,
Then whirl the wretch from high,
To bitter Scorn a sacrifice,
And grinning Infamy.
75   The stings of Falshood those shall try,
And hard Unkindness' alter'd eye,
That mocks the tear it forc'd to flow;
And keen Remorse with blood defil'd,
And moody Madness laughing wild
80   Amid severest woe.

Lo, in the vale of years beneath
A griesly troop are seen,
The painful family of Death,
More hideous than their Queen:
85   This racks the joints, this fires the veins,
That every labouring sinew strains,
Those in the deeper vitals rage:
Lo, Poverty, to fill the band,
That numbs the soul with icy hand,
90   And slow-consuming Age.

    To each his suff'rings: all are men,
Condemn'd alike to groan,
The tender for another's pain;
Th' unfeeling for his own.
95   Yet ah! why should they know their fate?
Since sorrow never comes too late,
And happiness too swiftly flies.
Thought would destroy their paradise.
No more; where ignorance is bliss,
100   'Tis folly to be wise.

SONNET ON THE DEATH OF
MR RICHARD WEST

In vain to me the smiling Mornings shine,
And redd'ning Phoebus lifts his golden fire:
The birds in vain their amorous descant join;
Or chearful fields resume their green attire:
5   These ears, alas! for other notes repine,
A different object do these eyes require.
My lonely anguish melts no heart but mine;
And in my breast the imperfect joys expire.
Yet Morning smiles the busy race to chear,
10   And new-born pleasure brings to happier men:
The fields to all their wonted tribute bear:
To warm their little loves the birds complain:
I fruitless mourn to him, that cannot hear,
And weep the more, because I weep in vain.

HYMN TO ADVERSITY

———Ζῆνα
Τὸν Φρονεῖν βροτοὺς ὁδώ-
σαντα, τῶ πάθει μαθὰν
Θέντα κυρίως ἔχειν
    ÆSCHYLUS, in Agamemnone. [176–7]

Daughter of Jove, relentless Power,
Thou Tamer of the human breast,
Whose iron scourge and tort'ring hour,
The Bad affright, afflict the Best!

5   Bound in thy adamantine chain
       The Proud are taught to taste of pain,
       And purple Tyrants vainly groan
       With pangs unfelt before, unpitied and alone.

       When first thy Sire to send on earth
10   Virtue, his darling Child, design'd,
       To thee he gave the heav'nly Birth,
       And bad to form her infant mind.
       Stern rugged Nurse! thy rigid lore
       With patience many a year she bore:
15   What sorrow was, thou bad'st her know,
       And from her own she learn'd to melt at others' woe.

       Scared at thy frown terrific, fly
       Self-pleasing Folly's idle brood,
       Wild Laughter, Noise, and thoughtless Joy,
20   And leave us leisure to be good.
       Light they disperse, and with them go
       The summer Friend, the flatt'ring Foe;
       By vain Prosperity received,
       To her they vow their truth, and are again believed.

25   Wisdom in sable garb array'd
       Immers'd in rapt'rous thought profound,
       And Melancholy, silent maid
       With leaden eye, that loves the ground,
       Still on thy solemn steps attend:
30   Warm Charity, the gen'ral Friend,
       With Justice to herself severe,
       And Pity, dropping soft the sadly-pleasing tear.

       Oh, gently on thy Suppliant's head,
       Dread Goddess, lay thy chast'ning hand!
35   Not in thy Gorgon terrors clad,
       Nor circled with the vengeful Band
       (As by the Impious thou art seen)
       With thund'ring voice, and threat'ning mien,
       With screaming Horror's funeral cry,
40   Despair, and fell Disease, and ghastly Poverty.

       Thy form benign, oh Goddess, wear,
       Thy milder influence impart,
       Thy philosophic Train be there
       To soften, not to wound my heart,
45   The gen'rous spark extinct revive,
       Teach me to love and to forgive,
       Exact my own defects to scan,
       What others are, to feel, and know myself a Man.

[HYMN TO IGNORANCE. A FRAGMENT]

Hail, Horrors, hail! ye ever gloomy bowers,
Ye gothic fanes, and antiquated towers,
Where rushy Camus' slowly-winding flood
Perpetual draws his humid train of mud:
5   Glad I revisit thy neglected reign,
Oh take me to thy peaceful shade again.
   But chiefly thee, whose influence breath'd from high
Augments the native darkness of the sky;
Ah Ignorance! soft salutary Power!
10   Prostrate with filial reverence I adore.
Thrice hath Hyperion roll'd his annual race,
Since weeping I forsook thy fond embrace.
Oh say, successful do'st thou still oppose
Thy leaden Ægis 'gainst our antient foes?
15   Still stretch, tenacious of thy right divine,
The massy sceptre o'er thy slumb'ring line?
And dews Lethean thro' the land dispense
To steep in slumbers each benighted sense?
If any spark of Wit's delusive ray
20   Break out, and flash a momentary day,
With damp, cold touch forbid it to aspire,
And huddle up in fogs the dangerous fire.
   Oh say—she hears me not, but careless grown,
Lethargic nods upon her ebon throne.
25   Goddess! awake, arise, alas my fears!
Can powers immortal feel the force of years?
Not thus of old, with ensigns wide unfurl'd,
She rode triumphant o'er the vanquish'd world;
Fierce nations own'd her unresisted might,
30   And all was Ignorance, and all was Night.
   Oh sacred Age! Oh Times for ever lost!
(The School-man's glory, and the Church-man's boast.)
For ever gone—yet still to Fancy new,
Her rapid wings the transient scene pursue,
35   And bring the buried ages back to view.
   High on her car, behold the Grandam ride
Like old Sesostris with barbaric pride;
* * * * a team of harness'd monarchs bend

* * * * *

ODE ON THE DEATH OF A FAVOURITE CAT, DROWNED IN A TUB OF GOLD FISHES

'Twas on a lofty vase's side,
Where China's gayest art had dy'd
   The azure flowers, that blow;
Demurest of the tabby kind,
5   The pensive Selima reclin'd,
   Gazed on the lake below.

Her conscious tail her joy declar'd;
The fair round face, the snowy beard,
   The velvet of her paws,
10   Her coat, that with the tortoise vies,
Her ears of jet, and emerald eyes,
   She saw; and purr'd applause.

Still had she gaz'd; but 'midst the tide
Two angel forms were seen to glide,
15   The Genii of the stream
Their scaly armour's Tyrian hue
Thro' richest purple to the view
   Betray'd a golden gleam.

The hapless Nymph with wonder saw:
20   A whisker first and then a claw,
   With many an ardent wish,
She stretch'd in vain to reach the prize.
What female heart can gold despise?
   What Cat's averse to fish?

25   Presumptuous Maid! with looks intent
Again she stretch'd, again she bent,
   Nor knew the gulf between.
(Malignant Fate sat by, and smil'd)
The slipp'ry verge her feet beguil'd,
30   She tumbled headlong in.

Eight times emerging from the flood
She mew'd to ev'ry watry God,
   Some speedy aid to send.
No Dolphin came, no Nereid stirr'd:
35   Nor cruel *Tom*, nor *Susan* heard.
   A Fav'rite has no friend!

From hence, ye Beauties, undeceiv'd,
Know, one false step is ne'er retriev'd,
　　And be with caution bold.
40　Not all that tempts your wand'ring eyes
And heedless hearts, is lawful prize;
　　Nor all, that glisters, gold.

[THE ALLIANCE OF EDUCATION AND GOVERNMENT]

ESSAY I

――*Πόταγ' ὦ γαθέ; τὰν γὰρ ἀοιδὰν*
Οὔτι πω εἰς Ἀΐδαν γε τὸν ἐκλελάθοντα φύλαξῖε.
THEOCRITUS [*Idylls* i 62–3]

As sickly Plants betray a niggard earth,
Whose barren bosom starves her gen'rous birth,
Nor genial warmth, nor genial juice retains
Their roots to feed, and fill their verdant veins:
5　And as in climes, where Winter holds his reign,
The soil, tho' fertile, will not teem in vain,
Forbids her gems to swell, her shades to rise,
Nor trusts her blossoms to the churlish skies:
So draw Mankind in vain the vital airs,
10　Unform'd, unfriended, by those kindly cares,
That health and vigour to the soul impart,
Spread the young thought, and warm the opening heart:
So fond Instruction on the growing powers
Of nature idly lavishes her stores,
15　If equal Justice with unclouded face
Smile not indulgent on the rising race,
And scatter with a free, tho' frugal hand
Light golden showers of plenty o'er the land:
But Tyranny has fix'd her empire there ⎫
20　To check their tender hopes with chilling fear, ⎬
And blast the blooming promise of the year. ⎭
　　This spacious animated scene survey,
From where the rolling Orb, that gives the day,
His sable sons with nearer course surrounds
25　To either pole, and life's remotest bounds.
How rude soe'er th' exteriour form we find,
Howe'er opinion tinge the varied mind,

Alike, to all the kind, impartial Heav'n
The sparks of truth and happiness has giv'n:
30   With sense to feel, with memory to retain,
They follow pleasure, and they fly from pain;
Their judgment mends the plan their fancy draws,
Th' event presages, and explores the cause;
The soft returns of gratitude they know,
35   By fraud elude, by force repell the foe;
While mutual wishes, mutual woes endear
The social smile and sympathetic tear.
   Say, then, thro' ages by what fate confin'd
To different climes seem different souls assign'd?
40   Here measur'd laws and philosophic ease
Fix, and improve the polish'd arts of peace.
There industry and gain their vigils keep,
Command the winds, and tame th' unwilling deep.
Here force and hardy deeds of blood prevail;
45   There languid pleasure sighs in every gale.
Oft o'er the trembling nations from afar
Has Scythia breath'd the living cloud of war;
And, where the deluge burst, with sweepy sway
Their arms, their kings, their gods were roll'd away.
50   As oft have issued, host impelling host,
The blue-eyed myriads from the Baltic coast.
The prostrate South to the Destroyer yields
Her boasted titles, and her golden fields:
With grim delight the Brood of winter view
55   A brighter day, and Heav'ns of azure hue,
Scent the new fragrance of the breathing rose,
And quaff the pendent vintage as it grows.
Proud of the yoke, and pliant to the rod,
Why yet does Asia dread a monarch's nod,
60   While European freedom still withstands
Th' encroaching tide, that drowns her lessening lands;
And sees far off with an indignant groan
Her native plains, and Empires once her own.
Can opener skies and suns of fiercer flame
65   O'erpower the fire, that animates our frame;
As lamps, that shed at eve a chearful ray,
Fade and expire beneath the eye of day?
Need we the influence of the Northern star
To string our nerves and steel our hearts to war?
70   And, where the face of nature laughs around,
Must sick'ning virtue fly the tainted ground?
Unmanly thought! what seasons can controul,
What fancied zone can circumscribe the soul,
Who, conscious of the source from whence she springs,
75   By reason's light, on resolution's wings,

Spite of her frail companion, dauntless goes
O'er Lybia's deserts and thro' Zembla's snows?
She bids each slumb'ring energy awake,
Another touch, another temper take,
80 Suspends th' inferior laws, that rule our clay:
The stubborn elements confess her sway;
Their little wants, their low desires, refine,
And raise the mortal to a height divine.
      Not but the human fabric from the birth
85 Imbibes a flavour of its parent earth.
As various tracts enforce a various toil,
The manners speak the idiom of their soil.
An iron-race the mountain-cliffs maintain,
Foes to the gentler genius of the plain:
90 For where unwearied sinews must be found
With side-long plough to quell the flinty ground,
To turn the torrent's swift-descending flood,
To brave the savage rushing from the wood,
What wonder, if to patient valour train'd
95 They guard with spirit, what by strength they gain'd?
And while their rocky ramparts round they see,
The rough abode of want and liberty,
(As lawless force from confidence will grow)
Insult the plenty of the vales below?
100 What wonder, in the sultry climes, that spread,
Where Nile redundant o'er his summer-bed
From his broad bosom life and verdure flings,
And broods o'er Ægypt with his wat'ry wings,
If with advent'rous oar and ready sail
105 The dusky people drive before the gale;
Or on frail floats to neighb'ring cities ride,
That rise and glitter o'er the ambient tide.
      *   *   *   *   *   *   *   *   *

[TOPHET]

Thus Tophet look'd, so grinn'd the brawling fiend,
Whilst frighted prelates bow'd, and call'd him friend.
Our mother-church, with half-averted sight,
Blush'd as she bless'd her grimly proselyte;
5 Hosannas rung thro' hell's tremendous borders,
And Satan's self had thoughts of taking orders.

ELEGY WRITTEN IN A COUNTRY CHURCH-YARD

The Curfew tolls the knell of parting day,
The lowing herd wind slowly o'er the lea,
The plowman homeward plods his weary way,
And leaves the world to darkness and to me.

5   Now fades the glimmering landscape on the sight,
And all the air a solemn stillness holds,
Save where the beetle wheels his droning flight,
And drowsy tinklings lull the distant folds:

Save that from yonder ivy-mantled tow'r
10   The mopeing owl does to the moon complain
Of such, as wand'ring near her secret bow'r,
Molest her ancient solitary reign.

Beneath those rugged elms, that yew-tree's shade,
Where heaves the turf in many a mould'ring heap,
15   Each in his narrow cell for ever laid,
The rude Forefathers of the hamlet sleep.

The breezy call of incense-breathing Morn,
The swallow twitt'ring from the straw-built shed,
The cock's shrill clarion, or the echoing horn,
20   No more shall rouse them from their lowly bed.

For them no more the blazing hearth shall burn,
Or busy housewife ply her evening care:
No children run to lisp their sire's return,
Or climb his knees the envied kiss to share.

25   Oft did the harvest to their sickle yield,
Their furrow oft the stubborn glebe has broke;
How jocund did they drive their team afield!
How bow'd the woods beneath their sturdy stroke!

Let not Ambition mock their useful toil,
30   Their homely joys, and destiny obscure;
Nor Grandeur hear with a disdainful smile,
The short and simple annals of the poor.

The boast of heraldry, the pomp of pow'r,
And all that beauty, all that wealth e'er gave,
35   Awaits alike th' inevitable hour.
The paths of glory lead but to the grave.

Nor you, ye Proud, impute to These the fault,
If Mem'ry o'er their Tomb no Trophies raise,
Where thro' the long-drawn isle and fretted vault
40   The pealing anthem swells the note of praise.

Can storied urn or animated bust
Back to its mansion call the fleeting breath?
Can Honour's voice provoke the silent dust,
Or Flatt'ry sooth the dull cold ear of Death?

45 Perhaps in this neglected spot is laid
Some heart once pregnant with celestial fire;
Hands, that the rod of empire might have sway'd,
Or wak'd to extasy the living lyre.

But Knowledge to their eyes her ample page
50   Rich with the spoils of time did ne'er unroll;
Chill Penury repress'd their noble rage,
And froze the genial current of the soul.

Full many a gem of purest ray serene,
The dark unfathom'd caves of ocean bear:
55 Full many a flower is born to blush unseen,
And waste its sweetness on the desert air.

Some village-Hampden, that with dauntless breast
The little Tyrant of his fields withstood;
Some mute inglorious Milton here may rest,
60   Some Cromwell guiltless of his country's blood.

Th' applause of list'ning senates to command,
The threats of pain and ruin to despise,
To scatter plenty o'er a smiling land,
And read their hist'ry in a nation's eyes,

65 Their lot forbad: nor circumscrib'd alone
Their growing virtues, but their crimes confin'd;
Forbad to wade through slaughter to a throne,
And shut the gates of mercy on mankind,

The struggling pangs of conscious truth to hide,
70   To quench the blushes of ingenuous shame,
Or heap the shrine of Luxury and Pride
With incense kindled at the Muse's flame.

Far from the madding crowd's ignoble strife,
Their sober wishes never learn'd to stray;
75 Along the cool sequester'd vale of life
They kept the noiseless tenor of their way.

Yet ev'n these bones from insult to protect
Some frail memorial still erected nigh,
With uncouth rhimes and shapeless sculpture deck'd,
80   Implores the passing tribute of a sigh.

Their name, their years, spelt by th' unletter'd muse,
The place of fame and elegy supply:
And many a holy text around she strews,
That teach the rustic moralist to die.

85   For who to dumb Forgetfulness a prey,
This pleasing anxious being e'er resign'd,
Left the warm precincts of the chearful day,
Nor cast one longing ling'ring look behind?

On some fond breast the parting soul relies,
90   Some pious drops the closing eye requires;
Ev'n from the tomb the voice of Nature cries,
Ev'n in our Ashes live their wonted Fires.

For thee, who mindful of th' unhonour'd Dead
Dost in these lines their artless tale relate;
95   If chance, by lonely contemplation led,
Some kindred Spirit shall inquire thy fate,

Haply some hoary-headed Swain may say,
'Oft have we seen him at the peep of dawn
Brushing with hasty steps the dews away
100   To meet the sun upon the upland lawn.

'There at the foot of yonder nodding beech
That wreathes its old fantastic roots so high,
His listless length at noontide would he stretch,
And pore upon the brook that babbles by.

105   'Hard by yon wood, now smiling as in scorn,
Mutt'ring his wayward fancies he would rove,
Now drooping, woeful wan, like one forlorn,
Or craz'd with care, or cross'd in hopeless love.

'One morn I miss'd him on the custom'd hill,
110   Along the heath and near his fav'rite tree;
Another came; nor yet beside the rill,
Nor up the lawn, nor at the wood was he;

'The next with dirges due in sad array
Slow thro' the church-way path we saw him born.
115   Approach and read (for thou can'st read) the lay,
Grav'd on the stone beneath yon aged thorn.'

THE EPITAPH

Here rests his head upon the lap of Earth
A Youth to Fortune and to Fame unknown.
Fair Science frown'd not on his humble birth,
120 *And Melancholy mark'd him for her own.*

Large was his bounty, and his soul sincere,
Heav'n did a recompence as largely send:
He gave to Mis'ry all he had, a tear,
He gain'd from Heav'n ('twas all he wish'd) a friend.

125 *No farther seek his merits to disclose,*
Or draw his frailties from their dread abode,
(There they alike in trembling hope repose,)
The bosom of his Father and his God.

A LONG STORY

In Britain's Isle, no matter where,
An ancient pile of building stands:
The Huntingdons and Hattons there
Employ'd the power of Fairy hands

5 To raise the cieling's fretted height,
Each pannel in achievements cloathing,
Rich windows that exclude the light,
And passages, that lead to nothing.

Full oft within the spatious walls,
10 When he had fifty winters o'er him,
My grave Lord-Keeper led the Brawls:
The Seal, and Maces, danc'd before him.

His bushy beard, and shoe-strings green,
His high-crown'd hat, and sattin-doublet,
15 Mov'd the stout heart of England's Queen,
Tho' Pope and Spaniard could not trouble it.

What, in the very first beginning!
Shame of the versifying tribe!
Your Hist'ry whither are you spinning?
20   Can you do nothing but describe?

A House there is, (and that's enough)
From whence one fatal morning issues
A brace of Warriors, not in buff,
But rustling in their silks and tissues.

25   The first came cap-a-pee from France
Her conqu'ring destiny fulfilling,
Whom meaner Beauties eye askance,
And vainly ape her art of killing.

The other Amazon kind Heaven
30   Had arm'd with spirit, wit, and satire:
But COBHAM had the polish given,
And tip'd her arrows with good-nature.

To celebrate her eyes, her air. . . .
Coarse panegyricks would but teaze her.
35   Melissa is her Nom de Guerre.
Alas, who would not wish to please her!

With bonnet blue and capucine,
And aprons long they hid their armour,
And veil'd their weapons bright and keen
40   In pity to the country-farmer.

Fame in the shape of Mr. P[ur]t
(By this time all the Parish know it)
Had told, that thereabouts there lurk'd
A wicked Imp they call a Poet,

45   Who prowl'd the country far and near,
Bewitch'd the children of the peasants,
Dried up the cows, and lam'd the deer,
And suck'd the eggs, and kill'd the pheasants.

My Lady heard their joint petition,
50   Swore by her coronet and ermine,
She'd issue out her high commission
To rid the manour of such vermin.

The Heroines undertook the task,
Thro' lanes unknown, o'er stiles they ventur'd,
55   Rap'd at the door, nor stay'd to ask,
But bounce into the parlour enter'd.

The trembling family they daunt,
They flirt, they sing, they laugh, they **tattle**,
Rummage his Mother, pinch his Aunt,
60   And up stairs in a whirlwind rattle.

Each hole and cupboard they explore,
Each creek and cranny of his chamber,
Run hurry-skurry round the floor,
And o'er the bed and tester clamber,

65   Into the Drawers and China pry,
Paper and books, a huge Imbroglio!
Under a tea-cup he might lie,
Or creased, like dogs-ears, in a folio.

On the first marching of the troops
70   The Muses, hopeless of his pardon,
Convey'd him underneath their hoops
To a small closet in the garden.

So Rumor says. (Who will, believe.)
But that they left the door a-jarr,
75   Where, safe and laughing in his sleeve,
He heard the distant din of war.

Short was his joy. He little knew,
The power of Magick was no fable.
Out of the window, whisk, they flew,
80   But left a spell upon the table.

The words too eager to unriddle
The Poet felt a strange disorder:
Transparent birdlime form'd the middle,
And chains invisible the border.

85   So cunning was the Apparatus,
The powerful pothooks did so move him,
That, will he, nill he, to the Great-house
He went, as if the Devil drove him.

Yet on his way (no sign of grace,
90   For folks in fear are apt to pray)
To Phœbus he prefer'd his case,
And beg'd his aid that dreadful day.

The Godhead would have back'd his **quarrel**,
But with a blush on recollection
95   Own'd, that his quiver and his laurel
'Gainst four such eyes were no protection.

The Court was sate, the Culprit there,
Forth from their gloomy mansions creeping
The Lady *Janes* and *Joans* repair,
100   And from the gallery stand peeping:

Such as in silence of the night
Come (sweep) along some winding entry
(*Styack* has often seen the sight)
Or at the chappel-door stand sentry;

105   In peaked hoods and mantles tarnish'd,
Sour visages, enough to scare ye,
High Dames of honour once, that garnish'd
The drawing-room of fierce Queen Mary!

The Peeress comes. The Audience stare,
110   And doff their hats with due submission:
She curtsies, as she takes her chair,
To all the People of condition.

The Bard with many an artful fib,
Had in imagination fenc'd him,
115   Disproved the arguments of *Squib*,
And all that *Groom* could urge against him.

But soon his rhetorick forsook him,
When he the solemn hall had seen;
A sudden fit of ague shook him,
120   He stood as mute as poor *Macleane*.

Yes something he was heard to mutter,
'How in the park beneath an old-tree
(Without design to hurt the butter,
Or any malice to the poultry,)

125   'He once or twice had pen'd a sonnet;
Yet hoped, that he might save his bacon:
Numbers would give their oaths upon it,
He ne'er was for a conj'rer taken.'

The ghostly Prudes with hagged face
130   Already had condemn'd the sinner.
My Lady rose, and with a grace——
She smiled, and bid him come to dinner.

'Jesu-Maria! Madam Bridget,
Why, what can the Vicountess mean?
135   (Cried the square Hoods in woful fidget)
The times are alter'd quite and clean!

Decorum's turn'd to mere civility;
Her air and all her manners shew it.
Commend me to her affability!
140   Speak to a Commoner and Poet!'

[*Here 500 Stanzas are lost.*]

And so God save our noble King,
And guard us from long-winded Lubbers,
That to eternity would sing,
And keep my Lady from her Rubbers.

STANZAS TO MR BENTLEY

In silent gaze the tuneful choir among,
    Half pleas'd, half blushing let the muse admire,
While Bentley leads her sister-art along,
    And bids the pencil answer to the lyre.
5   See, in their course, each transitory thought
    Fix'd by his touch a lasting essence take;
Each dream, in fancy's airy colouring wrought,
    To local symmetry and life awake!
The tardy rhymes that us'd to linger on,
10   To censure cold, and negligent of fame,
In swifter measures animated run,
    And catch a lustre from his genuine flame.
Ah! could they catch his strength, his easy grace,
    His quick creation, his unerring line;
15   The energy of Pope they might efface,
    And Dryden's harmony submit to mine.
But not to one in this benighted age
    Is that diviner inspiration giv'n,
That burns in Shakespear's or in Milton's page,
20   The pomp and prodigality of heav'n.
As when conspiring in the diamond's blaze,
    The meaner gems, that singly charm the sight,
Together dart their intermingled rays,
    And dazzle with a luxury of light.
25   Enough for me, if to some feeling breast
    My lines a secret sympathy *impart*;
And as their pleasing influence *flows confest*,
    A sigh of soft reflection *heave the heart*.

THE PROGRESS OF POESY
A PINDARIC ODE

Φωνᾶντα συνετοῖσιν· ἐς
Δὲ τὸ πᾶν ἑρμηνέων χατίζει.

Pindar, Olymp. II

I. 1.

 Awake, Æolian lyre, awake,
And give to rapture all thy trembling strings.
From Helicon's harmonious springs
A thousand rills their mazy progress take:
5 The laughing flowers, that round them blow,
Drink life and fragrance as they flow.
Now the rich stream of music winds along
Deep, majestic, smooth, and strong,
Thro' verdant vales, and Ceres' golden reign:
10 Now rowling down the steep amain,
Headlong, impetuous, see it pour:
The rocks, and nodding groves rebellow to the roar.

I. 2.

 Oh! Sovereign of the willing soul,
Parent of sweet and solemn-breathing airs,
15 Enchanting shell! the sullen Cares,
And frantic Passions hear thy soft controul.
On Thracia's hills the Lord of War,
Has curb'd the fury of his car,
And drop'd his thirsty lance at thy command.
20 Perching on the scept'red hand
Of Jove, thy magic lulls the feather'd king
With ruffled plumes, and flagging wing:
Quench'd in dark clouds of slumber lie
The terror of his beak, and light'nings of his eye.

I. 3.

25 Thee the voice, the dance, obey,
Temper'd to thy warbled lay.
O'er Idalia's velvet-green
The rosy-crowned Loves are seen
On Cytherea's day

30 With antic Sports, and blue-eyed Pleasures,
    Frisking light in frolic measures;
    Now pursuing, now retreating,
    Now in circling troops they meet:
    To brisk notes in cadence beating
35 Glance their many-twinkling feet.
    Slow melting strains their Queen's approach declare:
    Where'er she turns the Graces homage pay.
    With arms sublime, that float upon the air,
    In gliding state she wins her easy way:
40 O'er her warm cheek, and rising bosom, move
    The bloom of young Desire, and purple light of Love.

II. 1.

    Man's feeble race what Ills await,
    Labour, and Penury, the racks of Pain,
    Disease, and Sorrow's weeping train,
45 And Death, sad refuge from the storms of Fate!
    The fond complaint, my Song, disprove,
    And justify the laws of Jove.
    Say, has he giv'n in vain the heav'nly Muse?
    Night, and all her sickly dews,
50 Her Spectres wan, and Birds of boding cry,
    He gives to range the dreary sky:
    Till down the eastern cliffs afar
    Hyperion's march they spy, and glitt'ring shafts of war.

II. 2.

    In climes beyond the solar road,
55 Where shaggy forms o'er ice-built mountains roam,
    The Muse has broke the twilight-gloom
    To chear the shiv'ring Native's dull abode.
    And oft, beneath the od'rous shade
    Of Chili's boundless forests laid,
60 She deigns to hear the savage Youth repeat
    In loose numbers wildly sweet
    Their feather-cinctured Chiefs, and dusky Loves.
    Her track, where'er the Goddess roves,
    Glory pursue, and generous Shame,
65 Th' unconquerable Mind, and Freedom's holy flame.

II. 3.

    Woods, that wave o'er Delphi's steep,
    Isles, that crown th' Egæan deep,

Fields, that cool Ilissus laves,
Or where Mæander's amber waves
70   In lingering Lab'rinths creep,
How do your tuneful Echoes languish,
Mute, but to the voice of Anguish?
Where each old poetic Mountain
Inspiration breath'd around:
75   Ev'ry shade and hallow'd Fountain
Murmur'd deep a solemn sound:
Till the sad Nine in Greece's evil hour
Left their Parnassus for the Latian plains.
Alike they scorn the pomp of tyrant-Power,
80   And coward Vice, that revels in her chains.
When Latium had her lofty spirit lost,
They sought, oh Albion! next thy sea-encircled coast.

III.   1.

Far from the sun and summer-gale,
In thy green lap was Nature's Darling laid,
85   What time, where lucid Avon stray'd,
To Him the mighty Mother did unveil
Her aweful face: The dauntless Child
Stretch'd forth his little arms, and smiled.
This pencil take (she said) whose colours clear
90   Richly paint the vernal year:
Thine too these golden keys, immortal Boy!
This can unlock the gates of Joy;
Of Horrour that, and thrilling Fears,
Or ope the sacred source of sympathetic Tears.

III.   2.

95   Nor second He, that rode sublime
Upon the seraph-wings of Extasy,
The secrets of th' Abyss to spy.
He pass'd the flaming bounds of Place and Time:
The living Throne, the saphire-blaze,
100   Where Angels tremble, while they gaze,
He saw; but blasted with excess of light,
Closed his eyes in endless night.
Behold, where Dryden's less presumptuous car,
Wide o'er the fields of Glory bear
105   Two Coursers of ethereal race,
With necks in thunder cloath'd, and long-resounding pace.

III. 3.

Hark, his hands the lyre explore!
Bright-eyed Fancy hovering o'er
Scatters from her pictured urn
110   Thoughts, that breath, and words, that burn.
But ah! 'tis heard no more——
Oh! Lyre divine, what daring Spirit
Wakes thee now? tho' he inherit
Nor the pride, nor ample pinion,
115   That the Theban Eagle bear
Sailing with supreme dominion
Thro' the azure deep of air:
Yet oft before his infant eyes would run
Such forms, as glitter in the Muse's ray
120   With orient hues, unborrow'd of the Sun:
Yet shall he mount, and keep his distant way
Beyond the limits of a vulgar fate,
Beneath the Good how far—but far above the Great.

THE BARD

A PINDARIC ODE

Advertisement

The following Ode is founded on a Tradition current in Wales, that
EDWARD THE FIRST, when he compleated the conquest of that country,
ordered all the Bards, that fell into his hands, to be put to death.

I. 1.

'Ruin seize thee, ruthless King!
Confusion on thy banners wait,
Tho' fann'd by Conquest's crimson wing
They mock the air with idle state.
5   Helm, nor Hauberk's twisted mail,
Nor even thy virtues, Tyrant, shall avail
To save thy secret soul from nightly fears,
From Cambria's curse, from Cambria's tears!'
Such were the sounds, that o'er the crested pride
10   Of the first Edward scatter'd wild dismay,
As down the steep of Snowdon's shaggy side
He wound with toilsome march his long array.
Stout Glo'ster stood aghast in speechless trance:
To arms! cried Mortimer, and couch'd his quiv'ring lance.

Thomas Gray

I. 2.

15   On a rock, whose haughty brow
       Frowns o'er old Conway's foaming flood,
       Robed in the sable garb of woe,
       With haggard eyes the Poet stood;
       (Loose his beard, and hoary hair
20   Stream'd, like a meteor, to the troubled air)
       And with a Master's hand, and Prophet's fire,
       Struck the deep sorrows of his lyre.
       'Hark, how each giant-oak, and desert cave,
       Sighs to the torrent's aweful voice beneath!
25   O'er thee, oh King! their hundred arms they wave,
       Revenge on thee in hoarser murmurs breath;
       Vocal no more, since Cambria's fatal day,
       To high-born Hoel's harp, or soft Llewellyn's lay.

I. 3.

       'Cold is Cadwallo's tongue,
30   That hush'd the stormy main:
       Brave Urien sleeps upon his craggy bed:
       Mountains, ye mourn in vain
       Modred, whose magic song
       Made huge Plinlimmon bow his cloud-top'd head.
35   On dreary Arvon's shore they lie,
       Smear'd with gore, and ghastly pale:
       Far, far aloof th' affrighted ravens fail;
       The famish'd Eagle screams, and passes by.
       Dear lost companions of my tuneful art,
40   Dear, as the light that visits these sad eyes,
       Dear, as the ruddy drops that warm my heart,
       Ye died amidst your dying country's cries—
       No more I weep. They do not sleep.
       On yonder cliffs, a griesly band,
45   I see them sit, they linger yet,
       Avengers of their native land:
       With me in dreadful harmony they join,
       And weave with bloody hands the tissue of thy line.'

II. 1.

       'Weave the warp, and weave the woof,
50   The winding-sheet of Edward's race.
       Give ample room, and verge enough
       The characters of hell to trace.

Mark the year, and mark the night,
When Severn shall re-eccho with affright
55 The shrieks of death, thro' Berkley's roofs that ring,
Shrieks of an agonizing King!
She-Wolf of France, with unrelenting fangs,
That tear'st the bowels of thy mangled Mate,
From thee be born, who o'er thy country hangs
60 The scourge of Heav'n. What Terrors round him wait!
Amazement in his van, with Flight combined,
And sorrow's faded form, and solitude behind.

II. 2.

'Mighty Victor, mighty Lord,
Low on his funeral couch he lies!
65 No pitying heart, no eye, afford
A tear to grace his obsequies.
Is the sable Warriour fled?
Thy son is gone. He rests among the Dead.
The Swarm, that in thy noon-tide beam were born?
70 Gone to salute the rising Morn.
Fair laughs the Morn, and soft the Zephyr blows,
While proudly riding o'er the azure realm
In gallant trim the gilded Vessel goes;
Youth on the prow, and Pleasure at the helm;
75 Regardless of the sweeping Whirlwind's sway,
That, hush'd in grim repose, expects his evening-prey.

II. 3.

'Fill high the sparkling bowl,
The rich repast prepare,
Reft of a crown, he yet may share the feast:
80 Close by the regal chair
Fell Thirst and Famine scowl
A baleful smile upon their baffled Guest.
Heard ye the din of battle bray,
Lance to lance, and horse to horse?
85 Long Years of havock urge their destined course,
And thro' the kindred squadrons mow their way.
Ye Towers of Julius, London's lasting shame,
With many a soul and midnight murther fed,
Revere his Consort's faith, his Father's fame,
90 And spare the meek Usurper's holy head.
Above, below, the rose of snow,
Twined with her blushing foe, we spread:

The bristled Boar in infant-gore
Wallows beneath the thorny shade.
95   Now, Brothers, bending o'er th' accursed loom
Stamp we our vengeance deep, and ratify his doom.

III.   1.

'Edward, lo! to sudden fate
(Weave we the woof. The thread is spun.)
Half of thy heart we consecrate.
100   (The web is wove. The work is done.)
Stay, oh stay! nor thus forlorn
Leave me unbless'd, unpitied, here to mourn:
In yon bright track, that fires the western skies,
They melt, they vanish from my eyes.
105   But oh! what solemn scenes on Snowdon's height
Descending slow their glitt'ring skirts unroll?
Visions of glory, spare my aching sight,
Ye unborn Ages, crowd not on my soul!
No more our long-lost Arthur we bewail.
110   All-hail, ye genuine Kings, Britannia's Issue, hail!

III.   2.

'Girt with many a Baron bold
Sublime their starry fronts they rear;
And gorgeous Dames, and Statesmen old
In bearded majesty, appear.
115   In the midst a Form divine!
Her eye proclaims her of the Briton-Line;
Her lyon-port, her awe-commanding face,
Attemper'd sweet to virgin-grace.
What strings symphonious tremble in the air,
120   What strains of vocal transport round her play!
Hear from the grave, great Taliessin, hear;
They breathe a soul to animate thy clay.
Bright Rapture calls, and soaring, as she sings,
Waves in the eye of Heav'n her many-colour'd wings.

III.   3.

125   'The verse adorn again
Fierce War, and faithful Love,
And Truth severe, by fairy Fiction drest.
In buskin'd measures move

Pale Grief, and pleasing Pain,
130 With Horrour, Tyrant of the throbbing breast.
A Voice, as of the Cherub-Choir,
Gales from blooming Eden bear;
And distant warblings lessen on my ear,
That lost in long futurity expire.
135 Fond impious Man, think'st thou, yon sanguine cloud,
Rais'd by thy breath, has quench'd the Orb of day?
To-morrow he repairs the golden flood,
And warms the nations with redoubled ray.
Enough for me: With joy I see
140 The different doom our Fates assign.
Be thine Despair, and scept'red Care,
To triumph, and to die, are mine.'
He spoke, and headlong from the mountain's height
Deep in the roaring tide he plung'd to endless night.

ODE

[On the Pleasure arising from Vicissitude.]

Now the golden Morn aloft
Waves her dew-bespangled wing,
With vermil cheek, and whisper soft
She wooes the tardy Spring:
5   Till April starts, and calls around
The sleeping fragrance from the ground;
And lightly o'er the living scene
Scatters his freshest, tenderest green.

New-born flocks, in rustic dance,
10   Frisking ply their feeble feet;
Forgetful of their wintry trance
The birds his presence greet:
But chief, the Sky-Lark warbles high
His trembling thrilling extacy;
15   And, lessening from the dazzled sight,
Melts into air and liquid light.

Yesterday the sullen year
Saw the snowy whirlwind fly;
Mute was the music of the air,
20   The herd stood drooping by:

Their raptures now that wildly flow,
No yesterday, nor morrow know;
'Tis Man alone that joy descries
With forward, and reverted eyes.

25   Smiles on past Misfortune's brow
Soft Reflection's hand can trace;
And o'er the cheek of Sorrow throw
A melancholy grace;
While Hope prolongs our happier hour,
30   Or deepest shades, that dimly lower
And blacken round our weary way,
Gilds with a gleam of distant day.

Still, where rosy Pleasure leads,
See a kindred Grief pursue;
35   Behind the steps that Misery treads
Approaching Comfort view:
The hues of bliss more brightly glow,
Chastis'd by sabler tints of woe;
And blended form, with artful strife,
40   The strength and harmony of life.

See the Wretch, that long has tost
On the thorny bed of pain,
At length repair his vigour lost,
And breathe, and walk again:
45   The meanest floweret of the vale,
The simplest note that swells the gale,
The common sun, the air, the skies,
To Him are opening Paradise.

Humble Quiet builds her cell,
50   Near the source whence Pleasure flows;
She eyes the clear crystalline well,
And tastes it as it goes.
While far below the *madding* Croud
Where broad and turbulent it grows
55   They perish in the boundless deep.

Mark where Indolence, and Pride,
Go, softly rolling, side by side,
Their dull, but daily round:

[*Unfinished*]

THE FATAL SISTERS
AN ODE,

(From the Norse-Tongue,) in the Orcades of Thormodus Torfæus;
Hafniæ, 1697, Folio: and also in Bartholinus.

Now the storm begins to lower,
(Haste, the loom of Hell prepare,)
Iron-sleet of arrowy shower
Hurtles in the darken'd air.

5   Glitt'ring lances are the loom,
Where the dusky warp we strain,
Weaving many a Soldier's doom,
Orkney's woe, and *Randver*'s bane.

See the griesly texture grow,
10 ('Tis of human entrails made,)
And the weights, that play below,
Each a gasping Warriour's head.

Shafts for shuttles, dipt in gore,
Shoot the trembling cords along.
15 Sword, that once a Monarch bore,
Keep the tissue close and strong.

Mista black, terrific Maid,
Sangrida, and *Hilda* see,
Join the wayward work to aid:
20 'Tis the woof of victory.

Ere the ruddy sun be set,
Pikes must shiver, javelins sing,
Blade with clattering buckler meet,
Hauberk crash, and helmet ring.

25 (Weave the crimson web of war)
Let us go, and let us fly,
Where our Friends the conflict share,
Where they triumph, where they die.

As the paths of fate we tread,
30 Wading thro' th' ensanguin'd field:
Gondula, and *Geira*, spread
O'er the youthful King your shield.

We the reins to slaughter give,
Ours to kill, and ours to spare:
35   Spite of danger he shall live.
(Weave the crimson web of war.)

They, whom once the desart-beach
Pent within its bleak domain,
Soon their ample sway shall stretch
40   O'er the plenty of the plain.

Low the dauntless Earl is laid,
Gor'd with many a gaping wound:
Fate demands a nobler head;
Soon a King shall bite the ground.

45   Long his loss shall Eirin weep,
Ne'er again his likeness see;
Long her strains in sorrow steep,
Strains of Immortality!

Horror covers all the heath,
50   Clouds of carnage blot the sun.
Sisters, weave the web of death;
Sisters, cease, the work is done.

Hail the task, and hail the hands!
Songs of joy and triumph sing!
55   Joy to the victorious bands;
Triumph to the younger King.

Mortal, thou that hear'st the tale,
Learn the tenour of our song.
Scotland, thro' each winding vale
60   Far and wide the notes prolong.

Sisters, hence with spurs of speed:
Each her thundering faulchion wield;
Each bestride her sable steed.
Hurry, hurry to the field.

THE DESCENT OF ODIN
AN ODE,

*(From the Norse-Tongue,) in Bartholinus, de causis contemnendæ
mortis; Hafniæ, 1689, Quarto.*

Uprose the King of Men with speed,
And saddled strait his coal-black steed;
Down the yawning steep he rode,
That leads to HELA's drear abode.
5 Him the Dog of Darkness spied,
His shaggy throat he open'd wide,
While from his jaws, with carnage fill'd,
Foam and human gore distill'd:
Hoarse he bays with hideous din,
10 Eyes that glow, and fangs that grin;
And long pursues, with fruitless yell,
The Father of the powerful spell.
Onward still his way he takes,
(The groaning earth beneath him shakes,)
15 Till full before his fearless eyes
The portals nine of hell arise.

Right against the eastern gate,
By the moss-grown pile he sate;
Where long of yore to sleep was laid
20 The dust of the prophetic Maid.
Facing to the northern clime,
Thrice he traced the runic rhyme;
Thrice pronounc'd, in accents dread,
The thrilling verse that wakes the Dead;
25 Till from out the hollow ground
Slowly breath'd a sullen sound.

PR. What call unknown, what charms presume
To break the quiet of the tomb?
Who thus afflicts my troubled sprite,
30 And drags me from the realms of night?
Long on these mould'ring bones have beat
The winter's snow, the summer's heat,
The drenching dews, and driving rain!
Let me, let me sleep again.
35 Who is he, with voice unblest,
That calls me from the bed of rest?

O.   A Traveller, to thee unknown,
Is he that calls, a Warriour's Son.
Thou the deeds of light shalt know;
40   Tell me what is done below,
For whom yon glitt'ring board is spread,
Drest for whom yon golden bed.

PR.   Mantling in the goblet see
The pure bev'rage of the bee,
45   O'er it hangs the shield of gold;
'Tis the drink of *Balder* bold:
Balder's head to death is giv'n.
Pain can reach the Sons of Heav'n!
Unwilling I my lips unclose:
50   Leave me, leave me to repose.

O.   Once again my call obey.
Prophetess, arise, and say,
What dangers *Odin*'s Child await,
Who the Author of his fate.

55   PR.   In *Hoder*'s hand the Hero's doom:
His Brother sends him to the tomb.
Now my weary lips I close:
Leave me, leave me to repose.

O.   Prophetess, my spell obey,
60   Once again arise, and say,
Who th' Avenger of his guilt,
By whom shall *Hoder*'s blood be spilt.

PR.   In the caverns of the west,
By *Odin*'s fierce embrace comprest,
65   A wond'rous Boy shall *Rinda* bear,
Who ne'er shall comb his raven-hair,
Nor wash his visage in the stream,
Nor see the sun's departing beam;
Till he on *Hoder*'s corse shall smile
70   Flaming on the fun'ral pile.
Now my weary lips I close:
Leave me, leave me to repose.

O.   Yet a while my call obey.
Prophetess, awake, and say,
75   What Virgins these, in speechless woe,
That bend to earth their solemn brow,

That their flaxen tresses tear,
And snowy veils, that float in air.
Tell me, whence their sorrows rose:
80   Then I leave thee to repose.

PR.   Ha! no Traveller art thou,
King of Men, I know thee now,
Mightiest of a mighty line——

O.   No boding Maid of skill divine
85   Art thou, nor Prophetess of good;
But Mother of the giant-brood!

PR.   Hie thee hence, and boast at home,
That never shall Enquirer come
To break my iron-sleep again;
90   Till *Lok* has burst his tenfold chain.
Never, till substantial Night
Has reassum'd her ancient right;
Till wrap'd in flames, in ruin hurl'd,
Sinks the fabric of the world.

THE TRIUMPHS OF OWEN
A FRAGMENT

*From Mr Evans's Specimens of the Welch Poetry
London, 1764, Quarto.*

Owen's praise demands my song,
Owen swift, and Owen strong;
Fairest flower of Roderic's stem,
Gwyneth's shield, and Britain's gem.
5   He nor heaps his brooded stores,
Nor on all profusely pours;
Lord of every regal art,
Liberal hand, and open heart.

Big with hosts of mighty name,
10   Squadrons three against him came;
This the force of Eirin hiding,
Side by side as proudly riding,
On her shadow long and gay
Lochlin plows the watry way;

15   There the Norman sails afar
          Catch the winds, and join the war:
          Black and huge along they sweep,
          Burthens of the angry deep.
          Dauntless on his native sands
20   The Dragon-Son of Mona stands;
          In glitt'ring arms and glory drest,
          High he rears his ruby crest.
          There the thund'ring strokes begin,
          There the press, and there the din;
25   Talymalfra's rocky shore
          Echoing to the battle's roar.
          Where his glowing eye-balls turn,
          Thousand Banners round him burn.
          Where he points his purple spear,
30   Hasty, hasty Rout is there,
          Marking with indignant eye
          Fear to stop, and shame to fly.
          There Confusion, Terror's child,
          Conflict fierce, and Ruin wild,
35   Agony, that pants for breath,
          Despair and honourable Death.

[THE DEATH OF HOEL]
FROM THE WELCH

          Had I but the torrent's might,
          With headlong rage and wild affright
          Upon Deïra's squadrons hurl'd,
          To rush, and sweep them from the world!

5   Too, too secure in youthful pride
          By them my friend, my Hoel, died,
          Great Cian's Son: of Madoc old
          He ask'd no heaps of hoarded gold;
          Alone in Nature's wealth array'd,
10   He ask'd, and had the lovely Maid.

          To Cattraeth's vale in glitt'ring row
          Twice two hundred Warriors go;
          Every Warrior's manly neck
          Chains of regal honour deck,

15 Wreath'd in many a golden link:
    From the golden cup they drink
    Nectar, that the bees produce,
    Or the grape's extatic juice.
    Flush'd with mirth, and hope they burn:
20 But none from Cattraeth's vale return,
    Save Aëron brave, and Conan strong,
    (Bursting thro' the bloody throng)
    And I, the meanest of them all,
    That live to weep, and sing their fall.

[CARADOC]

Have ye seen the tusky Boar,
Or the Bull, with sullen roar,
On surrounding Foes advance?
So Carádoc bore his lance.

[CONAN]

    Conan's name, my lay, rehearse,
    Build to him the lofty verse,
    Sacred tribute of the Bard,
    Verse, the Hero's sole reward.
5   As the flame's devouring force;
    As the whirlwind in its course;
    As the thunder's fiery stroke,
    Glancing on the shiver'd oak;
    Did the sword of Conan mow
10 The crimson harvest of the foe.

[SKETCH OF HIS OWN CHARACTER]

Too poor for a bribe, and too proud to importune;
He had not the method of making a fortune:
Could love, and could hate, so was thought somewhat odd;
NO VERY GREAT WIT, HE BELIEV'D IN A GOD.
5   A Post or a Pension he did not desire,
But left Church and State to Charles Townshend and Squire.

THE CANDIDATE

When sly Jemmy Twitcher had smugg'd up his face,
With a lick of court white-wash, and pious grimace,
A wooing he went, where three sisters of old
In harmless society guttle and scold.
5   Lord! sister, says PHYSICK to LAW, I declare,
Such a sheep-biting look, such a pick-pocket air!
Not I for the Indies!—You know I'm no prude,—
But his nose is a shame,—and his eyes are so lewd!
Then he shambles and straddles so oddly—I fear—
10 No—at our time of life 'twould be silly, my dear.
        I don't know, says LAW, but methinks for his look
'Tis just like the picture in Rochester's book;
Then his character, *Phizzy*,—his morals—his life—
When she died, I can't tell, but he once had a wife;—
15 They say he's no Christian, loves drinking and whoring,
And all the town rings of his swearing and roaring,
His lying and filching, and Newgate-bird tricks;—
Not I; for a coronet, chariot and six.
        DIVINITY heard, between waking and dozing,
20 Her sisters denying, and Jemmy proposing:
From table she rose, with her bumper in hand,
She stroked up her belly, and stroked down her band—
What a pother is here about wenching and roaring!
Why David loved catches, and Solomon whoring:
25 Did not Israel filch from the Egyptians of old,
Their jewels of silver and jewels of gold?
The prophet of Bethel, we read, told a lie;
He drinks—so did Noah;—he swears—so do I:
To reject him for such peccadillos were odd:

30 Besides, he repents—for he talks about God—
    [*To Jemmy*]
    Never hang down your head, you poor penitent elf,
    Come buss me—I'll be Mrs *Twitcher* myself.
    Damn ye both for a couple of Puritan bitches!
    He's Christian enough that repents and that stitches.

ON L[OR]D H[OLLAND']S SEAT

Old and abandon'd by each venal friend,
    Here H[ollan]d took the pious resolution
To smuggle some few years, and strive to mend
    A broken character and constitution.
5 On this congenial spot he fix'd his choice;
    Earl Goodwin trembled for his neighb'ring sand,
Here sea-gulls scream, and cormorants rejoice,
    And mariners, though shipwreck'd, dread to land.
Here reigns the blust'ring North and blighting East,
10   No tree is heard to whisper, bird to sing;
Yet Nature cannot furnish out the feast,
    Art he invokes new horrors still to bring.
Now mould'ring fanes and battlements arise,
    Arches and turrets nodding to their fall,
15 Unpeopled palaces delude his eyes,
    And mimic desolation covers all.
'Ah!' said the sighing peer, 'had B[u]te been true,
    Nor [Shelburne's, Calcraft's, Rigby's] friendship vain,
Far other scenes than these had bless'd our view,
20   And realiz'd these ruins that we feign.
Purg'd by the sword, and beautify'd by fire,
    Then had we seen proud London's hated walls;
Owls should have hooted in St Peter's choir,
    And foxes stunk and litter'd in St Paul's.'

ODE FOR MUSIC

Air.

    'Hence, avaunt, ('tis holy ground)
    Comus, and his midnight-crew,

And Ignorance with looks profound,
And dreaming Sloth of pallid hue,
5   Mad Sedition's cry profane,
Servitude that hugs her chain,
Nor in these consecrated bowers
Let painted Flatt'ry hide her serpent-train in flowers.

Chorus.

'Nor Envy base, nor creeping Gain
10   Dare the Muse's walk to stain,
While bright-eyed Science watches round:
Hence, away, 'tis holy Ground!'

Recitative.

From yonder realms of empyrean day
Bursts on my ear th' indignant lay:
15   There sit the sainted Sage, the Bard divine,
The Few, whom Genius gave to shine
Through every unborn age, and undiscovered clime.
Rapt in celestial transport they,   (*accomp.*)
Yet hither oft a glance from high
20   They send of tender sympathy
To bless the place, where on their opening soul
First the genuine ardor stole.
'Twas *Milton* struck the deep-toned shell,
And, as the choral warblings round him swell,
25   Meek *Newton*'s self bends from his state sublime,
And nods his hoary head, and listens to the rhyme.

Air.

'Ye brown o'er-arching Groves,
That Contemplation loves,
Where willowy *Camus* lingers with delight!
30   Oft at the blush of dawn
I trod your level lawn,
Oft woo'd the gleam of *Cynthia* silver-bright
In cloisters dim, far from the haunts of Folly,
With Freedom by my Side, and soft-ey'd Melancholy.'

Recitative.

35　But hark! the portals sound, and pacing forth
　　With solemn steps and slow
　　High Potentates and Dames of royal birth
　　And mitred Fathers in long order go:
　　Great *Edward* with the lillies on his brow
40　From haughty *Gallia* torn,
　　And sad *Chatillon*, on her bridal morn
　　That wept her bleeding Love, and princely *Clare*,
　　And *Anjou*'s Heroïne, and the paler Rose,
　　The rival of her crown, and of her woes,
45　And either *Henry* there,
　　The murther'd Saint, and the majestic Lord,
　　That broke the bonds of *Rome*.
　　(Their tears, their little triumphs o'er,　　(*accomp.*)
　　Their human passions now no more,
50　Save Charity, that glows beyond the tomb)
　　All that on *Granta*'s fruitful plain
　　Rich streams of regal bounty pour'd,
　　And bad these aweful fanes and turrets rise,
　　To hail their *Fitzroy*'s festal morning come;
55　And thus they speak in soft accord
　　The liquid language of the skies.

Quartetto.

　　'What is Grandeur, what is Power?
　　Heavier toil, superior pain.
　　What the bright reward we gain?
60　The grateful mem'ry of the Good.
　　Sweet is the breath of vernal shower,
　　The bee's collected treasures sweet,
　　Sweet music's melting fall, but sweeter yet
　　The still small voice of Gratitude.'

Recitative.

65　Foremost and leaning from her golden cloud
　　The venerable *Marg'ret* see!
　　'Welcome, my noble Son, (she cries aloud)
　　To this, thy kindred train, and me:
　　Pleas'd in thy lineaments we trace
70　A *Tudor*'s fire, a *Beaufort*'s grace.

Thomas Gray

Air.

'Thy liberal heart, thy judging eye,
The flower unheeded shall descry,
And bid it round heaven's altars shed
The fragrance of it's blushing head:
75   Shall raise from earth the latent gem
To glitter on the diadem.

Recitative.

'Lo, *Granta* waits to lead her blooming band,
Not obvious, not obtrusive, She
No vulgar praise, no venal incense flings:
80   Nor dares with courtly tongue refin'd
Profane thy inborn royalty of mind:
She reveres herself and thee.
With modest pride to grace thy youthful brow
The laureate wreath, that *Cecil* wore, she brings,
85   And to thy just, thy gentle hand
Submits the Fasces of her sway,
While Spirits blest above and Men below
Join with glad voice the loud symphonious lay.

Grand Chorus.

'Thro' the wild waves as they roar
90   With watchful eye and dauntless mien
Thy steady course of honor keep,
Nor fear the rocks, nor seek the shore:
The Star of *Brunswick* smiles serene,
And gilds the horrors of the deep.'

William Collins (1721–59)

Collins was born at Chichester and educated at Winchester and Queen's and Magdalen Colleges, Oxford. He left Oxford on the strength of a legacy from his mother to live in London. His poetry was not well-received and he became dependent on the generosity of a nephew, but increasing melancholia and ultimate insanity led to his confinement. He died in Chichester, having been cared for by his sister, in 1759.

SONNET

When *Phœbe* form'd a wanton smile
  My soul! it reach'd not here!
Strange, that thy peace, thou trembler, flies
  Before a rising tear!

5   From midst the drops, my love is born,
  That o'er those eyelids rove:
Thus issued from a teeming wave
  The fabled queen of love.

PERSIAN ECLOGUES

THE PREFACE

It is with the Writings of Mankind, in some Measure, as with their Complexions or their Dress, each Nation hath a Peculiarity in all these, to distinguish it from the rest of the World.

    The Gravity of the Spaniard, and the Levity of the Frenchman, are as evident in all their Productions as in their Persons themselves; and the Stile of my Countrymen is as naturally Strong and Nervous as that of an Arabian or Persian is rich and figurative.

[205]

There is an Elegancy and Wildness of Thought which recommends all their Compositions; and our Genius's are as much too cold for the Entertainment of such Sentiments, as our Climate is for their Fruits and Spices. If any of these Beauties are to be found in the following Eclogues, I hope my Reader will consider them as an Argument of their being Original. I received them at the hands of a Merchant, who had made it his Business to enrich himself with the Learning, as well as the Silks and Carpets of the Persians. The little Information I could gather concerning their Author, was, That his Name was Mahamed, and that he was a Native of Tauris.

It was in that City that he died of a Distemper fatal in those Parts, whilst he was engag'd in celebrating the Victories of his favourite Monarch, the Great Abbas. As to the Eclogues themselves, they give a very just View of the Miseries, and Inconveniences, as well as the Felicities that attend one of the finest Countries in the East.

The Time of the Writing them was probably in the Beginning of Sha Sultan Hosseyn's Reign, the Successor of Sefi or Solyman the Second.

Whatever Defects, as, I doubt not, there will be many, fall under the Reader's Observation, I hope his Candour will incline him to make the following Reflections:

That the Works of Orientals contain many Peculiarities, and that thro' Defect of Language few European Translators can do them Justice.

ECLOGUE THE FIRST

SELIM: OR, THE SHEPHERD'S MORAL

Scene, a valley near Bagdat.

Time, the Morning.

Ye Persian Maids, attend your Poet's Lays,
And hear how Shepherds pass their golden Days:
Not all are blest, whom Fortune's Hand sustains
With Wealth in Courts, nor all that haunt the Plains:
5   Well may your Hearts believe the Truths I tell,
'Tis Virtue makes the Bliss where'er we dwell.

    Thus Selim sung; by sacred Truth inspir'd;
No Praise the Youth, but hers alone, desir'd:
Wise in himself, his meaning Songs convey'd
10   Informing Morals to the Shepherd Maid,

Or taught the Swains that surest Bliss to find,
What Groves nor Streams bestow, a virtuous Mind.

When sweet and odorous, like an Eastern Bride,
The radiant Morn resum'd her orient Pride,
15   When wanton Gales along the Valleys play,
Breathe on each Flow'r, and bear their Sweets away:
By Tigris' Wand'ring Waves he sate, and sung
This useful Lesson for the Fair and Young.

Ye Persian Dames, he said, to you belong,
20   Well may they please, the Morals of my Song;
No fairer Maids, I trust, than you are found,
Grac'd with soft Arts, the peopled World around!
The Morn that lights you, to your Loves supplies
Each gentler Ray delicious to your Eyes:
25   For you those Flow'rs her fragrant Hands bestow,
And yours the Love that Kings delight to know.
Yet think not these, all beauteous as they are,
The best kind Blessings Heav'n can grant the Fair!
Who trust alone in Beauty's feeble Ray,
30   Balsora's Pearls have more of Worth than they;
Drawn from the Deep, they sparkle to the Sight,
And, all-unconscious, shoot a lust'rous Light:
Such are the Maids, and such the Charms they boast,
By Sense unaided, or to Virtue lost.
35   Self-flattering Sex! your Hearts believe in vain
That Love shall blind, when once he fires the Swain;
Or hope a Lover by your Faults to win,
As Spots on Ermin beautify the Skin:
Who seeks secure to rule, be first her Care
40   Each softer Virtue that adorns the Fair,
Each tender Passion Man delights to find,
The lov'd Perfection of a female Mind.

Blest were the Days, when Wisdom held her Reign,
And Shepherds sought her on the silent Plain;
45   With Truth she wedded in the secret Grove,
The fair-eyed Truth, and Daughters bless'd their Love.

O haste, fair Maids, ye Virtues come away,
Sweet Peace and Plenty lead you on your Way!
The balmy Shrub for you shall love our Shore,
50   By Ind' excell'd or Araby no more.

Lost to our Fields, for so the Fates ordain,
The dear Deserters shall return again.
O, come thou, Modesty, as they decree,

The Rose may then improve her Blush by thee.
55	Here make thy Court amidst our rural Scene,
And Shepherd-Girls shall own Thee for their Queen.
With Thee be Chastity, of all afraid,
Distrusting all, a wise suspicious Maid;
But Man the most; not more the Mountain Doe
60	Holds the swift Falcon for her deadly Foe.
Cold is her Breast, like Flow'rs that drink the Dew,
A silken Veil conceals her from the View.
No wild Desires amidst thy Train be known,
But Faith, whose Heart is fix'd on one alone:
65	Desponding Meekness with her down-cast Eyes,
And friendly Pity full of tender Sighs;
And Love the last: By these your Hearts approve,
These are the Virtues that must lead to Love.

Thus sung the Swain, and Eastern Legends say,
70	The maids of Bagdat verify'd the Lay:
Dear to the Plains, the Virtues came along,
The Shepherds lov'd, and Selim bless'd his Song.

ECLOGUE THE SECOND

HASSAN; OR, THE CAMEL DRIVER

Scene, the desart

Time, Mid-day

In silent Horror o'er the Desart-Waste
The Driver Hassan with his Camels past.
One Cruise of Water on his Back he bore,
And his light Scrip contain'd a scanty Store:
5	A Fan of painted Feathers in his Hand,
To guard his shaded Face from scorching Sand.
The sultry Sun had gain'd the middle Sky,
And not a Tree, and not an Herb was nigh.
The Beasts, with Pain, their dusty Way pursue,
10	Shrill roar'd the Winds, and dreary was the View!
With desp'rate Sorrow wild th' affrighted Man
Thrice sigh'd, thrice strook his Breast, and thus began:
	Sad was the Hour, and luckless was the Day,
	When first from Schiraz' *Walls I bent my Way.*

15   Ah! little thought I of the blasting Wind,
     The Thirst or pinching Hunger that I find!
     Bethink thee, Hassan, where shall Thirst assuage,
     When fails this Cruise, his unrelenting Rage?
     Soon shall this Scrip its precious Load resign,
20   Then what but Tears and Hunger shall be thine?
     Ye mute Companions of my Toils, that bear
     In all my Griefs a more than equal Share!
     Here, where no Springs, in Murmurs break away,
     Or Moss-crown'd Fountains mitigate the Day:
25   In vain ye hope the green Delights to know,
     Which Plains more blest, or verdant Vales bestow.
     Here Rocks alone, and tasteless Sands are found,
     And faint and sickly Winds for ever howl around.
          Sad was the Hour, and luckless was the Day,
30   *When first from* Schiraz' *Walls I bent my Way.*

     Curst be the Gold and Silver which persuade
     Weak Men to follow far-fatiguing Trade.
     The Lilly-Peace outshines the silver Store,
     And Life is dearer than the golden Ore.
35   Yet Money tempts us o'er the Desart brown,
     To ev'ry distant Mart, and wealthy Town:
     Full oft we tempt the Land, and oft the Sea,
     And are we only yet repay'd by Thee?
     Ah! why this Ruin so attractive made,
40   Or why fond Man so easily betray'd?
     Why heed we not, while mad we haste along,
     The gentle Voice of Peace, or Pleasure's Song?
     Or wherefore think the flow'ry Mountain's Side,
     The Fountain's Murmurs, and the Valley's Pride,
45   Why think we these less pleasing to behold,
     Than dreary Desarts, if they lead to Gold?
          Sad was the Hour, and luckless was the Day,
          When first from Schiraz' *Walls I bent my Way.*

     O cease, my Fears! all frantic as I go,
50   When Thought creates unnumber'd Scenes of Woe,
     What if the Lion in his Rage I meet!
     Oft in the Dust I view his printed Feet:
     And fearful! oft, when Day's declining Light
     Yields her pale Empire to the Mourner Night,
55   By Hunger rous'd, he scours the groaning Plain,
     Gaunt Wolves and sullen Tygers in his Train:
     Before them Death with Shrieks directs their Way,
     Fills the wild Yell, and leads them to their Prey.
          Sad was the Hour, and luckless was the Day,
60   *When first from* Schiraz' *Walls I bent my Way.*

At that dead Hour the silent Asp shall creep,
If ought of rest I find, upon my Sleep:
Or some swoln Serpent twist his Scales around,
And wake to Anguish with a burning Wound.
65 Thrice happy they, the wise contented Poor,
From Lust of Wealth, and Dread of Death secure;
They tempt no Desarts, and no Griefs they find;
Peace rules the Day, where Reason rules the Mind.
Sad was the Hour, and luckless was the Day,
70 *When first from* Schiraz' *Walls I bent my Way.*

O hapless Youth! for she thy Love hath won,
The tender Zara, will be most undone!
Big swell'd my Heart, and own'd the pow'rful Maid,
When fast she dropt her Tears, and thus she said:
75 'Farewel the Youth whom Sighs could not detain,
Whom Zara's breaking Heart implor'd in vain;
Yet as thou go'st, may ev'ry Blast arise,
Weak and unfelt as these rejected Sighs!
Safe o'er the Wild, no Perils mayst thou see,
80 No Griefs endure, nor weep, false Youth, like me.'
O let me safely to the Fair return,
Say with a Kiss, she must not, shall not mourn.
Go teach my Heart to lose its painful Fears,
Recall'd by Wisdom's Voice, and Zara's Tears.

85 He said, and call'd on Heav'n to bless the Day,
When back to Schiraz' Walls he bent his Way.

ECLOGUE THE THIRD

ABRA; OR, THE GEORGIAN SULTANA

Scene, a forest

Time, the Evening

In Georgia's Land, where Tefflis' Tow'rs are seen,
In distant View along the level Green,
While Ev'ning Dews enrich the glitt'ring Glade,
And the tall Forests cast a longer Shade,
5 Amidst the Maids of Zagen's peaceful Grove,
Emyra sung the pleasing Cares of Love.

Of Abra first began the tender Strain,
Who led her Youth, with Flocks upon the Plain:
At Morn she came those willing Flocks to lead,
10   Where Lillies rear them in the wat'ry Mead;
From early Dawn the live-long Hours she told,
'Till late at silent Eve she penn'd the Fold.
Deep in the Grove beneath the secret Shade,
A various Wreath of od'rous Flow'rs she made:
15   Gay-motley'd Pinks and sweet Jonquils she chose,
The Violet-blue, that on the Moss-bank grows;
All-sweet to Sense, the flaunting Rose was there;
The finish'd Chaplet well-adorn'd her Hair.

Great Abbas chanc'd that fated Morn to stray,
20   By Love conducted from the Chace away;
Among the vocal Vales he heard her Song,
And sought the Vales and echoing Groves among:
At length he found, and woo'd the rural Maid,
She knew the Monarch, and with Fear obey'd.
25   *Be ev'ry Youth like Royal* Abbas *mov'd,*
And ev'ry Georgian *Maid like* Abra *lov'd.*

The Royal Lover bore her from the Plain,
Yet still her Crook and bleating Flock remain:
Oft as she went, she backward turn'd her View,
30   And bad that Crook, and bleating Flock Adieu.
Fair happy Maid! to other Scenes remove,
To richer Scenes of golden Pow'r and Love!
Go leave the simple Pipe, and Shepherd's Strain,
With Love delight thee, and with Abbas reign.
35   *Be ev'ry Youth like Royal* Abbas *mov'd,*
And ev'ry Georgian *Maid like* Abra *lov'd.*

Yet midst the Blaze of Courts she fix'd her Love,
On the cool Fountain, or the shady Grove;
Still with the Shepherd's Innocence her Mind
40   To the sweet Vale, and flow'ry Mead inclin'd,
And oft as Spring renew'd the Plains with Flow'rs,
Breath'd his soft Gales, and led the fragrant Hours,
With sure Return she sought the sylvan Scene,
The breezy Mountains, and the Forests green.
45   Her Maids around her mov'd, a duteous Band!
Each bore a Crook all-rural in her Hand:
Some simple Lay, of Flocks and Herds they sung,
With Joy the Mountain, and the Forest rung.
    Be ev'ry Youth like Royal Abbas *mov'd,*
50   *And ev'ry* Georgian *Maid like* Abra *lov'd.*

And oft the Royal Lover left the Care,
And Thorns of State, attendant on the Fair:
Oft to the Shades and low-roof'd Cots retir'd,
Or sought the Vale where first his Heart was fir'd;
55   A Russet Mantle, like a Swain, he wore,
And thought of Crowns and busy Courts no more.
    Be ev'ry Youth like Royal Abbas *mov'd,*
    And ev'ry Georgian *Maid like* Abra *lov'd.*

Blest was the Life, that Royal Abbas led:
60   Sweet was his Love, and innocent his Bed.
What if in Wealth the noble Maid excel;
The simple Shepherd Girl can love as well.
Let those who rule on Persia's jewell'd Throne,
Be fam'd for Love, and gentlest Love alone:
65   Or wreath, like Abbas, full of fair Renown,
The Lover's Myrtle, with the Warrior's Crown.

Oh happy Days! the Maids around her say,
Oh haste, profuse of Blessings, haste away!
    Be ev'ry Youth, like Royal Abbas, *moved*;
70   *And ev'ry* Georgian *Maid, like* Abra, *lov'd.*

ECLOGUE THE FOURTH

AGIB AND SECANDER: OR, THE FUGITIVES

Scene, a Mountain in Circassia

Time, Midnight

In fair Circassia, where to Love inclin'd,
Each Swain was blest, for ev'ry Maid was kind!
At that still Hour, when awful Midnight reigns,
And none, but Wretches, haunt the twilight Plains;
5   What Time the Moon had hung her Lamp on high,
And past in Radiance, thro' the cloudless Sky:
Sad o'er the Dews, two Brother Shepherds fled,
Where wild'ring Fear and desp'rate Sorrow led.
Fast as they prest their Flight, behind them lay
10   Wide ravag'd Plains, and Valleys stole away.
Along the Mountain's bending Sides they ran,
'Till faint and weak Secander thus began.

SECANDER

O stay thee, Agib, for my Feet deny,
No longer friendly to my Life, to fly.
15 Friend of my Heart, O turn thee and survey,
Trace our sad Flight thro' all its length of Way!
And first review that long-extended Plain,
And yon wide Groves, already past with Pain!
Yon ragged Cliff, whose dang'rous Path we try'd,
20 And last this lofty Mountain's weary Side!

AGIB

Weak as thou art, yet hapless must thou know
The Toils of Flight, or some severer Woe!
Still as I haste, the Tartar shouts behind,
And Shrieks and Sorrows load the sad'ning Wind:
25 In rage of Heart, with Ruin in his Hand,
He blasts our Harvests, and deforms our Land.
Yon Citron Grove, whence first in Fear we came,
Droops its fair Honours to the conqu'ring Flame:
Far fly the Swains, like us, in deep Despair,
30 And leave to ruffian Bands their fleecy Care.

SECANDER

Unhappy Land, whose Blessings tempt the Sword,
In vain, unheard, thou call'st thy Persian Lord!
In vain, thou court'st him, helpless to thine Aid,
To shield the Shepherd, and protect the Maid,
35 Far off in thoughtless Indolence resign'd,
Soft Dreams of Love and Pleasure sooth his Mind:
'Midst fair Sultanas lost in idle Joy,
No Wars alarm him, and no Fears annoy.

AGIB

Yet these green Hills, in Summer's sultry Heat,
40 Have lent the Monarch oft a cool Retreat,
Sweet to the Sight is Zabran's flow'ry Plain,
And once by Maids and Shepherds lov'd in vain!
No more the Virgins shall delight to rove,
By Sargis' Banks or Irwan's shady Grove:
45 On Tarkie's Mountain catch the cooling Gale,
Or breathe the Sweets of Aly's flow'ry Vale:

Fair Scenes! but ah no more with Peace possest,
With Ease alluring, and with Plenty blest.
No more the Shepherds' whit'ning Tents appear,
50 Nor the kind Products of a bounteous Year;
No more the Date with snowy Blossoms crown'd,
But Ruin spreads her baleful Fires around.

SECANDER

In vain Circassia boasts her spicy Groves,
For ever fam'd for pure and happy Loves:
55 In vain she boasts her fairest of the Fair,
Their Eyes' blue languish, and their golden Hair!
Those Eyes in Tears, their fruitless Grief must send,
Those Hairs the Tartar's cruel Hand shall rend.

AGIB

Ye Georgian Swains that piteous learn from far
60 Circassia's Ruin, and the Waste of War:
Some weightier Arms than Crooks and Staves prepare,
To shield your Harvests, and defend your Fair:
The Turk and Tartar like Designs pursue,
Fix'd to destroy, and stedfast to undo.
65 Wild as his Land, in native Deserts bred,
By Lust incited, or by Malice led,
The Villain-Arab, as he prowls for Prey,
Oft marks with Blood and wasting Flames the Way;
Yet none so cruel as the Tartar Foe,
70 To Death inur'd, and nurst in Scenes of Woe.

He said, when loud along the Vale was heard
A shriller Shriek, and nearer Fires appear'd:
Th' affrighted Shepherds thro' the Dews of Night
Wide o'er the Moon-light Hills renew'd their Flight.

AN EPISTLE:
ADDREST TO SIR *THOMAS HANMER*
ON HIS EDITION OF SHAKESPEAR'S WORKS

Sir,
While born to bring the Muse's happier Days,
A Patriot's Hand protects a Poet's Lays:

While nurst by you she sees her Myrtles bloom,
Green and unwither'd o'er his honour'd Tomb:
5   Excuse her Doubts, if yet she fears to tell
What secret Transports in her Bosom swell:
With conscious Awe she hears the Critic's Fame,
And blushing hides her Wreath at Shakespear's Name.
Hard was the Lot those injur'd Strains endur'd,
10   Unown'd by Science, and by Years obscur'd:
Fair Fancy wept; and echoing Sighs confest
A fixt Despair in ev'ry tuneful Breast.
Not with more Grief th' afflicted Swains appear
When wintry Winds deform the plenteous Year:
15   When ling'ring Frosts the ruin'd Seats invade
Where Peace resorted, and the Graces play'd.

Each rising Art by just Gradation moves,
Toil builds on Toil, and Age on Age improves.
The Muse alone unequal dealt her Rage,
20   And grac'd with noblest Pomp her earliest Stage.
Preserv'd thro' Time, the speaking Scenes impart
Each changeful Wish of Phædra's tortur'd Heart:
Or paint the Curse, that mark'd the Theban's Reign,
A Bed incestuous, and a Father slain.
25   With kind Concern our pitying Eyes o'erflow,
Trace the sad Tale, and own another's Woe.

To Rome remov'd, with Wit secure to please,
The Comic Sisters kept their native Ease.
With jealous Fear declining Greece beheld
30   Her own Menander's Art almost excell'd!
But ev'ry Muse essay'd to raise in vain
Some labour'd Rival of her Tragic Strain;
Ilissus' Laurels, tho' transferr'd with Toil,
Droop'd their fair Leaves, nor knew th' unfriendly Soil.

35   As Arts expir'd, resistless Dulness rose;
Goths, Priests, or Vandals,—all were Learning's Foes.
Till Julius first recall'd each exil'd Maid,
And Cosmo own'd them in th' Etrurian Shade:
Then deeply skill'd in Love's engaging Theme,
40   The soft Provencial pass'd to Arno's Stream:
With graceful Ease the wanton Lyre he strung,
Sweet flow'd the Lays—but Love was all he sung.
The gay Description could not fail to move;
For, led by Nature, all are Friends to Love.

45   But Heav'n, still various in its Works, decreed
The perfect Boast of Time should last succeed.

The beauteous Union must appear at length,
Of Tuscan Fancy, and Athenian Strength:
One greater Muse Eliza's Reign adorn,
50　And ev'n a Shakespear to her Fame be born!

Yet ah! so bright her Morning's op'ning Ray,
In vain our Britain hop'd an equal Day!
No second Growth the Western Isle could bear,
At once exhausted with too rich a Year.
55　Too nicely Johnson knew the Critic's Part;
Nature in him was almost lost in Art.
Of softer Mold the gentle Fletcher came,
The next in Order, as the Next in Name.
With pleas'd Attention 'midst his Scenes we find
60　Each glowing Thought, that warms the Female Mind;
Each melting Sigh, and ev'ry tender Tear,
The Lover's Wishes and the Virgin's Fear.
His ev'ry Strain the Smiles and Graces own;
But stronger Shakespear felt for Man alone:
65　Drawn by his Pen, our ruder Passions stand
Th' unrival'd Picture of his early Hand.

With gradual Steps, and slow, exacter France
Saw Art's fair Empire o'er her Shores advance:
By length of Toil, a bright Perfection knew,
70　Correctly bold, and just in all she drew.
Till late Corneille, with Lucan's spirit fir'd,
Breath'd the free Strain, as Rome and He inspir'd:
And classic Judgment gain'd to sweet Racine
The temp'rate Strength of Maro's chaster Line.

75　But wilder far the British Laurel spread,
And Wreaths less artful crown our Poet's Head.
Yet He alone to ev'ry Scene could give
Th' Historian's Truth, and bid the Manners live.
Wak'd at his Call I view, with glad Surprize,
80　Majestic Forms of mighty Monarchs rise.
There Henry's Trumpets spread their loud Alarms,
And laurel'd Conquest waits her Hero's Arms.
Here gentler Edward claims a pitying Sigh,
Scarce born to Honours, and so soon to die!
85　Yet shall thy Throne, unhappy Infant, bring
No Beam of Comfort to the guilty King?
The Time shall come, when Glo'ster's Heart shall bleed
In Life's last Hours, with Horror of the Deed:
When dreary Visions shall at last present
90　Thy vengeful Image, in the midnight Tent:
Thy Hand unseen the secret Death shall bear,
Blunt the weak Sword, and break th' oppressive Spear.

Where'er we turn, by Fancy charm'd, we find
Some sweet Illusion of the cheated Mind.
95   Oft, wild of Wing, she calls the Soul to rove
With humbler Nature, in the rural Grove;
Where Swains contented own the quiet Scene,
And twilight Fairies tread the circled Green:
Drest by her Hand, the Woods and Vallies smile,
100 And Spring diffusive decks th' *enchanted Isle.*

O more than all in pow'rful Genius blest,
Come, take thine Empire o'er the willing Breast!
Whate'er the Wounds this youthful Heart shall feel,
Thy Songs support me, and thy Morals heal!
105 There ev'ry Thought the Poet's Warmth may raise,
There native Music dwells in all the Lays.
O might some Verse with happiest Skill persuade
Expressive Picture to adopt thine Aid!
What wond'rous Draughts might rise from ev'ry Page!
110 What other Raphaels Charm a distant Age!

Methinks ev'n now I view some free Design,
Where breathing Nature lives in ev'ry Line:
Chast and subdu'd the modest Lights decay,
Steal into Shade, and mildly melt away.
115 —And see, where Anthony in Tears approv'd,
Guards the pale Relicks of the Chief he lov'd.
O'er the cold Corse the Warrior seems to bend,
Deep sunk in Grief, and mourns his murther'd Friend!
Still as they press, he calls on all around,
120 Lifts the torn Robe, and points the bleeding Wound.

But who is he, whose Brows exalted bear
A Wrath impatient, and a fiercer Air?
Awake to all that injur'd Worth can feel,
On his own Rome he turns th' avenging Steel.
125 Yet shall not War's insatiate Fury fall,
(So Heav'n ordains it) on the destin'd Wall.
See the fond Mother 'midst the plaintive Train
Hung on his Knees, and prostrate on the Plain!
Touch'd to the Soul, in vain he strives to hide
130 The Son's Affection, in the Roman's Pride:
O'er all the Man conflicting Passions rise,
Rage grasps the Sword, while Pity melts the Eyes.

Thus, gen'rous Critic, as thy Bard inspires,
The Sister Arts shall nurse their drooping Fires;
135 Each from his Scenes her Stores alternate bring,
Blend the fair Tints, or wake the vocal String:

Those Sibyl-Leaves, the Sport of ev'ry Wind,
(For Poets ever were a careless Kind)
By thee dispos'd, no farther Toil demand,
140   But, just to Nature, own thy forming Hand.

    So spread o'er Greece, th' harmonious Whole unknown,
Ev'n Homer's Numbers charm'd by Parts alone.
Their own Ulysses scarce had wander'd more,
By Winds and Water cast on ev'ry Shore:
145   When, rais'd by Fate, some former Hanmer join'd
Each beauteous Image of the boundless Mind:
And bad, like Thee, his Athens ever claim,
A fond Alliance with the Poet's Name.

A SONG FROM SHAKESPEAR'S CYMBELINE

SUNG BY GUIDERIUS AND ARVIRAGUS OVER FIDELE, SUPPOS'D TO BE DEAD

To fair Fidele's grassy Tomb
    Soft Maids and Village Hinds shall bring
Each op'ning Sweet, of earliest Bloom,
    And rifle all the breathing Spring.

5   No wailing Ghost shall dare appear
    To vex with Shrieks this quiet Grove;
But Shepherd Lads assemble here,
    And melting Virgins own their Love.

No wither'd Witch shall here be seen,
10   No Goblins lead their nightly Crew:
The Female Fays shall haunt the Green,
    And dress thy Grave with pearly Dew!

The Redbreast oft at Ev'ning Hours
    Shall kindly lend his little Aid:
15   With hoary Moss, and gather'd Flow'rs,
    To deck the Ground where thou art laid.

When howling Winds, and beating Rain,
    In Tempests shake the sylvan Cell:
Or midst the Chace on ev'ry Plain
20   The tender Thought on thee shall dwell.

Each lonely Scene shall thee restore,
  For thee the Tear be duly shed:
Belov'd till Life could charm no more;
  And mourn'd till Pity's self be dead.

SONG

THE SENTIMENTS BORROWED FROM SHAKESPEARE

Young Damon of the Vale is dead,
  Ye lowland hamlets moan,
A dewy turf lies o'er his head,
  And at his feet a stone.

5   His shroud, which Death's cold damps destroy,
  Of snow-white threads was made,
All mourn'd to see so sweet a boy
  In earth for ever laid.

Pale pansies o'er his corpse were plac'd,
10   Which, pluck'd before their time,
Bestrew'd the boy, like him to waste,
  And wither in their prime.

But will he ne'er return, whose tongue
  Cou'd tune the rural lay?
15   Ah, no! his bell of peace is rung,
  His lips are cold as clay.

They bore him out at twilight hour,
  The youth who lov'd so well:
Ah me! how many a true-love shower
20   Of kind remembrance fell!

Each maid was woe—but Lucy chief,
  Her grief o'er all was tried;
Within his grave she dropp'd in grief,
  And o'er her lov'd-one died.

WRITTEN ON A PAPER, WHICH CONTAINED A PIECE OF BRIDE CAKE: GIVEN TO THE AUTHOR BY A LADY

Ye curious hands, that hid from vulgar eyes,
  By search profane shall find this hallow'd cake,
With Virtue's awe forbear the sacred prize,
  Nor dare a theft for Love and Pity's sake!

5 This precious relick, form'd by magic power
  Beneath the shepherd's haunted pillow laid,
Was meant by Love to charm the silent hour,
  The secret present of a matchless maid.

The *Cyprian* queen, at Hymen's fond request,
10 Each nice ingredient chose with happiest art;
Fears, sighs, and wishes of th' enamour'd breast,
  And pains that please are mixt in every part.

With rosy hand the spicy fruit she brought
  From *Paphian* hills, and fair *Cythera*'s isle;
15 And temper'd sweet with these the melting thought,
  The kiss ambrosial and the yielding smile.

Ambiguous looks, that scorn and yet relent,
  Denials mild, and firm unalter'd truth,
Reluctant pride, and amorous faint consent,
20 And meeting ardours, and exulting youth,

Sleep, wayward God! hath sworn while these remain,
  With flattering dreams to dry his nightly tear,
And chearful Hope, so oft invok'd in vain,
  With fairy songs shall sooth his pensive ear.

25 If bound by vows to Friendship's gentle side,
  And fond of soul, thou hop'st an equal grace,
If youth or maid thy joys and griefs divide,
  O much intreated, leave this fatal place.

Sweet Peace, who long hath shunn'd my plaintive day,
30 Consents at length to bring me short delight,
Thy careless steps may scare her doves away,
  And Grief with raven note usurp the night.

ODE TO PITY

1

O thou, the Friend of Man assign'd,
With balmy Hands his Wounds to bind,
   And charm his frantic Woe:
When first *Distress* with Dagger keen
5   Broke forth to waste his destin'd Scene,
   His wild unsated Foe!

2

By *Pella*'s Bard, a magic Name,
By all the Griefs his Thought could frame,
   Receive my humble Rite:
10   Long, *Pity*, let the Nations view
Thy sky-worn Robes of tend'rest Blue,
   And Eyes of dewy Light!

3

But wherefore need I wander wide
To old *Ilissus*' distant Side,
15   Deserted Stream, and mute?
Wild *Arun* too has heard thy Strains,
And Echo, 'midst my native Plains,
   Been sooth'd by *Pity*'s Lute.

4

There first the Wren thy Myrtles shed
20   On gentlest *Otway*'s infant Head,
   To Him thy Cell was shown;
And while He sung the Female Heart,
With Youth's soft Notes unspoil'd by Art,
   Thy Turtles mix'd their own.

5

25   Come, *Pity*, come, by Fancy's Aid,
Ev'n now my Thoughts, relenting Maid,
   Thy Temple's Pride design:
Its Southern Site, its Truth compleat
Shall raise a wild Enthusiast Heat,
30   In all who view the Shrine.

6

There Picture's Toils shall well relate,
How Chance, or hard involving Fate,
   O'er mortal Bliss prevail:
The Buskin'd Muse shall near her stand,
35   And sighing prompt her tender Hand,
   With each disastrous Tale.

7

There let me oft, retir'd by Day,
In Dreams of Passion melt away,
   Allow'd with Thee to dwell:
40   There waste the mournful Lamp of Night,
Till, Virgin, Thou again delight
   To hear a *British* Shell!

ODE TO FEAR

Thou, to whom the World unknown
With all its shadowy Shapes is shown;
Who see'st appall'd th' unreal Scene,
While Fancy lifts the Veil between:
5   Ah *Fear!* Ah frantic *Fear!*
    I see, I see Thee near.
I know thy hurried Step, thy haggard Eye!
Like Thee I start, like Thee disorder'd fly,
For lo what *Monsters* in thy Train appear!
10   *Danger*, whose Limbs of Giant Mold
What mortal Eye can fix'd behold?
Who stalks his Round, an hideous Form,
Howling amidst the Midnight Storm,
Or throws him on the ridgy Steep
15   Of some loose hanging Rock to sleep:
And with him thousand Phantoms join'd,
Who prompt to Deeds accurs'd the Mind:
And those, the Fiends, who near allied,
O'er Nature's Wounds, and Wrecks preside;
20   Whilst *Vengeance*, in the lurid Air,
Lifts her red Arm, expos'd and bare:
On whom that rav'ning Brood of Fate,
Who lap the Blood of Sorrow, wait;

Who, *Fear*, this ghastly Train can see,
25   And look not madly wild, like Thee?

Epode

In earliest *Grece* to Thee with partial Choice,
    The Grief-full Muse addrest her infant Tongue;
The Maids and Matrons, on her awful Voice,
    Silent and pale in wild Amazement hung.

30 Yet He the Bard who first invok'd thy Name,
    Disdain'd in *Marathon* its Pow'r to feel:
For not alone he nurs'd the Poet's flame,
    But reach'd from Virtue's Hand the Patriot's Steel.

But who is He whom later Garlands grace,
35   Who left a-while o'er *Hybla*'s Dews to rove,
With trembling Eyes thy dreary Steps to trace,
    Where Thou and *Furies* shar'd the baleful Grove?

Wrapt in thy cloudy Veil th' *Incestuous Queen*
    Sigh'd the sad Call her Son and Husband hear'd,
40 When once alone it broke the silent Scene,
    And He the Wretch of *Thebes* no more appear'd.

O *Fear*, I know Thee by my throbbing Heart,
    Thy with'ring Pow'r inspir'd each mournful Line,
Tho' gentle *Pity* claim her mingled Part,
45   Yet all the Thunders of the Scene are thine!

Antistrophe

Thou who such weary Lengths hast past,
Where wilt thou rest, mad Nymph, at last?
Say, wilt thou shroud in haunted Cell,
Where gloomy *Rape* and *Murder* dwell?
50 Or in some hollow'd Seat,
'Gainst which the big Waves beat,
Hear drowning Sea-men's Cries in Tempests brought!
Dark Pow'r, with shudd'ring meek submitted Thought
Be mine, to read the Visions old,
55 Which thy awak'ning Bards have told:
And lest thou meet my blasted View,
Hold each strange Tale devoutly true;
Ne'er be I found, by Thee o'eraw'd,
In that thrice-hallow'd Eve abroad,

60   When Ghosts, as Cottage-Maids believe,
        Their pebbled Beds permitted leave,
        And *Gobblins* haunt from Fire, or Fen,
        Or Mine, or Flood, the Walks of Men!
          O Thou whose Spirit most possess
65   The sacred Seat of *Shakespear*'s Breast!
        By all that from thy Prophet broke,
        In thy Divine Emotions spoke:
        Hither again thy Fury deal,
        Teach me but once like Him to feel:
70   His *Cypress Wreath* my Meed decree,
        And I, O *Fear*, will dwell with *Thee!*

ODE TO SIMPLICITY

I

    O Thou by *Nature* taught,
    To breathe her genuine Thought,
In Numbers warmly pure, and sweetly strong:
    Who first on Mountains wild,
5   In *Fancy* loveliest Child,
Thy Babe, or *Pleasure*'s, nurs'd the Pow'rs of Song!

2

    Thou, who with Hermit Heart
    Disdain'st the Wealth of Art,
And Gauds, and pageant Weeds, and trailing Pall:
10   But com'st a decent Maid
    In *Attic* Robe array'd,
O chaste unboastful Nymph, to Thee I call!

3

    By all the honey'd Store
    On *Hybla*'s Thymy Shore,
15 By all her Blooms, and mingled Murmurs dear,
    By Her, whose Love-lorn Woe
    In Ev'ning Musings slow
Sooth'd sweetly sad *Electra*'s Poet's Ear:

4

By old *Cephisus* deep,
20   Who spread his wavy Sweep
In warbled Wand'rings round thy green Retreat,
    On whose enamel'd Side
    When holy *Freedom* died
No equal Haunt allur'd thy future Feet.

5

25   O Sister meek of Truth,
    To my admiring Youth,
Thy sober Aid and native Charms infuse!
    The Flow'rs that sweetest breathe,
    Tho' Beauty cull'd the Wreath,
30   Still ask thy Hand to range their order'd Hues.

6

While *Rome* could none esteem
But Virtue's Patriot Theme,
You lov'd her Hills, and led her Laureate Band:
    But staid to sing alone
35   To one distinguish'd Throne,
And turn'd thy Face, and fled her alter'd Land.

7

No more, in Hall or Bow'r,
The Passions own thy Pow'r,
Love, only Love her forceless Numbers mean:
40   For Thou hast left her Shrine,
    Nor Olive more, nor Vine,
Shall gain thy Feet to bless the servile Scene.

8

Tho' Taste, tho' Genius bless,
To some divine Excess,
45   Faints the cold Work till Thou inspire the whole,
    What each, what all supply,
    May court, may charm our Eye,
Thou, only Thou can'st raise the meeting Soul!

9

Of These let others ask,
50   To aid some mighty Task,
I only seek to find thy temp'rate Vale:
      Where oft my Reed might sound
      To Maids and Shepherds round,
And all thy Sons, O *Nature*, learn my Tale.

ODE ON THE POETICAL CHARACTER

I

As once, if not with light Regard,
I read aright that gifted Bard,
(Him whose School above the rest
His Loveliest *Elfin* Queen has blest.)
5   One, only One, unrival'd Fair,
Might hope the magic Girdle wear,
At solemn Turney hung on high,
The Wish of each love-darting Eye;

Lo! to each other Nymph in turn applied,
10   As if, in Air unseen, some hov'ring Hand,
Some chaste and Angel-Friend to Virgin-Fame,
      With whisper'd Spell had burst the starting Band,
It left unblest her loath'd dishonour'd Side;
      Happier hopeless Fair, if never
15   Her baffled Hand with vain Endeavour
Had touch'd that fatal Zone to her denied!
Young *Fancy* thus, to me Divinest Name,
      To whom, prepar'd and bath'd in Heav'n,
      The Cest of amplest Pow'r is giv'n:
20   To few the God-like Gift assigns,
      To gird their blest prophetic Loins,
And gaze her Visions wild, and feel unmix'd her Flame!

2

The Band, as Fairy Legends say,
Was wove on that creating Day,
25   When He, who call'd with Thought to Birth
Yon tented Sky, this laughing Earth,

And drest with Springs, and Forests tall,
And pour'd the Main engirting all,
Long by the lov'd *Enthusiast* woo'd;
30 Himself in some Diviner Mood,
Retiring, sate with her alone,
And plac'd her on his Saphire Throne;
The whiles, the vaulted Shrine around,
Seraphic Wires were heard to sound,
35 Now sublimest Triumph swelling,
Now on Love and Mercy dwelling;
And she, from out the veiling Cloud,
Breath'd her magic Notes aloud:
And Thou, Thou rich-hair'd Youth of Morn,
40 And all thy subject Life was born!
The dang'rous Passions kept aloof,
Far from the sainted growing Woof:
But near it sate Ecstatic *Wonder*,
List'ning the deep applauding Thunder:
75 And *Truth*, in sunny Vest array'd,
By whose the Tarsel's Eyes were made;
All the shad'wy Tribes of *Mind*,
In braided Dance their Murmurs join'd,
And all the bright uncounted *Pow'rs*,
50 Who feed on Heav'n's ambrosial Flow'rs.
Where is the Bard, whose Soul can now
Its high presuming Hopes avow?
Where He who thinks, with Rapture blind,
This hallow'd Work for Him design'd?

3

55 High on some Cliff, to Heav'n up-pil'd,
Of rude Access, of Prospect wild,
Where, tangled round the jealous Steep,
Strange Shades o'erbrow the Valleys deep,
And holy *Genii* guard the Rock,
60 Its Gloomes embrown, its Springs unlock,
While on its rich ambitious Head,
An *Eden*, like his own, lies spread.
I view that Oak, the fancied Glades among,
By which as *Milton* lay, His Ev'ning Ear,
65 From many a Cloud that drop'd Ethereal Dew,
Nigh spher'd in Heav'n its native Strains could hear:
On which that ancient Trump he reach'd was hung;
          Thither oft his Glory greeting,
          From *Waller's* Myrtle Shades retreating,
70 With many a Vow from Hope's aspiring Tongue,
My trembling Feet his guiding Steps pursue;

In vain— Such Bliss to One alone,
Of all the Sons of Soul was known,
And Heav'n, and *Fancy*, kindred Pow'rs,
75   Have now o'erturn'd th' inspiring Bow'rs,
Or curtain'd close such Scene from ev'ry future View.

ODE

Written in the beginning of the Year 1746.

How sleep the Brave, who sink to Rest,
By all their Country's Wishes blest!
When *Spring*, with dewy Fingers cold,
Returns to deck their hallow'd Mold,
5   She there shall dress a sweeter Sod,
Than *Fancy*'s Feet have ever trod.

By Fairy Hands their Knell is rung,
By Forms unseen their Dirge is sung;
There *Honour* comes, a Pilgrim grey,
10   To bless the Turf that wraps their Clay,
And *Freedom* shall a-while repair,
To dwell a weeping Hermit there!

ODE TO MERCY

Strophe.

O Thou, who sit'st a smiling Bride
By *Valour*'s arm'd and awful Side,
Gentlest of Sky-born Forms, and best ador'd:
    Who oft with Songs, divine to hear,
5   Win'st from his fatal Grasp the Spear,
And hid'st in Wreaths of Flow'rs his bloodless Sword!
    Thou who, amidst the deathful Field,
    By Godlike Chiefs alone beheld,
Oft with thy Bosom bare art found,
10 Pleading for him the Youth who sinks to Ground:

See, *Mercy*, see, with pure and loaded Hands,
Before thy Shrine my Country's Genius stands,
And decks thy Altar still, tho' pierc'd with many a Wound!

Antistrophe.

When he whom ev'n our Joys provoke,
15   The *Fiend of Nature* join'd his Yoke,
And rush'd in Wrath to make our Isle his Prey;
    Thy Form, from out thy sweet Abode,
    O'ertook Him on his blasted Road,
And stop'd his Wheels, and look'd his Rage away.

20   I see recoil his sable Steeds,
    That bore Him swift to Salvage Deeds,
Thy tender melting Eyes they own;
O Maid, for all thy Love to *Britain* shown,
    Where *Justice* bars her Iron Tow'r,
25   To Thee we build a roseate Bow'r,
Thou, Thou shalt rule our Queen, and share our
    Monarch's Throne!

ODE TO LIBERTY

Strophe.

Who shall awake the *Spartan* Fife,
    And call in solemn Sounds to Life,
The Youths, whose Locks divinely spreading,
    Like vernal Hyacinths in sullen Hue,
5 At once the Breath of Fear and Virtue shedding,
    Applauding *Freedom* lov'd of old to view?
What New *Alcæus*, Fancy-blest,
Shall sing the Sword, in Myrtles drest,
At *Wisdom*'s Shrine a-while its Flame concealing,
10 (What Place so fit to seal a Deed renown'd?)
    Till she her brightest Lightnings round revealing,
It leap'd in Glory forth, and dealt her prompted Wound!
    O Goddess, in that feeling Hour,
    When most its Sounds would court thy Ears,
15   Let not my Shell's misguided Pow'r,
    E'er draw thy sad, thy mindful Tears.

No, *Freedom*, no, I will not tell,
How *Rome*, before thy weeping Face,
With heaviest Sound, a Giant-statue, fell,
20   Push'd by a wild and artless Race,
From off its wide ambitious Base,
When Time his Northern Sons of Spoil awoke,
        And all the blended Work of Strength and Grace,
        With many a rude repeated Stroke,
25   And many a barb'rous Yell, to thousand Fragments broke.

Epode.

Yet ev'n, where'er the least appear'd,
Th' admiring World thy Hand rever'd;
Still 'midst the scatter'd States around,
Some Remnants of Her Strength were found;
30   They saw by what escap'd the Storm,
How wond'rous rose her perfect Form;
How in the great the labour'd Whole,
Each mighty Master pour'd his Soul!
For sunny *Florence*, Seat of Art,
35   Beneath her Vines preserv'd a part,
Till They, whom Science lov'd to name,
(O who could fear it?) quench'd her Flame.
And lo, an humbler Relick laid
In jealous *Pisa*'s Olive Shade!
40   See small *Marino* joins the Theme,
Tho' least, not last in thy Esteem:
Strike, louder strike th' ennobling Strings
To those, whose Merchant Sons were Kings;
To Him, who deck'd with pearly Pride,
45   In *Adria* weds his green-hair'd Bride;
Hail Port of Glory, Wealth, and Pleasure,
Ne'er let me change this *Lydian* Measure:
Nor e'er her former Pride relate,
To sad *Liguria*'s bleeding State.
50   Ah no! more pleas'd thy Haunts I seek,
On wild *Helvetia*'s Mountains bleak:
(Where, when the favor'd of thy Choice,
The daring Archer heard thy Voice;
Forth from his Eyrie rous'd in Dread,
55   The rav'ning *Eagle* northward fled.)
Or dwell in willow'd Meads more near,
With Those to whom thy Stork is dear:
Those whom the Rod of *Alva* bruis'd,
Whose Crown a *British* Queen refus'd!

60 The Magic works, Thou feel'st the Strains,
  One holier Name alone remains;
  The perfect Spell shall then avail,
  Hail Nymph, ador'd by *Britain*, Hail!

Antistrophe.

  Beyond the Measure vast of Thought,
65 The Works, the Wizzard *Time* has wrought!
   The *Gaul*, 'tis held of antique Story,
  Saw *Britain* link'd to his now adverse Strand,
   No Sea between, nor Cliff sublime and hoary,
  He pass'd with unwet Feet thro' all our Land.
70   To the blown *Baltic* then, they say,
    The wild Waves found another way,
  Where *Orcas* howls, his wolfish Mountains rounding;
   Till all the banded West at once 'gan rise,
  A wide wild Storm ev'n Nature's self confounding,
75 With'ring her Giant Sons with strange uncouth Surprise.
    This pillar'd Earth so firm and wide,
     By Winds and inward Labors torn,
    In Thunders dread was push'd aside,
     And down the should'ring Billows born.
80 And see, like Gems, her laughing Train,
   The little Isles on ev'ry side,
  Mona, once hid from those who search the Main,
   Where thousand Elfin Shapes abide,
  And *Wight* who checks the west'ring Tide,
85 For Thee consenting Heav'n has each bestow'd,
  A fair Attendant on her sov'reign Pride:
   To Thee this blest Divorce she ow'd,
  For thou hast made her Vales thy lov'd, thy last Abode!

Second Epode.

  Then too, 'tis said, an hoary Pile,
90 'Midst the green Navel of our Isle,
  Thy Shrine in some religious Wood,
  O Soul-enforcing Goddess stood!
  There oft the painted Native's Feet,
  Were wont thy Form celestial meet:
95 Tho' now with hopeless Toil we trace
  Time's backward Rolls, to find its place;
  Whether the fiery-tressed *Dane*,
  Or *Roman*'s self o'erturn'd the Fane,

Or in what Heav'n-left Age it fell,
100   'Twere hard for modern Song to tell.
Yet still, if Truth those Beams infuse,
Which guide at once, and charm the Muse,
Beyond yon braided Clouds that lie,
Paving the light-embroider'd Sky:
105   Amidst the bright pavilion'd Plains,
The beauteous *Model* still remains.
There happier than in Islands blest,
Or Bow'rs by Spring or *Hebe* drest,
The Chiefs who fill our *Albion*'s Story,
110   In warlike Weeds, retir'd in Glory,
Hear their consorted *Druids* sing
Their Triumphs to th' immortal String.

How may the Poet now unfold,
What never Tongue or Numbers told?
115   How learn delighted, and amaz'd,
What Hands unknown that Fabric rais'd?
Ev'n now before his favor'd Eyes,
In *Gothic* Pride it seems to rise!
Yet *Græcia*'s graceful Orders join,
120   Majestic thro' the mix'd Design;
The secret Builder knew to chuse,
Each sphere-found Gem of richest Hues:
Whate'er Heav'n's purer Mold contains,
When nearer Suns emblaze its Veins;
125   There on the Walls the *Patriot*'s Sight,
May ever hang with fresh Delight,
And, grav'd with some Prophetic Rage,
Read *Albion*'s Fame thro' ev'ry Age.

Ye Forms Divine, ye Laureate Band,
130   That near her inmost Altar stand!
Now sooth Her, to her blissful Train
Blithe *Concord*'s social Form to gain:
Concord, whose Myrtle Wand can steep
Ev'n *Anger*'s blood-shot Eyes in Sleep:
135   Before whose breathing Bosom's Balm,
Rage drops his Steel, and Storms grow calm;
Her let our Sires and Matrons hoar
Welcome to *Britain*'s ravag'd Shore,
Our Youths, enamour'd of the Fair,
140   Play with the Tangles of her Hair,
Till in one loud applauding Sound,
The Nations shout to Her around,
O how supremely art thou blest,
Thou, Lady, Thou shalt rule the West!

ODE, TO A LADY ON THE DEATH OF COLONEL ROSS IN THE ACTION OF FONTENOY

1

While, lost to all his former Mirth,
Britannia's Genius bends to Earth,
    And mourns the fatal Day:
While stain'd with Blood he strives to tear
5   Unseemly from his Sea-green Hair
       The Wreaths of chearful *May:*

2

The Thoughts which musing Pity pays,
And fond Remembrance loves to raise,
    Your faithful Hours attend:
10   Still Fancy to Herself unkind,
Awakes to Grief the soften'd Mind,
       And points the bleeding Friend.

3

By rapid *Scheld*'s descending Wave
His Country's Vows shall bless the Grave,
15   Where'er the Youth is laid:
That sacred Spot the Village Hind
With ev'ry sweetest Turf shall bind,
       And Peace protect the Shade.

4

Blest Youth, regardful of thy Doom,
20   Aërial Hands shall build thy Tomb,
       With shadowy Trophies crown'd:
Whilst *Honor* bath'd in Tears shall rove
To sigh thy Name thro' ev'ry Grove,
       And call his Heros round.

5

The warlike Dead of ev'ry Age,
25   Who fill the fair recording Page,
       Shall leave their sainted Rest:

                And, half-reclining on his Spear,
                Each wond'ring Chief by turns appear,
30   To hail the blooming Guest.

                               6

                Old *Edward*'s Sons, unknown to yield,
                Shall croud from *Cressy*'s laurell'd Field,
                    And gaze with fix'd Delight:
                Again for *Britain*'s Wrongs they feel,
35   Again they snatch the gleamy Steel,
                    And wish th' avenging Fight.

                               7

                But lo where, sunk in deep Despair,
                Her Garments torn, her Bosom bare,
                    Impatient *Freedom* lies!
40   Her matted Tresses madly spread,
                To ev'ry Sod, which wraps the Dead,
                    She turns her joyless Eyes.

                               8

                Ne'er shall she leave that lowly Ground,
                Till Notes of Triumph bursting round
45   Proclaim her Reign restor'd:
                Till *William* seek the sad Retreat,
                And bleeding at her sacred Feet,
                    Present the sated Sword.

                               9

                If, weak to sooth so soft an Heart,
50   These pictur'd Glories nought impart,
                    To dry thy constant Tear:
                If yet, in Sorrow's distant Eye,
                Expos'd and pale thou see'st him lie,
                    Wild War insulting near:

                              10

55   Where'er from Time Thou court'st Relief,
                The Muse shall still, with social Grief,
                    Her gentlest Promise keep:
                Ev'n humble *Harting*'s cottag'd Vale
                Shall learn the sad repeated Tale,
60   And bid her Shepherds weep.

ODE TO EVENING

If ought of Oaten Stop, or Pastoral Song,
May hope, chaste *Eve*, to sooth thy modest Ear,
    Like thy own solemn Springs,
    Thy Springs, and dying Gales,
5 O *Nymph* reserv'd, while now the bright-hair'd Sun
Sits in yon western Tent, whose cloudy Skirts,
    With Brede ethereal wove,
    O'erhang his wavy Bed:
Now Air is hush'd, save where the weak-ey'd Bat,
10 With short shrill Shriek flits by on leathern Wing,
    Or where the Beetle winds
    His small but sullen Horn,
As oft he rises 'midst the twilight Path,
Against the Pilgrim born in heedless Hum:
15   Now teach me, *Maid* compos'd,
    To breathe some soften'd Strain,
Whose Numbers stealing thro' thy darkning Vale,
May not unseemly with its Stillness suit,
    As musing slow, I hail
20   Thy genial lov'd Return!
For when thy folding Star arising shews
His paly Circlet, at his warning Lamp
    The fragrant *Hours*, and *Elves*
    Who slept in Flowers the Day,
25 And many a *Nymph* who wreaths her Brows with Sedge,
And sheds the fresh'ning Dew, and lovelier still,
    The *Pensive Pleasures* sweet
    Prepare thy shadowy Car.
Then lead, calm *Vot'ress* where some sheety Lake
30 Cheers the lone Heath, or some time-hallowed Pile,
    Or upland Fallows grey
    Reflect its last cool Gleam.
But when chill blustring Winds, or driving Rain,
Forbid my willing Feet, be mine the Hut,
35   That from the Mountain's Side,
    Views Wilds, and swelling Floods,
And Hamlets brown, and dim-discover'd Spires,
And hears their simple Bell, and marks o'er all
    Thy Dewy Fingers draw
40   The gradual dusky Veil.
While *Spring* shall pour his Show'rs, as oft he wont,
And bathe thy breathing Tresses, meekest *Eve!*
    While *Summer* loves to sport,
    Beneath thy ling'ring Light:

45   While sallow *Autumn* fills thy Lap with Leaves,
      Or *Winter* yelling thro' the troublous Air,
           Affrights thy shrinking Train,
           And rudely rends thy Robes.
      So long, sure-found beneath the sylvan Shed,
50   Shall *Fancy*, *Friendship*, *Science*, rose-lipp'd *Health*,
           Thy gentlest Influence own,
           And love thy fav'rite Name!

ODE TO PEACE

1

      O Thou, who bad'st thy Turtles bear
      Swift from his Grasp thy golden Hair,
           And sought'st thy native Skies:
      When *War*, by Vultures drawn from far,
5   To *Britain* bent his Iron Car,
           And bad his Storms arise!

2

      Tir'd of his rude tyrannic Sway,
      Our Youth shall fix some festive Day,
           His sullen Shrines to burn:
10   But Thou who hear'st the turning Spheres,
      What Sounds may charm thy partial Ears,
           And gain thy blest Return!

3

      O *Peace*, thy injur'd Robes up-bind,
      O rise, and leave not one behind
15   Of all thy beamy Train:
      The *British* Lion, Goddess sweet,
      Lies stretch'd on Earth to kiss thy Feet,
           And own thy holier Reign.

4

      Let others court thy transient Smile,
20   But come to grace thy western Isle,
           By warlike *Honour* led!
      And, while around her Ports rejoice,
      While all her Sons adore thy Choice,
           With Him for ever wed!

THE MANNERS. AN ODE

Farewell, for clearer Ken design'd,
The dim-discover'd Tracts of Mind:
Truths which, from Action's Paths retir'd,
My silent Search in vain requir'd!
5   No more my Sail that Deep explores,
No more I search those magic Shores,
What Regions part the World of Soul,
Or whence thy Streams, *Opinion*, roll:
If e'er I round such Fairy Field,
10   Some Pow'r impart the Spear and Shield,
At which the Wizzard *Passions* fly,
By which the Giant *Follies* die!
    Farewell the Porch, whose Roof is seen,
Arch'd with th' enlivening Olive's Green:
15   Where *Science*, prank'd in tissued Vest,
By *Reason*, *Pride*, and *Fancy* drest,
Comes like a Bride so trim array'd,
To wed with *Doubt* in *Plato*'s Shade!
    Youth of the quick uncheated Sight,
20   Thy Walks, *Observance*, more invite!
O Thou, who lov'st that ampler Range,
Where Life's wide Prospects round thee change,
And with her mingling Sons ally'd,
Throw'st the prattling Page aside:
25   To me in Converse sweet impart,
To read in Man the native Heart,
To learn, where Science sure is found,
From Nature as she lives around:
And gazing oft her Mirror true,
30   By turns each shifting Image view!
Till meddling *Art's* officious Lore,
Reverse the Lessons taught before,
Alluring from a safer Rule,
To dream in her enchanted School;
35   Thou Heav'n, whate'er of Great we boast,
Hast blest this social Science most.
    Retiring hence to thoughtful Cell,
As *Fancy* breathes her potent Spell,
Not vain she finds the charmful Task,
40   In Pageant quaint, in motley Mask,
Behold before her musing Eyes,
The countless *Manners* round her rise;
While ever varying as they pass,
To some *Contempt* applies her Glass:

45 With these the *white-rob'd Maids* combine,
    And those the laughing *Satyrs* join!
    But who is He whom now she views,
    In Robe of wild contending Hues?
    Thou by the Passions nurs'd, I greet
50 The comic Sock that binds thy Feet!
    O *Humour*, Thou whose Name is known,
    To *Britain*'s favor'd Isle alone:
    Me too amidst thy Band admit,
    There where the young-eyed healthful *Wit*,
55 (Whose Jewels in his crisped Hair
    Are plac'd each other's Beams to share,
    Whom no Delights from Thee divide)
    In Laughter loos'd attends thy Side!
        By old *Miletus* who so long
60 Has ceas'd his Love-inwoven Song:
    By all you taught the *Tuscan* Maids,
    In chang'd *Italia*'s modern Shades:
    By Him, whose *Knight*'s distinguish'd Name
    Refin'd a Nation's Lust of Fame;
65 Whose Tales ev'n now, with Echos sweet,
    Castilia's *Moorish* Hills repeat:
    Or Him, whom *Seine*'s blue Nymphs deplore,
    In watchet Weeds on *Gallia*'s Shore,
    Who drew the sad *Sicilian* Maid,
70 By Virtues in her Sire betray'd:
        O Nature boon, from whom proceed
    Each forceful Thought, each prompted Deed;
    If but from Thee I hope to feel,
    On all my Heart imprint thy Seal!
75 Let some retreating Cynic find,
    These oft-turn'd Scrolls I leave behind,
    The *Sports* and I this Hour agree,
    To rove thy Scene-full World with Thee!

THE PASSIONS. AN ODE FOR MUSIC

    When Music, Heav'nly Maid, was young,
    While yet in early *Greece* she sung,
    The Passions oft to hear her Shell,
    Throng'd around her magic Cell,
5   Exulting, trembling, raging, fainting,
    Possest beyond the Muse's Painting;

By turns they felt the glowing Mind,
Disturb'd, delighted, rais'd, refin'd.
Till once, 'tis said, when all were fir'd,
10   Fill'd with Fury, rapt, inspir'd,
From the supporting Myrtles round,
They snatch'd her Instruments of Sound,
And as they oft had heard a-part
Sweet Lessons of her forceful Art,
15   Each, for Madness rul'd the Hour,
Would prove his own expressive Pow'r.

First *Fear* his Hand, its Skill to try,
   Amid the Chords bewilder'd laid,
And back recoil'd he knew not why,
20   Ev'n at the Sound himself had made.

Next *Anger* rush'd, his Eyes on fire,
   In Lightnings own'd his secret Stings,
In one rude Clash he struck the Lyre,
   And swept with hurried Hand the Strings.

25 With woful Measures wan *Despair*
   Low sullen Sounds his Grief beguil'd,
A solemn, strange, and mingled Air,
   'Twas sad by Fits, by Starts 'twas wild.

But Thou, O *Hope*, with Eyes so fair,
30   What was thy delightful Measure?
Still it whisper'd promis'd Pleasure,
   And bad the lovely Scenes at distance hail!
Still would Her Touch the Strain prolong,
   And from the Rocks, the Woods, the Vale,
35 She call'd on Echo still thro' all the Song;
   And where Her sweetest Theme She chose,
   A soft responsive Voice was heard at ev'ry Close,
And *Hope* enchanted smil'd, and wav'd Her golden Hair.

And longer had She sung,—but with a Frown,
40   *Revenge* impatient rose,
He threw his blood-stain'd Sword in Thunder down,
    And with a with'ring Look,
The War-denouncing Trumpet took,
And blew a Blast so loud and dread,
45 Were ne'er Prophetic Sounds so full of Woe.
    And ever and anon he beat
    The doubling Drum with furious Heat;
   And tho' sometimes each dreary Pause between,
    Dejected *Pity* at his Side,

50   Her Soul-subduing Voice applied,
          Yet still He kept his wild unalter'd Mien,
      While each strain'd Ball of Sight seem'd bursting from his Head.
          Thy Numbers, *Jealousy*, to nought were fix'd,
            Sad Proof of thy distressful State,
55   Of diff'ring Themes the veering Song was mix'd,
            And now it courted *Love*, now raving call'd on *Hate*.

      With Eyes up-rais'd, as one inspir'd,
      Pale *Melancholy* sate retir'd,
      And from her wild sequester'd Seat,
60   In Notes by Distance made more sweet,
      Pour'd thro' the mellow *Horn* her pensive Soul:
            And dashing soft from Rocks around,
            Bubbling Runnels join'd the Sound;
      Thro' Glades and Glooms the mingled Measure stole,
65   Or o'er some haunted Stream with fond Delay,
            Round an holy Calm diffusing,
            Love of Peace, and lonely Musing,
      In hollow Murmurs died away.

      But O how alter'd was its sprightlier Tone!
70   When *Chearfulness*, a Nymph of healthiest Hue,
          Her Bow a-cross her Shoulder flung,
          Her Buskins gem'd with Morning Dew,
      Blew an inspiring Air, that Dale and Thicket rung,
          The Hunter's Call to *Faun* and *Dryad* known!
75   The Oak-crown'd *Sisters*, and their chast-eye'd *Queen*,
          Satyrs and sylvan Boys were seen,
          Peeping from forth their Alleys green;
      Brown *Exercise* rejoic'd to hear,
          And *Sport* leapt up, and seiz'd his Beechen Spear.

80   Last came *Joy*'s Ecstatic Trial,
      He with viny Crown advancing,
          First to the lively Pipe his Hand addrest,
      But soon he saw the brisk awak'ning Viol,
          Whose sweet entrancing Voice he lov'd the best.
85   They would have thought who heard the Strain,
          They saw in *Tempe*'s Vale her native Maids,
            Amidst the festal sounding Shades,
      To some unwearied Minstrel dancing,
          While as his flying Fingers kiss'd the Strings,
90   Love fram'd with *Mirth*, a gay fantastic Round,
      Loose were Her Tresses seen, her Zone unbound,
          And HE amidst his frolic Play,
      As if he would the charming Air repay,
      Shook thousand Odours from his dewy Wings.

95 O *Music*, Sphere-descended Maid,
    Friend of Pleasure, *Wisdom*'s Aid,
    Why, Goddess, why to us deny'd?
    Lay'st Thou thy antient Lyre aside?
    As in that lov'd *Athenian* Bow'r,
100 You learn'd an all-commanding Pow'r,
    Thy mimic Soul, O Nymph endear'd,
    Can well recall what then it heard.
    Where is thy native simple Heart,
    Devote to Virtue, Fancy, Art?
105 Arise as in that elder Time,
    Warm, Energic, Chaste, Sublime!
    Thy Wonders in that God-like Age,
    Fill thy recording *Sister*'s Page——
    'Tis said, and I believe the Tale,
110 Thy humblest *Reed* could more prevail,
    Had more of Strength, diviner Rage,
    Than all which charms this laggard Age,
    Ev'n all at once together found,
    Cæcilia's mingled World of Sound——
115 O bid our vain Endeavors cease,
    Revive the just Designs of *Greece*,
    Return in all thy simple State!
    Confirm the Tales Her Sons relate!

ODE OCCASIONED BY THE DEATH OF MR. THOMSON

ADVERTISEMENT

The Scene of the following STANZAS is suppos'd to lie on the *Thames* near *Richmond*.

Haec tibi semper erunt, et cum solennia vota reddemus Nymphis, et cum lustrabimus agros——Amavit nos quoque Daphnis.
                                    VIRG. Bucol. Eclog. v [74–5]

I

    In yonder Grave a Druid lies
        Where slowly winds the stealing Wave!
    The Year's best Sweets shall duteous rise
        To deck it's Poet's sylvan Grave!

II

In yon deep Bed of whisp'ring Reeds
  His airy Harp shall now be laid,
That He, whose Heart in Sorrow bleeds,
  May love thro' Life the soothing Shade.

III

Then Maids and Youths shall linger here,
  And while it's Sounds at distance swell,
Shall sadly seem in Pity's Ear
  To hear the Woodland Pilgrim's Knell.

IV

Remembrance oft shall haunt the Shore
  When Thames in Summer-wreaths is drest,
And oft suspend the dashing Oar
  To bid his gentle Spirit rest!

V

And oft as Ease and Health retire
  To breezy Lawn, or Forest deep,
The Friend shall view yon whit'ning Spire,
  And 'mid the varied Landscape weep.

VI

But Thou, who own'st that Earthy Bed,
  Ah! what will ev'ry Dirge avail?
Or Tears, which Love and Pity shed
  That mourn beneath the gliding Sail!

VII

Yet lives there one, whose heedless Eye
  Shall scorn thy pale Shrine glimm'ring near?
With Him, Sweet Bard, may Fancy die,
  And Joy desert the blooming Year.

VIII

But thou, lorn Stream, whose sullen Tide
  No sedge-crown'd Sisters now attend,
Now waft me from the green Hill's Side
  Whose cold Turf hides the buried Friend!

IX

And see, the Fairy Valleys fade,
    Dun Night has veil'd the solemn View!
35 —Yet once again, Dear parted Shade
    Meek Nature's Child again adieu!

X

The genial Meads assign'd to bless
    Thy Life, shall mourn thy early Doom,
Their Hinds, and Shepherd-Girls shall dress
40   With simple Hands thy rural Tomb.

XI

Long, long, thy Stone and pointed Clay
    Shall melt the musing Briton's Eyes,
O! Vales, and Wild Woods, shall He say
    In yonder Grave Your Druid lies!

AN ODE ON THE
POPULAR SUPERSTITIONS OF THE
HIGHLANDS OF SCOTLAND
CONSIDERED AS THE SUBJECT OF POETRY

I

H[ome], Thou return'st from Thames, whose Naiads long
    Have seen Thee ling'ring with a fond delay
'Mid those soft Friends, whose hearts some future day
    Shall melt perhaps to hear thy Tragic Song
5 Go not unmindfull of that cordial Youth
    Whom long endear'd thou leav'st by Lavant's side
Together let us wish Him lasting truth
    And Joy untainted with his destin'd Bride.
Go! nor regardless, while these Numbers boast
10   My short-liv'd bliss, forget my social Name
But think far-off how on the Southern coast
    I met thy Friendship with an equal Flame!
Fresh to that soil thou turn'st, whose ev'ry Vale
    Shall prompt the Poet, and his Song demand;
15   To Thee thy copious Subjects ne'er shall fail.
    Thou need'st but take the Pencil to thy Hand
And paint what all believe who own thy Genial Land.

2

There must Thou wake perforce thy Doric Quill,
   'Tis Fancy's Land to which thou set'st thy Feet,
20   Where still, tis said, the Fairy People meet
Beneath each birken Shade, on mead or Hill.
    There each trim Lass that skims the milky store
    To the swart Tribes their creamy Bowl allots,
By Night They sip it round the cottage Door
25 While airy Minstrels warble jocund notes.
    There ev'ry Herd by sad experience knows
      How wing'd with fate their Elf-shot arrows fly
When the Sick Ewe her summer food foregoes
    Or, stretch'd on Earth, the Heart-smit Heifers lie!
30 Such airy Beings awe th'untutor'd Swain;
    Nor Thou, tho' learn'd, his homelier thoughts neglect.
Let thy sweet Muse the rural faith sustain;
    These are the Themes of simple sure Effect
That add new conquests to her boundless reign
35 And fill with double force her heart commanding Strain.

3

Ev'n yet preserv'd how often may'st thou hear,
   Where to the Pole the Boreal Mountains run,
   Taught by the Father to his list'ning Son
Strange lays whose pow'r had charm'd a Spenser's Ear.
40   At Ev'ry Pause, before thy Mind possest,
Old Runic Bards shall seem to rise around
    With uncouth Lyres, in many-colour'd Vest,
    Their matted Hair with boughs fantastic crown'd
Whether thou bidst the well-taught Hind repeat
45   The Choral Dirge that mourns some Chieftain brave,
When ev'ry shrieking Maid her bosom beat
    And strew'd with choicest herbs his scented Grave
Or whether sitting in the Shepherd's Shiel
    Thou hear'st some sounding Tale of War's alarms
50 When at the Bugle's call with fire and steel
    The sturdy Clans pour'd forth their bonny Swarms
And hostile Brothers met to prove each other's Arms.

4

'Tis thine to sing how, framing hideous Spells,
   In Skye's lone Isle the gifted Wizzard Seer
55 Lodg'd in the Wintry cave with *Fate's fell spear*
Or in the depth of Uist's dark forests dwells

How they, whose Sight such dreary dreams engross,
    With their own Visions oft astonished droop,
When o'er the watry strath or quaggy Moss
60   They see the gliding Ghosts unbodied troop
Or if in Sports or on the festive Green
    Their *destined* glance some fated Youth descry
Who now perhaps in lusty Vigour seen
    And rosy health shall soon lamented die.
65 For them the viewless Forms of Air obey
    Their bidding heed, and at their beck repair.
They know what Spirit brews the stormfull day
    And heartless, oft like moody Madness stare
To see the Phantom train their secret work prepare!

[*Stanza 5 and part of stanza 6 are missing*]

95 What tho far off from some dark dell espied
    His glimm'ring Mazes cheer th'excursive sight,
 Yet turn, ye Wandrers, turn your steps aside
    Nor chuse the Guidance of that faithless light!
For watchfull, lurking mid th' unrustling Reed,
100   At those mirk hours the wily Monster lies
And listens oft to hear the passing Steed
    And frequent round him rolls his sullen Eyes
If Chance his savage wrath may some weak wretch surprise.

7

Ah luckless Swain, o'er all unblest indeed!
105 Whom late bewilder'd in the dank dark Fen
Far from his Flocks and smoaking Hamlet then!
    To that sad spot *where hums the sedgy weed*:
On him enrag'd the Fiend in angry mood
    Shall never look with Pity's kind concern
110 But instant furious rouse the whelming Flood
O'er its drown'd Banks, forbidding all return;
    Or if he meditate his wish'd Escape
    To some dim Hill that seems uprising near,
To his faint Eye the grim and griesly Shape
115 In all its Terrors clad shall wild appear.
Mean time the watry Surge shall round him rise,
    Pour'd sudden forth from ev'ry swelling source.
What now remains but Tears and hopeless sighs?
    His Fear-shook limbs have lost their Youthly force
120 And down the waves he floats a pale and breathless Corse.

8

For him in vain his anxious Wife shall wait
 Or wander forth to meet him on his way,
 For him in vain at to-fall of the Day
His Bairns shall linger at the unclosing Gate.
125 Ah ne'er shall he return—Alone, if Night
 Her travell'd limbs in broken slumbers steep
With dropping Willows drest his mournfull Sprite
 Shall visit sad perhaps her silent Sleep,
Then He perhaps with moist and watry hand
130 Shall fondly seem to press her shudd'ring cheek
And with his blue swoln face before her stand
 And, shivring cold, these piteous accents speak:
'Pursue, dear Wife, thy daily toils pursue
At Dawn, or dusk, industrious as before,
135 Nor e'er of me one hapless thought renew,
 While I lie weltring on the osier'd Shore
Drown'd by the Kaelpie's wrath, nor e'er shall aid thee more.'

9

Unbounded is thy range; with varied style
 Thy Muse may like those feath'ry tribes which spring
140 From their rude Rocks extend her skirting wing
 Round the moist Marge of each cold Hebrid Isle
To that hoar Pile which still its ruin shows.
 In whose small vaults a Pigmie-Folk is found,
Whose Bones the Delver with his Spade up-throws
145 And culls them wondring from the hallow'd Ground!
Or thither, where beneath the show'ry west
 The mighty Kings of three fair Realms are laid,
Once Foes perhaps, together now they rest;
 No Slaves revere them, and no Wars invade:
150 Yet frequent now at Midnight's solemn hour
 The rifted Mounds their yawning cells unfold
And forth the Monarchs stalk with sovreign Pow'r
In pageant Robes, and wreath'd with sheeny Gold
And on their twilight tombs aerial council hold.

10

155 But O, o'er all, forget not Kilda's race
 On whose bleak rocks which brave the wasting tides
 Fair Nature's Daughter, Virtue, yet abides!
Go just, as they, their blameless Manners trace!
 Then to my Ear transmit some gentle Song
160 Of those whose Lives are yet sincere and plain,

Their bounded walks the ragged Cliffs along
  And all their Prospect but the wintry main.
With sparing Temp'rance at the needful Time
They drain the sainted Spring, or Hunger-prest,
165 Along th'Atlantic Rock undreading climb
  And of its Eggs despoil the Solan's nest.
Thus blest in primal Innocence they live
  Sufficed and happy with that frugal fare
Which tastefull Toil and hourly Danger give.
170 Hard is their shallow Soil, *and bleak* and bare
Nor ever vernal Bee was heard to murmur there!

11

Nor needst thou blush that such false Themes engage
  Thy gentle Mind of fairer stores possest,
For not alone they touch the Village Breast,
175 But fill'd in elder Time th' historic page.
  There Shakespeare's Self with evry Garland crown'd
In musing hour his wayward Sisters found
  And with their terrors drest the magic Scene!
From them he sung, when mid his bold design
180 Before the Scot afflicted and aghast
The shadowy Kings of Banquo's fated line
  Thro' the dark cave in gleamy Pageant past.
Proceed nor quit the tales which simply told
  Could once so well my answering Bosom pierce,
185 Proceed, in forcefull sounds and Colours bold
  The native Legends of thy Land rehearse;
To such adapt thy Lyre, and suit thy pow'rfull Verse.

12

In Scenes like these which, daring to depart
  From sober Truth, are still to Nature true
190 And call forth fresh delights to Fancy's view,
Th' heroic Muse employ'd her Tasso's Art!
How have I trembled, when at Tancred's stroke
  Its gushing Blood the gaping Cypress pour'd,
When each live Plant with mortal accents spoke
195 And the wild Blast up-heav'd the vanish'd Sword.
How have I sate where pip'd the pensive Wind
  To hear his harp by British Fairfax strung,
Prevailing Poet, whose undoubting Mind
  Believ'd the magic Wonders which he sung!
200 Hence at each Sound Imagination glows
Hence his warm lay with softest Sweetness flows.

Melting it flows, pure, num'rous, strong and clear
And fills th'impassion'd heart, and lulls th'harmonious Ear.

13

All Hail, ye Scenes that o'er my soul prevail
205   Ye *splendid* Firths and Lakes which far away
Are by smooth Annan fill'd, or past'ral Tay
Or Don's romantic Springs, at distance hail!
The Time shall come, when I perhaps may tread
Your lowly Glens, o'erhung with spreading Broom,
210 Or o'er your stretching Heaths by Fancy led,
Then will I dress once more the faded Bow'r
Where Jonson sate in Drummond's *classic* Shade
Or crop from Tiviot's dale each *lyric Flower*
And mourn on Yarrow Banks, *where Willy's laid.*
215 Meantime, ye Pow'rs, that on the plains which bore
The cordial Youth, on Lothian's plains attend
Where'er he dwell, on Hill or lowly Muir
To him I lose your kind protection lend
And touch'd with Love, like Mine, preserve my absent Friend.

Notes

JONATHAN SWIFT

p. 1. Humble Petition of Frances Harris. 1. *Lady Betty* Germaine, daughter of the Earl of Berkeley, Lord Justice of Ireland, to whom Swift was private chaplain from 1699 to 1701. Mrs Harris was one of her gentle-women, and the other Lord Justice (of the title) was the Earl of Galway.
23. *Mrs Dukes*, wife of a footman.
24. *Whittle*, the Earl of Berkeley's valet.
27. *Collway*, a corruption of 'Galway'.
28. *Dromedary* Drogheda, one of the Earl of Berkeley's successors as Lord Justice.
30. *Cary*, Clerk of the kitchen.
45. *Bedlam*, where lunatics were confined.
48. *Cunning Man*, fortune-teller.

p. 4. Baucis and Philemon. Baucis and Philemon were poor cottagers who, unawares, entertained Zeus and Hermes, as a reward for which their cottage was turned into a temple and they became priest and priestess. They died at the same hour in old age and were changed into trees with inter-twining branches. (See Ovid, *Metamorphoses* VIII. 618ff.)
65. *Jack*, a spit.
106. Swift preached an amusing sermon on 'Sleeping in Church'.
132. The parson was entitled to a tithe-pig, just as he had claim to a tithe (or one-tenth) of all other produce of his parish.
133. *Dissenters*, Nonconformists.
134. *Right Divine*, strictly the claim made by some kings, the Stuarts especially, that they ruled as the appointees of God. There may here be a pun, referring to the parson's rights as the representative of God.
140. *Colberteen*, a kind of open lace.
144. *Grogram*, a coarse fabric of silk, mohair and wool, sometimes stiffened with gum.

p. 8. A Description of the Morning. 16. Prisoners had to pay for certain privileges, such as special accommodation.

p. 8. Cadenus and Vanessa. Cadenus is intended to represent Swift, the word being an anagram of Decanus (Lat. for Dean), whilst Vanessa was Esther Vanhomrigh. The poem was written in 1713 but not published until after her death, in 1727.
2. *Cyprian Queen*, Venus.
72. *Deponents*, persons making legal depositions on oath.
96. *Graces*, the goddesses, usually three, in Greek mythology who personified loveliness.
107. *Fleta's, Bractons, Cokes*, Fleta was a Latin treatise on English law (*c.* 1290); Henry Bracton (*d.* 1268) was a commentator; and Sir Edward Coke (1552–1634) wrote the *Institutes* (or Coke upon Littleton).
109. *Ovid Book the Second*, the desertion of Phyllis by Demophöon, *Heroides* II.
111. *Dido*, Queen of Carthage, loved and deserted by Aeneas, *Aeneid* IV.
112. *Tibullus* (?48–19 B.C.) wrote love poems addressed to Delia.

114. Abraham Cowley (1618–67), *The Mistress* (1647); Edmund Waller (1606–87) wrote poems addressed to Sacharissa, *Poems*, 1645.

122. *Demur, Imparlance and Essoign*, legal terms for objection, petition for delay and excuse for non-appearance respectively.

126. *Clio*, the muse of history.

136. *Lucina*, goddess of childbirth.

155. *Amaranthine*, unfading.

157. *Titan*, the sun.

187. *Pallas*, or Minerva, goddess of wisdom.

372. *Montaigne*, Michel de (1533–92), French essayist.

417. See above, 'Baucis and Philemon', l. 140.

431. *Ombre*, card-game. Cf. Pope, *The Rape of the Lock*, III, 25–100.

483. *Plutarch* (46–120?); *Moralia* were essays that formed a model for those of Montaigne and Bacon.

581. *Grand-Monde*, the fashionable world.

673. *Bite*, trick.

839. A legal phrase, commanding the parties concerned to appear before the queen (or her judicial representatives) on the last day of March.

p. 28. Horace, Lib. 2. Sat. 6. This poem was completed by Pope and published in 1728.

10. Swift always wanted to be able to settle in England, and in this line shows his preference for the southern half of England.

15. *Lewis*, Erasmus, secretary to Harley (see below).

26. *Levee*, reception by the monarch or a great lord.

27. *Pound*, a place of confinement.

29. *Ribbons*, showing political allegiances.

55. *Bolingbroke*, Henry St John, 1st Viscount (1678–1751), Tory politician and philosopher.

65. *Harley*, Robert, 1st Earl of Oxford, Tory minister, with Bolingbroke led the Government from 1710 to 1713.

74. Alexander Pope (1688–1744), Thomas Parnell (1679–1718), John Gay (1685–1732), Swift's friends and fellow-poets. See, e.g., 'Verses on the Death of Dr Swift', ll. 47, 52, 207, 438.

80. *Charing Cross*, where royal proclamations were (and are) read.

p. 31. On Stella's Birthday, 1718/19. 1. Stella [Hester Johnson] was, in fact, thirty-eight at that time.

p. 34. A Satirical Elegy on the Death of a Late Famous General Marlborough died on 16 June 1722. Swift never forgave him for the immense private fortune which he derived from his military career. He once described him as being 'as covetous as hell and ambitious as the prince of it.'

p. 35. Stella's Birthday, March 13, 1726/7. Stella died less than a year later on 28 January 1727/8.

74. *Janus*, the two-headed god.

p. 37. The Furniture of a Woman's Mind. 2. *Scarlet-Coat*, soldier.

59. *Mrs Harding*, a printer, wife of the man who printed Swift's *Drapier's Letters* and who was prosecuted for doing so.

p. 39. Verses on the Death of Dr Swift. 1. *Rochefoucault*, François, Duc de la Rochefoucauld (1613–80), *Maximes* (1665).

47, 52. See above, 'Horace, Lib. 2. Sat. 6.' l. 74.

55. John *ARBUTHNOT* (1667–1735) wrote the greater part of the *Memoirs*

of Martinus Scriblerus and collaborated with Pope, Swift and Gay. Cf. l. 208 below.

59. *ST JOHN.* See under '*Bolingbroke*', 'Horace, Lib. 2. Sat. 6.' l. 55. Cf. also ll. 196, 209, 377 below. *PULTNEY,* Sir William, Earl of Bath, friend and, later, opponent of Walpole. Cf. l. 194 below.

117. *Tropes,* ironic use of words.

165. *Grub-Street,* the abode of hack writers. Cf. 'On Poetry', l. 58.

168. Swift in the *Drapier's Letters* (1724) attacked the monopoly given to Wood to manufacture coins for Ireland.

179–88. According to Swift's notes, the Queen promised him a gift of medals which were never sent. She saw a piece of Indian plaid cloth which Swift had sent to Henrietta Howard, Countess of Suffolk and Lady of the Bedchamber to the Queen and also mistress of George II, liked it and took it. She asked Swift to send more, which he did, but neither paid him nor gave him the medals, but treated him, in fact, with contempt.

189. Francis *Chartres* (1675–1732), gambler and rogue. Swift calls him an 'infamous scoundrel' and refers to his trial 'at seventy' for rape.

189, 192. *Sir Robert* Walpole (1676–1745), Prime Minister 1715–17 and 1721–1742. Cf. 'On Poetry', ll. 187, 441.

197. *Curl[l],* Edmund (1675–1747), bookseller and pamphleteer, attributed some of his publications to Swift who disowned them. In l. 202 Swift refers to Curll's publishing the 'lives, letters and last wills and testaments of the nobility and ministers of state as well as of all the rogues who are hanged at Tyburn'. Cf. Pope, *Dunciad* I. 40, with its ironic reference to Curll's obscene publications, and II. 57 ff.

200. *Tibbalds, Moore and Cibber,* 'three stupid verse writers in London' (Swift's note). Lewis Theobald (1688–1744) in *Shakespeare Restored* exposed the weakness of Pope's edition, for which he became the satiric hero of *The Dunciad.* By the time Pope revised this poem he had been passed over for the Laureateship in favour of Colley Cibber (1671–1757) (cf. also l. 270), actor and playwright, as a result of which Cibber replaced Theobald as hero in the revised *Dunciad.* For James Moore (Smythe) (1702–34), see *Dunciad,* II. 50 and Pope's note in the first version at II. 46. All three are mentioned together by Pope, *Epistle to Dr Arbuthnot,* ll. 372–3.

230. *Vole,* to win all the tricks.

253. *Lintot,* Bernard (1675–1736), a more reputable bookseller. See below, 'On Poetry', l. 107; and *Dunciad,* II. 53ff.

258. *Duck Lane,* in Little Britain, London, where old books were sold.

272. *Stephen Duck* (1705–56), 'thresher-poet', noticed by Queen Caroline, became Rector of Byfleet.

274. *Craftsman,* a periodical begun in 1726, anti-Walpole, to which Swift, Bolingbroke, Arbuthnot and possibly Pope contributed.

278. *Henl[e]y,* John (1692–1706), known as 'Orator' Henley. Cf. *Dunciad* II. 370, III. 199 and *Epistle to Dr Arbuthnot,* l. 98.

281. *Wo[o]lston,* Thomas (1670–1733), published works in the Deist controversy, chiefly against the credibility of Scriptural miracles. Contrary to what Swift says in l. 290, he did not receive a pension. See below, 'On Poetry', l. 494.

300. *Rose* Tavern, Drury Lane.

346. Psalm 146:3.

349. *Irish Senate,* that is, the Irish Parliament.

355. Reference to the attempt in England in 1713 to discover by the offer of a reward the author of *The Public Spirit of the Whigs* and in Ireland in 1724 the author of the fourth of *The Drapier's Letters,* both by Swift.

378. *ORMOND*, James Butler, 2nd Duke of (1665–1745), Lord Lieutenant of Ireland, 1713, but later supported Jacobites. For *Oxford*, see *Harley*, 'Horace, Lib. 2, Sat. 6', l. 65.

381. Queen Anne died in 1714.

383. *dangerous Faction*, the Whigs who came to power and continued therein throughout Swift's life. In a note he criticized them for their indiscriminate bestowal of ecclesiastical preferment, their maltreatment of Ireland and their general graft and corruption. Walpole, their leader, is said to have believed that 'every man has his price'.

385. The original Solemn *League and Cov'nant* (1643) was that between the English Puritans and the Scottish Presbyterians to resist what they believed to be the Catholicizing tendencies of Charles I.

398, 400. After the succession of George I and the triumph of the Whigs Swift sought refuge first at Letcombe (Berkshire) before going to Ireland, 'the land of slaves and fens'.

412. Wood. See l. 168 above.

421. Whitshed, William, Lord Chief Justice of Ireland, presided over the prosecution of the printer of Swift's *Proposal for the Universal Use of Irish Manufacture* (1720) and attempted by sending back the jury nine times to secure a verdict of 'Guilty'. He likewise dismissed an unco-operative jury which refused to make a presentment of Swift's *Seasonable Advice* (1724), written during the *Drapier's Letters* controversy. He is the object of Swift's satire in 'Verses on the upright Judge' and 'Whitshed's Motto on his Coach'.

424. *Scroggs*, Sir William (1623–83), Lord Chief Justice, imposed severe penalties on victims of Titus Oates's plot against Roman Catholics.

Tressilian, Sir Robert (*d.* 1388), tried peasant leader John Ball; ultimately hanged for treason.

435. *Exile*, as Swift always regarded his life in Ireland.

449. The Irish Parliament met only every two years. Swift suggests that the members return to their homes to oppress the peasantry with heavy exactions.

453. *go Snacks*, share with   *Rapparees*, freebooter soldiers who plundered the Protestants in Ireland.

484. Swift did, in fact, leave his wealth to found such a hospital.

p. 51. **A Beautiful Young Nymph Going to Bed.**   41. *Bridewell and the Compter*, prisons for vagrants and loose women.

63. *Issue-Peas* were placed in surgical issues to keep up irritation.

p. 53. **On Poetry.**   3. Edward *Young* (1683–1765), *The Universal Passion* (collected as *The Love of Fame*, 1728).

36. *Bridewell*, see above, 'A Beautiful Young Nymph Going to Bed', l. 41.

41. *Phoebus*, god of the sun.

56. *Cibber*, see above, 'Verses on the Death of Dr Swift', l. 200. The Poet Laureate received £100 per annum. Cf. also ll. 305, 396 below.

58. *Grubstreet*, see above, 'Verses on the Death of Dr Swift', l. 165, and below, ll. 346, 357.

85. *Aurora*, goddess of the dawn.

107. *Lintot*, see above, 'Verses on the Death of Dr Swift', l. 253.

117. *Will's*, coffee-house frequented by men of letters.

162. The *South-Sea* Bubble in 1720 was a scramble for highly speculative stock in which the market eventually collapsed with widespread ruin among investors.

187. *Sir Bob*, see above, 'Verses on the Death of Dr Swift', ll. 189, 192.

211. *Charon* ferried the souls of the dead over the river Styx.

213. *Cerberus*, the three-headed dog which guarded the entrance to Hades.

244, 247. *Unities* are explained by *Aristotle* (384–322 B.C.) in his *Poetics*.

245. *Horace* (65–8 B.C.), Roman lyric poet and satirist, wrote the *Ars Poetica*.

249. *Rymer*, Thomas (1641–1713), neo-classical critic, wrote *A Short View of Tragedy* (1692), in which he criticized Shakespeare's *Othello*.

250. *Dennis*, John (1657–1734) emphasized the importance of passion in poetic expression in *The Grounds of Criticism in Poetry* (1704). 'Wise' is, of course, ironic.

Bossu, René le (1631–80), wrote *Traité du poème épique* (1675).

251. *Dryden*, John (1631–1700), playwright, poet and critic. The reference is to the prefaces which he attached to several of his plays and collections of poems, but his best-known critical work is the *Essay of Dramatic Poesy* (1668).

256, 261. *Longinus* (1st cent. A.D.) wrote a treatise 'On the Sublime', translated by Nicholas *Boileau* (1636–1711). Dryden revised a translation of Boileau into English. Longinus was also translated by one of Pope's victims in *The Dunciad*, Leonard Welsted (1688–1747).

264. *Battus* is meant for Dryden.

280. *Augusta Trinobantum*, the ancient name for London.

300–4. Some of the less salubrious parts of London.

301–3. *Bavius* and *Maevius* were poetasters attacked in Virgil, *Eclogue* III. 90, and *Tigellius* a musician satirized by Horace, *Satires* I. ii. 3, iii. 4.

307, 308. *Gay*, *Pope*, see above, 'Horace', Lib. 2. Sat. 6', l. 74. The disgrace refers to the prohibition of Gay's opera, *Polly* (1728).

309. *Young*, see l. 3 above. He received a pension from Walpole, to whom he addressed *The Instalment*.

319. *Hobbes*, Thomas (1588–1679), political philosopher, wrote *Leviathan* (1651) with its anarchic view of human nature and belief in the need for strong government.

329. *Parnassus*, the mount of the Muses.

369. *Flecknoe*, Richard (d. 1678?), the type of bad poets, satirized by Marvell and in 'MacFlecknoe' indirectly by Dryden.

Howard, Edward (1624–?1700).

372. *Blackmore*, Sir Richard (1654–1729). Cf. *Dunciad* II, 261, 302.

376. *Great Poet*, William Luckyn Grimston (1683–1756), Viscount G. (1719), wrote a play, *The Lawyer's Fortune*, or *Love in a Hollow Tree*.

394. *Welsted*, Leonard (1688–1747). Cf. *Dunciad* II. 207–10, III. 169–172 and see above, ll. 256, 261.

397. *Concannen*, Matthew (1701–49), was patronized by Swift and subsequently slandered him. Cf. *Dunciad* II. 138, 299.

399. *Moor[e]*. See above, 'Verses on the Death of Dr Swift', l. 200.

411. These lines with their ironic praise of George II compare with Pope's 'Epistle to Augustus', *Imitations of Horace*.

421. Rivers of India.

429. *Iülus*, Frederick, Prince of Wales.

440. *William*, Duke of Cumberland, later to obtain doubtful fame for his victory over the Jacobites at Culloden in 1746.

441. *Minister of State*, Walpole. See 'Verses on the Death of Dr Swift', l. 189.

444. *Atlas* was said to hold the earth on his shoulders.

446. *Fabius* (Cunctator), who held off Hannibal's attacks during the Punic Wars by means of delaying actions.

461. Reference to decoration as a Knight of the Garter.

473. *Lewis*, Louis XIV of France.

488. *Butter-weight*, formerly eighteen ounces to the pound, and therefore good weight.

494. *Woolston*. See above, 'Verses on the Death of Dr Swift', l. 281.

SAMUEL JOHNSON

p. 65. **On a Lady's presenting a Sprig** . . . . The gentleman was Morgan Graves.

p. 66. **To Miss Hickman** . . . Dorothy Hickman was a relative by marriage of Johnson's.

9. Cf. Dryden, *Alexander's Feast*. Timotheus was a musician of Thebes.

p. 66. **London.** Juvenal's third satire is an account of the dangers and misery of life in Rome. The motto from *Satire* I. 30–1 reads: Who is so tolerant of this unjust city, so iron-hearted that he can restrain himself?

2. *THALES*, said by Johnson's biographer, Hawkins, to be Savage, but this was denied by Boswell.

8. *true Briton* was the name of a periodical essay run by the Duke of Wharton, enemy of Walpole, exiled in 1729.

38. *Science*, knowledge.

50. The blanks have never been filled.

51. *Pensions*, 'pay given to a state hireling for treason to his country'—Johnson, *Dictionary*.

54. *Pirates* refers to Spain's attempts to regulate traffic with her American possessions, which led after vacillation by Walpole, to the War of Jenkins' Ear (1739), so-called after Jenkins produced his ear, slit off by the Spaniards, in the House of Commons.

58. *Lottery*, run by the Government, common in the 18th century.

59. *warbling Eunuchs*, the castrati of Italian opera.

licens'd Stage. The Licensing Act (1737) required plays to be licensed by the Lord Chamberlain before performance.

72. *Gazetteer*, the official newspaper of Walpole's Government, founded 1735.

84. *Orgilio* suggests pomposity and pride.

86. *Marlborough*, see above, Swift, 'A Satirical Elegy on the Death of A Late Famous General'.

Villiers, George, 2nd Duke of Buckingham (1628–87). 'Zimri' in Dryden, *Absalom and Achitophel*. See also Pope, 'Of the Use of Riches', ll. 299–314.

98. The attack on France equates with Juvenal's condemnation of Greece.

99. *Edward* III, victor of Crécy.

108. The English and French modes of execution.

120. *Henry* V, victor of Agincourt.

124. *supple*, flattering.

143. *Dog-days* from about 3 July to 11 August when the dog-star (Sirius) was in the ascendant.

150. *Balbo*, a stammerer.

151. *gropes*, takes hold of.

161. *snarling Muse*, Satire.

173. Spain laid claim to Georgia at this time.

203. *Dome*, building.

204. *boroughs* with the right to return Members of Parliament, some so small as not to have any inhabitants.

211. *Severn* . . . *Trent*, one roughly the boundary with Wales, the other dividing the north and south of England.

227. *sleeps on Brambles*, be extremely impatient.

234. *Flambeau*, a lighted torch carried in front of noblemen.

242. *Tyburn*, the place of public execution in London.

245. *Ways and Means*, 'a cant term in the House of Commons for methods of raising money'—Johnson.

247. The King's travels to Hanover were a source of public criticism, especially as it was thought that their purpose was to visit his mistresses.

252. *Special Juries* consisted of members possessed of considerable means and were used in trials for sedition.

p. 72. **To Posterity.** This attack on Walpole is a translation of a Latin poem which Johnson pretended had been found on an inscription in Norfolk.

6. *Ground*, shore.

7. *scarlet Reptiles*, red-coat soldiers, a description illustrating Johnson's and the Tories' dislike of a standing army.

16. *change their Kings*, Johnson's fear of revolution.

17. *Bear . . . Moon*, Russia, Turkey.

18. *Lilies*, France.

19. *Lyon*, Britain.

21. *inviolable Bloom*, lily.

23. *tortured Sons*, see above, 'London', l. 54.

24. *lewd Embrace*, see above, 'London', l. 247.

25. *Horse*, the white horse, emblem of the House of Hanover.

p. 73. **Prologue to Garrick's 'Lethe'.** This play was performed on 15 April 1740.

p. 73. **Translation of the Epitaph on Hanmer.** Sir Thomas Hanmer (1677–1746) was Speaker of the House of Commons and edited Shakespeare (1744). See also below, Collins, 'An Epistle addressed to Sir Thomas Hanmer'.

p. 77. **An Ode.** 4. *gales*, breezes.

p. 79. **Prologue, spoken by Mr Garrick.** 9. *Jonson*, Ben (1572–1637), whose plays followed the classical rules more closely than those of most of his contemporaries.

16. *lasting Tomb*, the Pyramids.

17. *Wits of Charles*, the Restoration dramatists.

36. *Faustus*, a popular subject for the farces or 'after-pieces'. Cf. Pope, *Dunciad* III. 308.

42. Aphra *Behn* (?1640–89), Tom *Durfey* (1653–1723).

46. *Hunt* fought and defeated Hawksley at Broughton's Amphitheatre on 11 June 1746.

Mahomet, a rope-dancer at Covent Garden in 1746.

50. *Bubbles* has overtones of financial speculation.

p. 80. **The Vanity of Human Wishes.** 46. *Gales*, see above, 'Spring', l. 4.

49. *Democritus*, Greek philosopher (*c.* 500 B.C.).

84. *Palladium*, the statue of Pallas, guardian of Troy.

93. *Remonstrance*, the Grand Remonstrance was a petition to Charles I presented in 1641 against alleged oppressions.

97. *Septennial Ale*, used for bribing the voters at the seven-yearly parliamentary elections.

99. *Wolsey*, Thomas (?1475–1530), cardinal, chancellor of England and archbishop of York, whose fall proceeded largely from his inability to secure the Pope's agreement for a divorce from Catharine of Aragon for Henry VIII. He retired to Cawood, his archiepiscopal palace, before he was finally arrested.

125. *Villiers*, George, 1st Duke of Buckingham, minister to Charles II.
130. *Harley*, Robert, Earl of Oxford, see above, Swift, 'Horace, Lib. 2. Sat. 6', l. 65.
131. *Wentworth*, Thomas, Earl of Strafford (1593–1641), minister to Charles I, executed after impeachment by Parliament.
Hyde, Edward, Earl of Clarendon (1609–74), minister to Charles II, banished 1667. His daughter, Anne, married the Duke of York (later James II).
139. *Bodley*, Thomas (1545–1613), founder of the Bodleian Library, Oxford. *Dome*, house.
140. *Bacon's Mansion*, the reputed study of Roger Bacon (?1214–94) at Grandpont (Folly Bridge), Oxford, demolished in 1779.
162. *tardy Bust* of Milton (1608–74) placed in Westminster Abbey in 1737.
164. *Lydiat*, Thomas (1572–1646), Oxford mathematician and biblical scholar, who is reputed to have lived in poverty.
Galileo, Galilei (1564–1642)'s last years were afflicted by ill-health and blindness.
168. *Laud*, Thomas (1573–1645), archbishop of Canterbury, impeached and executed by Parliament for his support of Charles I.
179. *rapid Greek*, Alexander the Great.
182. *Danube or the Rhine*, references to the Wars of the Austrian Succession (1743–8) and the Spanish Succession (1702–13).
187. *Wreaths* of triumph.
188. *Debt*, National Debt.
192. *Swedish Charles*, Charles XII (1682–1718) defeated Frederick IV of Denmark and deposed Augustus II of Poland (l. 200) but was himself defeated by Peter the Great of Russia at Pultowa (l. 210) and died in the attack on Frederikshald (Norway) (l. 220).
224. *Persia's Tyrant*, Xerxes, defeated by a small Greek force at Thermopylae. *Bavaria's Lord*, Charles Albert, later Charles VII, defeated in the War of the Austrian Succession by Maria Theresa (l. 245).
279. *last*, most recent.
313. *Lydia's Monarch*, Croesus.
317. *Marlborough* suffered a stroke in 1716 but lived on, paralysed, till 1722.
318. *Swift* was certified a lunatic in 1742 and died in 1745.
321. *Vane*, Anne (1705–36), mistress of Frederick, Prince of Wales.
322. *Sedley*, Catherine (1657–1717), mistress of the Duke of York, later James II, created Countess of Dorchester.

p. 88. **A New Prologue to 'Comus'.** Milton's masque (1634) was produced at Drury Lane for the benefit of his grand-daughter, Mrs Elizabeth Foster, on 5 April 1750.
4. *Augustan Times*, considered the high point of Roman civilization.
23. *Bust*, see above, 'Vanity of Human Wishes', l. 162.
24. *circulating Gold*, commemorative medals.

p. 89. **The Ant.** 11. *artful*, skilful.

p. 90. **Prologue to 'The Good-Natur'd Man'.** Goldsmith's comedy was produced at Covent Garden on 29 January 1768.
7. *Caesar's pilot* was forced to sail into a storm. See Lucan, *Pharsalia*, V. 539.
22. *Crispin*, patron saint of shoemakers and therefore a name applied to men of this craft.

p. 90. **[Epitaph on Hogarth].** William Hogarth, the painter, died in 1771.
3. *curious*, meticulous.

p. 91. **[To Mrs Thrale].** Mrs Hester Thrale (1741–1821), friend of Johnson.
1. *Oft in danger*, a reference to her several dangerous pregnancies.

p. 91. **[Lines on Thomas Warton's Poems].** Thomas Warton (1728–90) is associated with Collins as a precursor of the Romantic Movement in poetry.

p. 92. **Prologue to 'A Word to the Wise'.** Hugh Kelly (1739–77)'s play was produced at Covent Garden in 1777 for the benefit of his widow and children.
2. *hooted from the stage* in 1770.
4. Cf. Pope's Homer, *Iliad*, VII. 485.

p. 93. **[Anacreon, Ode ix.].** The Greek poet, Anacreon (*fl.* 540 B.C.).
44. *pye*, magpie.

p. 94. **A Short Song of Congratulation.** 4. *Sir John* Lade (1759–1838), son of Thrale's sister, married Laetitia Darby, former mistress of the highwayman, Jack Rann, and of Frederick Augustus, Duke of York, and squandered his fortune, thus fulfilling Johnson's prediction.

p. 95. **On the Death of Dr Robert Levet.** Levet (1706–82) was one of the dependants whom Johnson sheltered.
7. *Officious*, full of good works. *innocent*, not hurtful.
28. Cf. Matthew 25: 14–30.

p. 96. **Translation of Horace, Odes, Book IV. vii.** 15. *Priam*, King of Troy when it was sacked by the Greeks.
21. *Torquatus*, the addressee of Horace's poem, of whom nothing is known.
22. *Minos*, the judge in Hades of the dead.
25. *Hyppolytus* was put to death by his father Theseus as a result of his stepmother Phaedra's unjust accusations of his sexual designs upon her. In one tradition Diana had him restored to life.
27. *Theseus* helped his friend Pirithous to carry Proserpine from Hades. Pluto fastened them to a rock, from which Theseus was rescued by Hercules.

OLIVER GOLDSMITH

p. 97. **[Prologue of Laberius].** Decimus Laberius (106–43 B.C.), a Roman knight and writer of mimes, was compelled by Caesar late in life to appear as an actor in competition with a young freedman, also a mime-writer. See Macrobius, *Saturnalia* II. vii.

p. 98. **The Gift.** Bow Street was the residence of actresses and prostitutes.

p. 99. **An Elegy on . . . Mrs Mary Blaize.** 26. *Kent-Street* was inhabited by beggars.

p. 102. **[Description of an Author's Bedchamber].** 3. *Calvert . . . Parsons*, London brewers.
4. *Drury-Lane* was frequented by prostitutes.
11. *game of goose*, a board game played with dice with squares containing geese which allowed a player to proceed several places and other squares containing other symbols which caused him to be sent back a number of places.

12. *rules* of life supposed to have been found in Charles I's study after his death.

14. *Prince William*, see above, Collins, 'Ode . . . on the Death of Colonel Ross', l. 46.

p. 109. **The Captivity.**   The captivity is that of the Jews in Babylon from 587 to 539 B.C.

182. *Zedekiah*, last King of Judah, revolted against Nebuchadnezzar (2 *Kings* 25 and 2 *Chronicles* 36).

252. *Cyrus*, King of Persia, conquered Babylon in 539 B.C.

p. 121. **The Traveller.**   2. *Scheld*, see above, Collins, 'Ode . . . on the Death of Colonel Ross', l. 13.   *Po*, river whose course runs across Northern Italy.

3. *Carinthian*, inhabitant of one of the southern provinces of Italy.

5. *Campania*, the Roman Campagna.

84. *Idra*, various places have been suggested, but the most probable is Idria, a mining town in a valley of the Austrian Alps (see *The Poems of Gray, Collins and Goldsmith*, ed. R. Lonsdale, 1969, p. 636).   *Arno*, river of Italy running through Florence and Pisa.

105. *Appennine*, mountain-range in Northern Italy.

253. *gestic*, relating to bodily movement.

276. *frieze*, coarse, warm cloth.

277. *cheer*, food.

320. *Hydaspis*, river of the Punjab.

387–8. These lines may refer to Clive's victories in India (e.g. Plassey, 1757), or just more generally to English aggrandizement in that sub-continent.

411. *Oswego*, river running between Lakes Oneida and Ontario (Canada).

429–34, 437–8. were contributed by Johnson.

436. *Luke's iron crown*, it was not Luke Dosa, but his brother George (*d.* 1514), leader of a peasant rising, who was made to sit on a red-hot iron throne, wear a red-hot iron crown and hold a red-hot iron sceptre as punishment for being proclaimed king by his followers.

Damien's bed of steel, Robert Damiens (1715–57) was chained to an iron bed as part of the tortures preceding his execution for the attempted assassination of Louis XV.

p. 131. **A New Simile.**   6. *Took's Pantheon*, a schoolbook, with illustrations, telling the stories of the gods and heroes, a translation from the French by Andrew Tooke.

33. *caducis*, Mercury's rod, a touch from which induced sleep.

36. *poppy water*, used as a soporific.

p. 132. **Verses in Reply to . . . Dr Baker's.**   10. *duds*, clothes.

11. *Horneck*, Mrs Hannah, mother of Mary, Catherine and Charles, see below, ll. 14, 17, 18.   *Nesbitt*, Mrs Susannah, sister of Johnson's friend and patron, Henry Thrale.

12. *Baker*, Dr (later Sir) George (1722–1809), physician to George III.

13. *Kauffman*, Angelica (1741–1807), painter.

14. *Jessamy bride*, Mary Horneck   *jessamy*, fashionable. Mary Horneck did not marry until several years after this poem was written (about 1769).

16. *Reynoldses two*, Sir Joshua (1723–92), President of the Royal Academy, and his sister Frances (1729–1807) who also painted.

17. *Little Comedy*, Catherine Horneck.

18. *Captain in lace*, Charles Horneck had just purchased an ensignship in the Foot Guards. He later became a general.

p. 133. **[Epilogue to 'The Sister'].** This comedy by Mrs Charlotte Lennox (1770–1840) was performed at Covent Garden in mid-February, 1768, but was a failure.

16. *Patriots*, in its pejorative sense 'a factious disturber of the government' (Johnson).

17. *Hebe*, daughter of Zeus and Hera, associated with perpetual youth.

p. 134. **The Deserted Village.** 25. *simply*, naïvely.

122. *vacant*, carefree.

142. *passing*, very.

209. *terms*, days on which rents, wages and the like were payable.

210. *gauge*, calculate the capacity of various vessels for containing liquids, usually alcoholic.

232. *rules—game of goose*, see above, 'Description of an Author's Bedchamber', ll. 11–12.

248. *mantling*, frothing.

316. *artist*, workman.

318. *black gibbet* at Tyburn.

344. *Altama*, river in Georgia (U.S.A.).

418. *Torno* (Tornea), river in Sweden.

p. 144. **The Haunch of Venison.** Robert Nugent, Lord Clare (later Earl Nugent) (1702–88), held minor posts in government from 1760 to 1782. Goldsmith stayed with him in 1770 and 1771.

14. *Bounce*, a boasting lie.

21. *Reynolds*, see above, 'Verses in Reply to . . . Dr Baker's', l. 16.

24. *Monroe*, Dorothy, niece of the Earl of Ely, a renowned beauty.

27. *Howard*, &c. Only *Hiff* (Paul Hifferman, 1719–77) has been definitely identified in this group of minor writers.

29. *Higgins*, possibly Captain Higgins who helped Goldsmith in his fight with Evans, a bookseller, over the latter's publication of an offensive letter.

49. *Burke*, Edmund (1729–97), statesman and writer.

55. *Mile-end* in Stepney, London.

60. This line was taken from a letter of Henry Frederick, Duke of Cumberland, to Lady Grosvenor, produced during his trial for adultery with her in 1770.

72. *Thrale*, Henry, brewer and friend of Johnson.

82. *swinging*, large.

p. 147. **[Prologue to 'Zobeide'].** This play, a tragedy, was written by Joseph Cradock (1742–1826) and first performed at Covent Garden in December 1771.

5. *Botanists*, Joseph Banks (1743–1820) and Daniel Solanda (1736–82) accompanied Captain Cook on his voyage to Tahiti in 1769.

8. *hoity-toity*, haughty.

11. *Scythian*, Cradock's play was adapted from one by Voltaire set in Scythia.

p. 148. **Threnodia Augustalis.** This work was performed at a memorial concert for Augusta, Princess Dowager of Wales and mother of George III, in February 1772.

225. *Edward* III.

p. 156. **[First Epilogue for 'She Stoops to Conquer'].** 20. *dangle*, 'to follow a woman without asking the question' (Grose, *Classical Dictionary of the Vulgar Tongue*).

21. *mump*, mumble.

31. *macaroni*, foppish.

32. *friseurs*, hairdressers. *nosegays*, perfumes.
36. *Heinelle*, Anna-Frederica (1752–1808), danced at the King's Theatre in 1773.
57. *crack*, boast.

p. 158. **[Second Epilogue to 'She Stoops . . .'].** 9–10. The theatres opened at 5 p.m., but Foote's was an exception. His puppet-show at the Haymarket opened at noon.
15. *Macaronis*, see above, 'First Epilogue . . .', l. 31.
25. *Mohawk*, derived from Red Indian tribes, to describe aristocratic ruffians in the early eighteenth century.
46. *Heinele*, see above, 'First Epilogue . . .', l. 36.
48. *Che faro*, aria in Gluck's *Orfeo*, performed at the King's Theatre in March 1773. *Nancy Dawson*, possibly a song named after the Covent Garden dancer of that name.

p. 160. **Epilogue spoken by Mr Lee Lewis.** Charles Lee Lewis (1740–1803), well known as Harlequin in pantomime, played the part of Young Marlow in *She Stoops to Conquer*. The epilogue was spoken at Covent Garden on 7 May 1773.
5. *pyebald vest*, the criss-cross colours of the harlequin.
7. *visionary birth*, fantastic creation.
15–18. contain references to the spectacular devices of the pantomime stage.
21. Cf. *King Lear* III. 4. 113.
24. Cf. *Richard III* V. 3. 177.

p. 161. **Retaliation.** Written as an answer to Garrick's 'epitaph': Here lies Nolly Goldsmith, for shortness call'd Noll,/Who wrote like an angel, but talk'd like poor Poll. It commemorates fellow-members of St James's Coffee House and was left incomplete at Goldsmith's death in 1774.
1. *Scarron*, Paul (1610–60), French comic writer.
5. *Dean*, Thomas Barnard (1728–1806), Dean of Derry. See l. 23.
6. *Burke*, Edmund, see above, 'The Haunch of Venison', l. 49 and also l. 29 below.
7. *Will*, William Burke (1730–98), M.P. See l. 43.
8. *Dick*, Richard Burke (1703–94), brother of Edmund. See l. 51.
9. *Cumberland*, Richard (1732–1811), dramatist. See l. 61.
10. *Douglas*, Dr John (1721–1807), later Bishop of Carlisle and Salisbury. See l. 79.
11. *Garrick*, David (1717–69), actor and theatre manager of Drury Lane. See l. 93.
14. *Ridge*, John (*c.* 1728–76), lawyer. *Reynolds*, see above, 'Verses in Reply to . . . Dr Baker's'.
15. *Hickey*, Joseph (*c.* 1714–94), lawyer. See l. 125.
34. *Towns[h]end*, Thomas (1733–1800), M.P.
55. *keep up the ball*, maintain the conversation.
62. *Terence*, the Roman dramatist, an exemplar of 'sentimental' comedy.
68. *rout*, fashionable party.
86. *Dodds*, William Dodd (1729–77), popular preacher, executed for forgery. *Kenricks*, William Kenrick (*c.* 1725–79), lectured at the Devil's Tavern on Shakespeare.
87. *Macpherson*, James (1736–96) wrote *Ossian* which he claimed to have discovered and translated from the Gaelic.
89. *Lauder*, William, attributed to Milton borrowings from the Latin which were, in fact, found in a Latin translation of *Paradise Lost* itself. *Bower*,

Archibald (1686–1766), a Roman Catholic who falsely claimed to have been converted to the faith of the Church of England.

115. *Kellys*, Hugh Kelly, see above, Johnson, 'Prologue to Kelly's *A Word to the Wise*'. *Woodfalls*, William Woodfall (1746–1803), actor, journalist and critic.

118. *be-roscius'd*, Roscius, famous comic actor of the Roman stage.

124. *Beaumonts and Bens*, Francis Beaumont (*c.* 1584–1616) and Ben Jonson (1572–1637), Jacobean comic playwrights.

135. *burn ye*, a greeting among the lower classes in Ireland in the eighteenth century.

THOMAS GRAY

p. 165. **Ode on the Spring.** 1. *Hours*, attendants on Venus in the Homeric Hymns.

2. *VENUS* is here V. Genetrix, goddess of natural life and growth.

p. 166. **Ode on a Distant Prospect of Eton College.** The prospect was from Gray's uncle's house at Stoke Poges. The poet had been at school at Eton.

Epigraph: I am a man, a sufficient excuse for being unhappy.

4. *Henry* VI, founder of Eton.

p. 169. **Sonnet on the Death of West.** Richard West (1716–42), a friend of Gray, wrote Anglo-Latin poetry.

p. 169. **Hymn to Adversity.** Epigraph: Zeus who leads mortals in the way of understanding and has made it a fixed law that wisdom comes through suffering.

35. *Gorgons* were able to turn whatever they gazed on to stone.

36. *vengeful Band*, Furies.

p. 171. **[Hymn to Ignorance].** 3. *Camus*, the river Cam which flows through Cambridge.

11. *Hyperion*, the Titan who controlled the sun's course.

14. *Ægis*, a heavy shield used by the gods.

37. *Sesostris*, Egyptian king in Greek legend who conquered parts of Africa and Asia.

p. 172. **Ode on the Death of a Favourite Cat.** 34. *Dolphin* rescued Arion from the sea.

35. *Nereid*. Sabrina was carried to Nereus' hall, Milton, *Comus*, l. 835.

p. 173. **[The Alliance of Education and Government].** Epigraph: Begin, my friend, for be sure, you cannot take your song to Hades, where all things are forgotten.

67. *eye of day*, the sun.

77. *Zembla*, islands north of Russia.

101. *redundant*, overflowing.

107. *ambient*, surrounding.

p. 175. **[Tophet].** An attack on the Revd Henry Etough, Rector of Therfield (Herts), formerly a dissenter (hence 'proselyte', l. 4), who was known for his fund of scandalous information about prominent and influential people.

1. *Tophet*, a phonetic anagram of Etough, was the place outside Jerusalem where sacrifices to Moloch took place.

p. 176. **Elegy . . . in a Country Churchyard.**   1. *Curfew*, bell rung in the evening and originally stemming from William the Conqueror's edict requiring the extinguishing of fires and lights at the time of curfew.
90. *pious*, attentive to one's obligations to near-relations, especially parents.
119. *Science*, learning generally.

p. 179. **A Long Story.**   2–3. *ancient pile*, manor-house of Stoke Poges, built by the Earls of Huntingdon and subsequently owned by Queen Elizabeth's minister, Sir Christopher Hatton, Lord Chancellor.
6. *achievements*, heraldic decorations given for distinguished actions.
11. *Lord Keeper*, Hatton was Lord Chancellor. *Brawls*, an old-fashioned dance.
12. *Seal, and Maces*, the insignia of the Lord Chancellor.
16. *Pope and Spaniard*, Queen Elizabeth was excommunicated by Pius V in 1570 and the Spanish Armada attacked England in 1588.
23. *A brace of Warriors*, the first of whom (l. 25) is Lady Schaub, the other (l. 29), Miss Henrietta Speed, niece of Lady Cobham (l. 31), who lived at the manor-house at Stoke Poges.
37. *capucine*, a coat consisting of cloak and hood and resembling that worn by the capuchin monks.
41. *P[ur]t*, Robert, Fellow of King's College, Cambridge, taught at Eton.
80. *spell*, note left by Lady Schaub.
99. *Lady Janes and Joans*, ghosts of the manor-house.
103. *Styack*, actually Tyack, the housekeeper.
115. *Squib[b]*, James, groom of the chamber.
116. *Groom*, the steward.
120. *Macleane*, James, convicted highwayman, executed in 1750, who sought to speak at his trial but found himself unable to do so.
144. *Rubbers* of whist or other card-games.

p. 183. **Stanzas to Mr Bentley.**   3. *Bentley*, Richard (1708–81), illustrated Gray's poems.
26–8. The words in italics, the manuscript having been torn, were supplied by Mason in 1775.

p. 184. **The Progress of Poesy.**   Epigraph: Vocal to the wise, but as for the crowd they need interpreters.
3. The subject and simile, as usual with Pindar, are united. The various sources of poetry, which gives life and lustre to all it touches, are here described; its quiet majestic progress enriching every subject (otherwise dry and barren) with a pomp of diction and luxuriant harmony of numbers; and its more rapid irresistible course, when swoln and hurried away by the conflict of tumultuous passions. (Gray.)   *Helicon*, a mountain, sacred to the Muses, with the springs of Hippocrene and Aganippe.
9. *Ceres*, goddess of the crops.
13. Power of harmony to curb the turbulent sallies of the soul. (Gray.)
15. *shell*, lyre.
17. *Lord of War*, Mars, who was associated in classical literature with Thrace.
21. *feather'd king*, the eagle.
25. Power of harmony to produce all the graces of motion in the body. (Gray.)
27. *Idalia*, a town in Crete where Aphrodite (Venus) was worshipped.
29. *Cytherea*. After her birth in the sea Aphrodite was said to have landed on Cythera, an island off Laconia.
37. *Graces*, personified loveliness.

42. To compensate the real and imaginary ills of life, the Muse was given to Mankind by the same Providence that sends the Day by its cheerful presence to dispel the gloom and terrors of the Night. (Gray.)

53. *Hyperion*, see above, 'Hymn to Ignorance', l. 11.

54. Extensive influence of poetic Genius over the remotest and most uncivilized nations . . . (Gray).

63. *Goddess*, Muse of poetry.

66. Progress of Poetry from Greece to Italy, and from Italy to England . . . (Gray).

Delphi, shrine of Apollo, god of poetry, on Mount Parnassus.

68. *Ilissus* and 69. *Mæander*, rivers of Greece.

77. *sad Nine*, the Muses.

78. *Latian*, Roman.

84. *Nature's Darling*, Shakespeare.

86. *mighty Mother*, Cybele, goddess of the powers of nature.

95. *He*, Milton.

98-9. Cf. *Ezekiel* 1 : 20, 26, 28.

113. *he*, Gray.

115. *Theban Eagle*, Zeus's bird, associated with the true poetic gift in Pindar, *Olympian Odes* II. 88, which Gray quoted in the epigraph to the poem.

p. 187. **The Bard.** Gray, relying on Carte's *General History of England*, believed that Edward I in his conquest of Wales exterminated the bards.

8. *Cambria*, Wales.

13. *Gloster*, Gilbert de Clare (1243–95), 8th Earl, son-in-law of Edward I, one of the Lords of the Marches, the lands on the borders of England and Wales.

14. *Mortimer* identified by Gray as Edmond de Mortimer, but actually it was Roger de Mortimer (?1231–1282) who took part in the Welsh campaigns.

28-33. These names do not appear to refer to actual bards.

34. *Plinlimmon*, mountain in mid-Wales.

35. *Arvon*, the shores of the mainland opposite Anglesey.

56. *agonizing King*, Edward II was murdered at Berkeley Castle in 1327.

57. *She-Wolf of France*, Isabella, wife of Edward II and mistress of Mortimer, who engineered the King's death.

63. *Mighty Victor*, Edward III.

67. *sable Warriour*, Edward the Black Prince, son of Edward III.

74. *Youth . . . Pleasure . . .* , the reign of Richard II (1377–99).

83. *din of battle*, The Wars of the Roses.

87-8. *Towers of Julius*, the Tower of London, where Henry VI and the young princes (Edward and his brother) were murdered.

89. *Consort*, Margaret of Anjou, wife of Henry VI.

90. *meek Usurper*, Henry VI, of the illegitimate line of Lancaster.

91-2. *rose of snow . . . blushing foe*, the white and red roses of York and Lancaster, referring to the Wars of the Roses.

93. *bristled Boar*, the badge of Richard III, who was responsible for the deaths of the princes in the Tower.

99. *Half of thy heart*, Eleanor of Castile, wife of Edward I, who predeceased him.

109. *Arthur*, believed in Welsh legend to be still alive in fairy-land.

110. *genuine Kings*, the Tudors were of Welsh descent.

115. *Form divine*, Elizabeth I.

121. *Taliessin*, chief of the bards, flourished in the sixth century.

124. *eye of Heav'n*, the sun.

128. *buskin'd*, tragic. Gray's note names Shakespeare.
131. *Voice*, Milton.

p. 193. **The Fatal Sisters.**   The poem derives ultimately from the (allegedly prophetic) account of the Battle of Clontarf (1014) in the *Darraðar Ljoð*, later incorporated in the Latin commentaries of Bartholin (1689) and Torfaeus (1697). Sictryg, King of Dublin, and Sigurd, Earl of Orkney, opposed the former's father-in-law, Brian, King of Munster, who lost his life in the battle which also brought severe damage to his opponents' forces. Gray in his preface speaks of a native of Caithness seeing and following several figures who enter an opening in the rocks. They are the fatal sisters who work on a loom, their weft consisting of human entrails (l. 10), the warp of spears (l. 5), the shuttles swords (l. 13) and the weights human heads (ll. 11–12).
8. *Orkney*, Sigurd (see above).   *Randver's bane*, Odin, killer of Randver.
17–18, 31. Names of several of the Valkyries, messenger maidens of Odin, who killed heroes selected for death in battle and a place in Valhalla.
32. *youthful King*, Sictryg (see above).
41. *dauntless Earl*, Sigurd.
45. *Eirin*, Ireland.

p. 195. **The Descent of Odin.**   The story of Balder is found in Bartholin's work (see above, 'The Fatal Sisters').
1. *King of Men*, Odin.
2. *steed*, Sleipner.
4. *HELA*, goddess of death, presiding over Nifleimr (or Hell).
5. *Dog*, Garm, guardian of the entrance to the underworld.
46. *Balder* was proof against all harmful things except the mistletoe which Lok, the evil god, placed in the hand of blind Hoder to throw at Balder.
65. *Rinda* bore Vali, begotten by Odin, to avenge Balder's death.
75. *Virgins*, probably Norns, or Scandinavian Fates.
90. *Lok*, see above, l. 46.

p. 197. **The Triumphs of Owen.**   This and the three following poems were based on Latin translations of Welsh poems made by Evan Evans.
1, 3, 4. *Owen*, prince of North Wales (Gwyneth) (1137–70), descended from *Roderic*.
10. *Squadrons three* points to the sea-battle off Tal-y-Moelfre (1157) when three fleets of Henry II were defeated.
14. *Lochlin*, Denmark.
15. *Norman*, Norwegian.
20. *Dragon*. The red dragon was the device of Cadwallader.   *Mona*, Anglesey.
25. *Talymalfra*, see above, l. 10.

p. 198. **[The Death of Hoel].**   For the original, see above, 'The Triumphs of Owen'. The event referred to is the Battle of Catterick about 603 A.D. when the Gododdin, a tribe of North Britain, were defeated.
3. *Deïra*, Saxon kingdom in north-east Yorkshire.
6, 7, 21. The figures mentioned have not been identified.
11. *Cattraeth*, Catterick.

p. 200. **[Sketch of His Own Character].**   6. *Charles Townshend* (1725–67), Secretary at War 1761.   *Squire*, Dr Samuel (1713–66), chaplain to the Duke of Newcastle, Dean of Bristol 1761.

p. 200. **The Candidate.**   This poem refers to the contest for the High Stewardship of Cambridge University in 1764 between the Tory candidate, the profligate Earl of Sandwich, and the Whig, unattractive Lord Royston (later Lord Hardwicke), who was eventually after a lawsuit declared elected.

1. *Jemmy Twitcher*, the Earl of Sandwich.
2. *white-wash* was used as a cosmetic for whitening the skin.
3. *three sisters*, the Faculties of Medicine, Law and Divinity.
4. *guttle*, to gorge.
6. *sheep-biting*, sneaking.
8. *his nose*, possibly a reference to damage as a result of venereal disease.
12. *Rochester*, John Wilmot (1647–80), also a profligate, from whom Sandwich was descended.
14. *wife*. Sandwich's wife was confined for insanity, but was also said to have been kept in confinement after her recovery.
17. *Newgate-bird*, thief confined in Newgate Prison.
24. *David ... Solomon* refer to David as psalmist and to Solomon's 700 concubines.
25–6. *Israel*. The Jews borrowed of the Egyptians before embarking on the exodus (*Exodus* 12 : 35–6).
27. *prophet of Bethel*'s story is found in 1 *Kings* 13 : 11–19.
28. *Noah*'s drunkenness is described in *Genesis* 9 : 21.
34. *stitches*, a vulgar term for sexual intercourse.

p. 201. **On L[or]d H[olland']s Seat.** 2. *H[olland]*, Henry Fox, 1st Baron (1705–74), amassed a huge fortune as Paymaster-General (1757–65). Gray puns on the family name in the last line.
6. *Goodwin*. Goodwin Sands, dangerous sandbanks off the Kent coast, traditionally the remains of an island which belonged to Earl Godwin in the 11th century.
17. *Bute*, 3rd Earl of, Prime Minister (1760–3), who dismissed Holland.
18. *Shelburne*, 2nd Earl of, suggested that Holland would resign if he was given a peerage. *Rigby*, Richard, left Holland to follow the Duke of Bedford. *Calcraft*, John, deserted Holland for Pitt.
23. *St Peter's*, Westminster Abbey.

p. 201. **Ode for Music.** This ode was written for the installation of the Duke of Grafton, the Prime Minister, as Chancellor of Cambridge University, on 1 July 1769.
21. *place*, Cambridge.
23. *Milton* was an undergraduate at Christ's College.
25. *Newton* was a scholar and later Fellow of Trinity College.
32. *Cynthia*, the moon.
39. *Edward* III founded King's Hall, later incorporated with others to form Trinity College. The *lilies* were those of France which Edward quartered with the leopards of England on his crest.
41. *sad Chatillon*, Marie de Castillon, founder of Pembroke Hall (later College). The tradition, here referred to, of her husband's death in a tournament on their wedding-day is inaccurate.
42. *Clare*, Elizabeth de Burgh, Countess of, daughter of Gilbert de Clare and grand-daughter of Edward I, re-founded Clare Hall (later College).
43. *Anjou's Heroine*, Margaret, wife of Henry VI, founded Queen's College. *paler Rose*, Elizabeth Woodville, wife of Edward IV (of the Yorkist line) re-founded the college.
45. *either Henry*, Henry VI founded King's College and Henry VIII was an extensive benefactor to Trinity College.
47. *broke the bonds of Rome*, Henry VIII's part in the English Reformation.
51. *Granta*, the upper reaches of the river Cam.

54. *Fitzroy*, the family name of the Duke of Grafton, see above, introductory sentence.

66, 70. *Marg'ret* Beaufort, wife of Edmund Tudor, Earl of Richmond, and mother of Henry VII, founded Christ's and St John's Colleges. Grafton was descended from her illegitimately through Charles II.

84. *Cecil*, William, Lord Burleigh, Chancellor of Cambridge in the reign of Elizabeth I.

86. *Fasces*, bundles of rods signifying consular authority in ancient Rome.

93. *Star of Brunswick*, George III, descended from the Duke of Brunswick, Elector of Hanover.

WILLIAM COLLINS

p. 205. **Persian Eclogues.** I. 30. *Balsora*, the Persian Gulf.
II. 14. *Schiraz* or Sheraz.
III. 1. *Tefflis*, capital of Eastern Georgia.
IV. 44, 45. *Irvan* and *Tarkie* (Tarku), Persian cities.

p. 214. **An Epistle . . . to Hanmer.** For Hanmer, see above, Johnson, 'Translation of the Epitaph on Hanmer'.

22. *Phaedra*, see above, Johnson, 'Translation of Horace, Odes, Book IV, vii', l. 25. The story is dramatized in Euripides' *Phaedra*.

23. *Curse*, Oedipus's unwitting murder of his father and marriage with his mother to be found in Sophocles' *Oedipus Tyrannus*.

30. *Menander* (*c.* 342–292 B.C.) wrote Greek 'New Comedy'. His successors in Rome (l. 27) were Plautus and Terence.

33. *Ilissus*, river of Athens, and thus associated with Greek tragedy.

37. *Julius* II, pope (1503–1513), friend of Raphael and Michel Angelo.

38. *Cosmo* or Cosimo de Medici (1389–1464), patron of the arts in Florence.

40. *Provincial* troubadours of the 13th century.

55, 57. *Jo[h]nson*, Ben and *Fletcher*, John, comic dramatists of the early 17th century.

71. *Corneille*, Pierre (1606–84), French tragic dramatist, influenced by *Lucan* (39–65), Roman epic poet.

73. *Racine*, Jean (1639–99), also French tragic dramatist.

74. *Maro*, one of the names of Virgil.

81–2. *Henry* V, in which Shakespeare describes the victory of Agincourt.

83–92. *gentler Edward*, Edward V, the boy-king, whose murder was encompassed by Gloucester (l. 85) (later Richard III), enacted in Shakespeare's *Richard III*.

97–8. *Swains . . . twilight Fairies* in *A Midsummer Night's Dream*.

100. *enchanted Isle* of *The Tempest*.

110. *Raphael* (1483–1520), Italian painter.

115. *Anthony in tears* over Caesar's body, *Julius Caesar*, III. 2.

121, 124. *he*, Coriolanus, especially in *Coriolanus* V. 3.

137. *Sibyl-Leaves*, the verses of the sibyl (in Virgil, *Aeneid* VI) were blown about by the wind.

142. *Homer's Numbers* were said to have been collected by Pisistratus, who ruled Athens in sixth century B.C.

p. 218. **A Song from Shakespear's Cymbeline.** The song refers to 'Fear no more the heat of the sun' in *Cymbeline*, IV. 2, of which scenes there are echoes of ll. 218–20 (ll. 3–4), 276–9 (ll. 5–6, 9–10), 217 (l. 11), 224–9 (ll. 13–16).

p. 219. **Song . . . from Shakespeare.** This song is based mainly on Ophelia's mad song in *Hamlet* IV. 5, which is echoed in ll. 3–4 (*Hamlet* IV. 5. 29–32), 5–6 (l. 35), 13–16 (ll. 191–5), 17 (l. 164) and 19 (l. 39).
1. *Damon*, a conventional name for a shepherd in poetry.

p. 220. **Written on a Paper . . . Bride Cake.** 6. *shepherd*, i.e., the poet.
9. *Cyprian queen*, Venus. *Hymen*, goddess of marriage.
14. *Paphian*, Paphos (Cyprus) was claimed, with Cythera, as the place where Venus landed after her birth in the sea.

p. 221. **Ode to Pity.** 7. *Pella's Bard*, Euripides who died at Pella, 406 B.C.
14. *Ilissus*, see above, 'An Epistle to Hanmer', l. 33.
16. *Arun*, birthplace of Thomas Otway (1652–85), writer of tragedies.
34. *Buskin'd Muse*, Tragedy.

p. 222. **Ode to Fear.** 22. *rav'ning Brood*, referring to the chorus preceding the avenging murder of Clytemnestra in Sophocles' *Electra*.
30. *Bard*, Aeschylus (525–456 B.C.), Greek tragic dramatist, fought at Marathon, 490 B.C.
34. *He*, Sophocles (496–406 B.C.).
35. *Hybla*, Sicilian town famous for its honey.
37. *baleful Grove*, dedicated to the Furies, the setting in Sophocles' *Oedipus Coloneus*.
38. *Incestuous Queen*, Jocasta, who unwittingly married her son, Oedipus, in *Oedipus Tyrannus*.
59. *thrice-hallow'd Eve*, Hallowe'en (31 October).
70. *Cypress Wreath*, the garland of the tragic poet.

p. 224. **Ode to Simplicity.** 14. *Hybla*, see above, 'Ode to Fear', l. 35.
16. *Her*, the nightingale.
18. *Electra's Poet*, here Sophocles (though both he and Euripides wrote on Electra).
19. *Cephisus*, river flowing near Athens.
22. *enamel'd*, beautified with various colours.

p. 226. **Ode on the Poetical Character.** 3. *Him*, Edmund Spenser (1552–1599), author of *The Faerie Queene*.
6. *magic Girdle*, symbol of chastity in marriage, lost by Florimel, won by the false Florimel who was unable to fasten it (*Faerie Queene*, IV–V).
16. *Zone*, girdle.
19. *Cest*, girdle.
29. *Enthusiast*, Fancy (l. 17).
32–4. Cf. *Ezekiel* 1 : 26–28.
46. *Tarsel*, male hawk.
62. *Eden*. Cf. *Paradise Lost* IV.
69. *Waller*, Edmund (1606–87), first of the Augustan poets. *myrtle*, sacred to Venus and representative therefore of love.

p. 228. **Ode to Mercy.** 16. *our Isle his Prey*, the Jacobite uprising of 1745.
26. *share our Monarch's Throne*, Collins' belief that George II might pardon the three Scottish rebel noblemen, the Earls of Kilmarnock and Cromartie and Lord Balmerino, on trial for their support of Charles in the Jacobite uprising.

p. 229. **Ode to Liberty.** 1. *the Spartan Fife*, possibly a reference to Tyrtaeus, who wrote songs to encourage the Spartans in the Second Messenian War (*c.* 690 B.C.).

7. *Alcaeus* (8th cent. B.C.). Collins quotes and attributes to him some lines from an Athenian national song which, however, refers to events in the sixth century B.C.

9. *Wisdom's Shrine* was where the attempted assassination referred to in the lines quoted by Collins took place.

36. *They,* the Medici family. *Science,* knowledge.

39. *Pisa,* rival city of Florence and annexed by the latter.

40. *Marino,* the republic of San Marino.

43. *those,* the Venetians.

44. *Him,* the Doge of Venice.

45. *weds . . . Bride,* the annual ceremony symbolizing the marriage of the city of Venice with the sea.

47. *Lydian Measure* was apparently soft and soothing.

49. *Liguria,* Genoa, taken by the French in 1684 and re-captured by the Austrians in 1746.

51. *Helvetia,* Switzerland, where the *daring archer* (l. 53), William Tell, led the insurrection against the Austrians, whose ensign was the *eagle* (l. 55).

57. *Those,* the Dutch.

59. *British Queen,* Elizabeth I, who refused the crown of the Netherlands (or United Provinces).

72. *Orcas,* the far north of Scotland.

82. *Mona,* Isle of Man. Collins' note refers to a mermaid's rejection by a young man with whom she had become enamoured, in revenge for which she is said to have enveloped the island in mist, thus making it inaccessible to ships.

108. *Hebe,* goddess of youth.

p. 233. **Ode . . . on the Death of Colonel Ross.**   The lady to whom this poem is addressed may have been Elizabeth Goddard. The subject of the poem was Captain (not Colonel) Charles Ross of Balnagown, Ross-shire, for which county he was also Member of Parliament. Fontenoy was fought on 11 May 1745.

13. *Scheld,* river rising in Northern France and flowing through Belgium.

32. *Crecy,* where the Black Prince, son of Edward III, fought almost exactly 400 years before in 1346.

46. *William,* Duke of Cumberland, victor of Culloden which marked the total overthrow of the Jacobites. Lines 37–48 were inserted in 1746 as a compliment to him and then removed in 1748.

48. *Harting* (Sussex) where Miss Goddard may have lived.

p. 236. **Ode to Peace.** 1. *Turtles,* doves.

3. *sought'st thy native Skies,* Astraea, goddess of justice, fled from earth to the sky when evil appeared among men after the Golden Age.

p. 237. **The Manners.**   'Manners' in the title refers to behaviour, motivation and impulse of characters.

13. *Porch,* a public walk in the agora of Athens where the Stoic philosophy was taught.

14. *Olive,* sacred to Athena, goddess of Athens.

50. *comic Sock,* light shoe worn by comic actors in the classical theatre.

59. *Miletus,* Aristides of (2nd cent. B.C.), writer of short love-stories.

61. *you,* probably Boccaccio (1313–75), who lived in Florence.

63. *Him,* Cervantes (1547–1616), author of *Don Quixote.*

67. *Him,* Le Sage (1667–1747), author of *Gil Blas.*

68. *watchet*, light blue.

69. *sad Sicilian Maid*, Blanche, in love with the King of Sicily but forced by her father to marry someone else—a narrative to be found in *Gil Blas*.

75. *Cynic*, philosophers who were contemptuous of worldly pleasure.

p. 238. The Passions. 75. *Queen*, Diana, goddess of chastity, famed as a huntress.

86. *Tempe's Vale* between the mountains Olympus and Ossa.

108. *recording Sister*, Clio, the muse of history.

114. *Cæcilia*, patron saint of music.

p. 241. Ode . . . the Death of Thomson. Epigraph: These rites are yours for ever, both when we pay the Nymphs our solemn vows and when we purify the fields—Daphnis also loved us.

1. *Druid* or prophet-poet; here James Thomson (1700–48), author of *The Seasons*.

6. *airy Harp*, the Aeolian harp which produces musical sounds when air passes through it.

19. *Spire* of Richmond Church.

p. 243. Ode on the Popular Superstitions of the Highlands. 1. *H[ome]*, John (1722–1808), Scottish clergyman and, later, playwright.

4. *Tragic Song*, possibly Home's play, *Agis*, rejected by Garrick.

5. *cordial Youth*, Thomas Barrow of Edinburgh, who with Home fought against the Jacobite rebels at Falkirk and with him was captured and escaped.

6. *Lavant*, the river which ran through Chichester.

8. *destin'd Bride*, Mary Downer of Chichester.

18. *Doric*, rustic.

37. *Boreal*, northern.

41. *Runic*, Scottish (not Scandinavian).

48. *Shiel*, herdsman's summer-hut.

55. *Fate's fell spear*. These and other italicized words and phrases are possibly the insertions of Home's friend, Alexander Carlyle, who read the poem from a draft which he possessed to the Royal Society of Edinburgh in 1784.

59. *strath*, flat land adjoining water.

100. *Monster*, kelpie (l. 137) or spirit of the waters.

126. *travell'd*, wearied.

155. *Kilda*, the remotest of the Hebrides and here celebrated as a place of primitive virtue.

166. *Solan*, gannet.

191. *Tasso* wrote *Gerusalemme Liberata* (1593), to incidents in which the following lines refer.

197. *Fairfax*, Edward, translated Tasso (1600).

198. *Prevailing*, powerful.

212. *Drummond*, William, of Hawthornden (1585–1649), with whom Jonson stayed and had conversations.

213. *Tiviot* or Teviot, river in Roxburghshire.

214. *Yarrow*, river in Selkirkshire. Carlyle's inserted phrase suggests that he had in mind William Hamilton of Bangour's poem, 'The Braes of Yarrow'.

216. *Lothian*, where Edinburgh is situated.

217. *Muir*, moor.

Index of First Lines